American Averages

AMAZING FACTS OF EVERYDAY LIFE

Mike Feinsilber
William B. Mead

DOLPHIN BOOKS
Doubleday & Company, Inc.
Garden City, New York   1980

Library of Congress Cataloging in Publication Data

Feinsilber, Mike.
American averages.

Bibliography: p. 397
1. National characteristics, American—Miscellanea.
I. Mead, William B., joint author.   II. Title.
E169.02.F45   973
ISBN 0-385-17176-4 (pbk.)
Library of Congress Catalog Card Number 79–8567

To Doris Feinsilber and Jenny Mead,
who are by no means average.

Special acknowledgments

Beulah Land, U. S. Bureau of the Census
Dr. David B. P. Goodman
Sandra Surber Smith, National Center for Health Statistics
Barbara B. Crandall
Jean Jones, American Psychiatric Association
Fred D. Lindsey
Professor John P. Robinson
U. S. Department of Agriculture
Barbara L. McBride, Food Marketing Institute
Peggy Grant, U. S. Postal Service
Professor Richard Stevens
State Farm Insurance Companies
Paul Dickson
Dan Rapoport
Gerard Helferich

Contents

load . . . The American bureaucrat . . . Lunch hours and coffee
breaks . . . Who gets overtime? Who gets stock options? . . . Who
totes a briefcase home and who works weekends? . . . How much
we like (or hate) our jobs and our bosses . . . Does your plumber
really make more than you do? . . . Does your pay measure up?
. . . The lot of the career woman.

10 FOOD AND DRINK 283

Exactly what we eat, to the last carrot . . . Our favorite candy
bars . . . Who cooked last night's dinner . . . Eating at the ball
park . . . The backyard barbecue . . . Fat people . . . How much
the average person your age and height weighs . . . How many
dieters keep it off . . . Eating out . . . At McDonald's . . . The
national sweet tooth . . . Grown at home and proud of it . . . The
chemicals we eat . . . Exactly what we drink, to the last harvey
wallbanger . . . Coffee, pop, and mother's milk . . . Youth at
the bar . . . Drinking customs . . . Meet your average drunk . . .
Six-pack America . . . A portrait of the average bourbon drinker
. . . Who drinks wine.

11 WHEELS 320

The family car and its color, age, cost, mileage, make, recalls,
repairs, options, driver . . . Vacation dreams and realities . . .
Who commutes and how . . . How kids get to school . . . By plane,
train, bus . . . The good and bad motels . . . The average
conventioneer.

12 HAVING FUN 341

What we do for fun . . . How often we go to the flicks . . . What we
watch on TV, and what we did before there was any . . . Who
smokes pot . . . The jogging American . . . Casey Stengel, the
average manager . . . Boating, camping, swimming, sailing, skiing,
and the boomerang . . . Women athletes are gaining on men . . .
Boy Scouts, culture vultures, and stamp collectors . . . What the
average big leaguer makes in baseball, football, hockey, and
basketball . . . The tube and the tot . . . How many games of
Monopoly . . . The average play on an average day in the National
Football League.

13 LORD KNOWS WHAT ELSE   374

The average day's weather across America . . . The life span of the
average aardvark, toad, swan, honey bee, and other living things . . .
The average U.S. President . . . Who robs banks . . . Your average
dog and cat . . . How hard the wind blows in Chicago . . . Crime
and weather . . . The weatherman's batting average . . . Middle
America, exactly . . . The average American Indian . . . What
makes Iowa so average.

Introduction

This book is the reverse of the *Guinness Book of World Records*. If you're outstanding, look for yourself there. The rest of us are in here.

This book will tell you how many Americans believe in the Devil, keep up with astrology, wear uniforms to work, enjoy oral sex, dip snuff, and have sweaty hands. You will learn that the average baby pees a pint a day, that the average American goes to bed earlier on Thursday than on any other night, and that Rutherford B. Hayes was as average a President as you're likely to find.

The average, when you stop to think about it, is a funny concept. Nothing is so commonplace, yet so full of surprises. Although "average" describes all of us, it describes none of us.

In fact, if you can find the average American, stuff him, mount him, and charge people a quarter to look at him. Or her. He will resist the label; no one considers himself ordinary, common, garden variety, or run of the mill. Politicians have stopped talking about "the common man," because every voter counts himself out of that crowd. We Americans don't want to be average, and we don't want the average man or woman to write our books, share our beds, or marry our children.

But though none of us wants to *be* the average American, we all want to know him. He defines the national character, etches the routines of everyday life. It is the average, not the exceptional, that reveals whether we as a people are charitable or greedy, diligent or lazy, prim or prurient.

Averages also give us a benchmark to measure ourselves against. Do you sleep, earn, owe, work, jog, make love, eat, laugh, loaf, or sweat more than average? Turn these pages and you'll find out.

We have measured the average American in bed, in church, at the table, and on the bathroom scale. Every year, he swallows 215 aspirins, 50 bananas, and 374 beers. His dog weighs 32 pounds. He is home sick from work 6 days a year, takes off another 3 days, and even on the job goofs off 45 minutes a day.

Because facts about the average American are constantly popping up, we're continuing to collect our data. If you come across something pertinent, we'd appreciate it if you'd share it with us. Our address is 5154 34th Street NW, Washington, D.C. 20008.

Finally, did you know that about half the people in America are below average?

Not you. Not us.

Them.

> *Mike Feinsilber*
> *William B. Mead*

Every normal person, in fact, is only normal on the average.

—SIGMUND FREUD

In the average man is curled
The hero stuff that rules the world.
—SAM WALTER FOSS, American farmer, news-
paperman, humorist, and poet, 1858–1911

AMERICAN AVERAGES

1 On an Average Day in America

10,930,000 cows are milked.
500 million cups of coffee are drunk.
80 million people hear Muzak.
Schoolchildren ride 12,720,000 miles on school buses.
10,205 people give blood.
1,253 people are arrested on marijuana charges.
1 of every 6 Americans sits down with a good book.
$54,794 is spent to fight dandruff.
10,000 people take their first airplane ride.
205 animals are buried in pet cemeteries.
3 million people go to the movies.
Bricklayers lay 22,741,000 bricks.
180 women are raped, 53 people are murdered, 1,108 people are robbed, and 2,618 cars are stolen.
Amateurs take 19,178,000 snapshots.
9,077 babies are born, including about 360 twins or triplets. 1,282 of them are illegitimate. Between 16 and 27 of them were conceived through artificial insemination.

4 square miles of good farmland are taken over for housing, roads, or shopping centers.

2,466 children are bitten by dogs.

4,109 people parachute from airplanes for the fun of it.

Government inspectors seize 718 pounds of meat that travelers are trying to sneak into the United States.

679 million telephone conversations occur, 50 million of which are long-distance.

5,962 couples wed, and before the sun sets 2,986 couples divorce.

Drunk drivers do $18 million worth of damage.

U.S. rivers discharge 1.3 million tons of sediment.

The typical American spends 2 hours reading, if you count signboards, labels, and the daily mail.

41 million people go to school.

People smoke 1.6 billion cigarettes.

People drink 90 million cans of beer.

48,800 rural mail carriers drive 2.2 million miles.

Every one of us produces nearly 6 pounds of garbage.

1,644 people buy hearing aids.

1,370 men undergo vasectomies.

1,169,863 people take a taxi.

176,810,950 eggs are laid.

56,000 animals are turned over to animal shelters; 36,986 dogs and cats are put to death in these establishments.

$10 million is spent on advertising.

191,952 clothespins are manufactured.

5,041 people observe their 65th birthday.

2,740 kids run away from home.

Motorists pay $4,036,000 in tolls.

214,795 hogs are slaughtered.

11,419,178 people take a bus, and 3,943,000 take a subway, elevated, or commuter train; another 147,671 ride a trolley.

10 doctors are disciplined by state medical boards.

21,000 gallons of oil are spilled from tankers and barges.

438 immigrants become U.S. citizens.

88 million people watch prime-time TV.

2,740 teen-agers get pregnant.

240 patents are issued.

1 American in 8 has a beer.

3,425 carloads of grain are sent to market.

63,288 cars crash, killing 129 people.

8 children swallow toys and are taken to hospital emergency rooms.

Fires kill 32 people, and damage 1,855 houses, 434 apartment buildings, 94 school and college buildings, 83 hospitals and nursing homes, 326 stores and offices, 65 restaurants and taverns, 142 factories, 177 warehouses, and 82 farm buildings.

38,690 people go to hear a major symphony orchestra.

28 mailmen are bitten by dogs.

2 billion $1.00 bills are in circulation.

Tobacco chewers chew up 1.3 million packages of the stuff.

Industry generates nearly 1 pound of hazardous waste for every person in America.

230 people are arrested for stealing cars.

1.1 million people are in the hospital.

3,231 women have abortions.

3 bike riders are killed in accidents; 15 people drown.

The U. S. Postal Service sells 90 million stamps, handles 320 million pieces of mail, and delivers 833,000 packages.

180,000 people buy a new radio.

5,200 people die, 1,070 of them from cancer.

1,885,000 people go to sleep in a hotel or motel.

2,008 tons of disposable plastics—dry-cleaning bags, Styrofoam cups, plastic plates, and the like—are thrown out.

Americans buy 3,287 sets of encyclopedias.

The average motorist drives 24 miles.

2 Life, Death, and the Average Body

How long will you live? At the turn of the century, 1 American in 25 reached age 65. Today, 1 in 5 does. And by the year 2000, 1 American in 5 will be 65 or older.

On average, a newborn baby in the United States can expect to live 72 years and 10 months. Not bad. A baby born in 1900 had only 48 years to live. Babies born in 1940 could expect 63 years of life.

Babies are fragile. Of every 1,000 babies born in the United States, 14 die before their first birthday, most of them before they are 1 month old. A newborn babe is less likely to survive the coming year than a 64-year-old.

But after that first year, things get better. On your first birthday, based on average life expectancies, you have longer to live than you did on the day you were born.

And the longer you stay alive, the greater chance you have of exceeding that initial expectancy of 72 years, 10 months.

At age 10, you can expect to live another 64 years, to the age of 74.

When you are 29, you pick up another year, to age 75.

At 55, you have 23 years to go, and at 62, your life prospects bloom into the 80s. The average 75-year-old can look forward to an 85th birthday—but not an 86th.

People 85 or older—the government lumps them all together —have another 6 years to go, on average.

Actually, things are a few years better than that for women and a few years worse for men. Baby girls can expect to live to age 76½—7½ years longer than baby boys.

That's why widows outnumber widowers in the United States, 3 to 1.

The longer a man lives, the more he narrows that 7½-year gap. But the woman never yields the advantage.

Race makes a difference, too, but not as much as sex. On average, whites in the United States live 5 years longer than "all others," as the government calls them. Life expectancy at birth is 77.3 years for a white girl, 72.6 years for a nonwhite girl, 69.7 years for a white boy, and 64.1 years for a nonwhite boy. A black baby is twice as likely to die before age 5 as a white baby.

Among really old folks, the "others" surpass the whites. On average, a nonwhite woman 85 or older has 9 years to live, nearly 3 years more than a white woman of the same age. A man 85 or older lives another 7 years if he is not white but only 5 years if he is white.

You are more likely to die in March than in any other month, and least likely to die in August.

You can look up your age on this chart and tell how much longer you have to live, assuming that you are average. The figures were compiled by the National Center for Health Statistics, a government agency.

Age	Years to live		Age	Years to live	
	MALE	FEMALE		MALE	FEMALE
Newborn	69.0	76.7	8	62.5	70.0
1	69.2	76.7	9	61.5	69.0
2	68.3	75.8			
3	67.3	74.8	10	60.5	68.0
4	66.4	73.9	11	59.5	67.0
5	65.4	72.9	12	58.6	66.0
6	64.4	71.9	13	57.6	65.0
7	63.5	70.9	14	56.6	64.1

Age	Years to live		Age	Years to live	
	MALE	FEMALE		MALE	FEMALE
15	55.7	63.1	50	24.2	30.1
16	54.7	62.1	51	23.4	29.2
17	53.8	61.1	52	22.6	28.4
18	52.9	60.2	53	21.9	27.5
19	51.9	59.2	54	21.1	26.7
			55	20.4	25.8
20	51.0	58.2	56	19.6	25.0
21	50.1	57.3	57	18.9	24.2
22	49.2	56.3	58	18.2	23.4
23	48.3	55.4	59	17.5	22.6
24	47.4	54.4			
25	46.5	53.4	60	16.8	21.8
26	45.6	52.5	61	16.2	21.0
27	44.7	51.5	62	15.5	20.3
28	43.8	50.5	63	14.9	19.5
29	42.8	49.6	64	14.3	18.8
			65	13.7	18.0
30	41.9	48.6	66	13.1	17.3
31	41.0	47.6	67	12.6	16.6
32	40.1	46.7	68	12.0	15.2
33	39.2	45.7	69	11.5	15.1
34	38.2	44.8			
35	37.3	43.8	70	10.9	14.4
36	36.4	42.9	71	10.4	13.7
37	35.5	41.9	72	9.9	13.1
38	34.6	41.0	73	9.5	12.4
39	33.6	40.0	74	9.0	11.8
			75	8.6	11.2
40	32.7	39.1	76	8.2	10.7
41	31.9	38.2	77	7.8	10.1
42	31.0	37.3	78	7.4	9.6
43	30.1	36.3	79	7.1	9.1
44	29.2	35.4			
45	28.4	34.5	80	6.8	8.7
46	27.5	33.6	81	6.5	8.2
47	26.7	32.7	82	6.2	7.8
48	25.9	31.8	83	5.9	7.3
49	25.0	31.0	84	5.6	6.9
			85	5.3	6.6

The knife and you. Every year, 1 of every 11 Americans undergoes surgery.

Of every 50 operations, 43 are "elective." That means the patient decides whether to go through with it.

Of every 650 patients, 1 fails to survive.

The unswelled head. The average man would take a hat size 7⅛ or smaller, if he wore a hat. Men's heads are the only parts of their bodies that haven't grown bigger for generations.

The middle age. In 1970, the median age in the United States was 27.9 years—half the people were younger than that, and half were older. By 1977, it had advanced to 29.4 years.

The population by age. According to projections by the U.S. Bureau of the Census, the average American will be 30 in 1980, 32 in 1985, 34 in 1990, 36 in 1995, and 37 in the year 2000.

Here's a breakdown by age group of 100 average Americans:

Age	1976	1985	2000
Under 5	7	7	6
5 to 13	15	12	12
14 to 17	8	6	6
18 to 24	13	12	9
25 to 34	15	17	14
35 to 44	11	14	17
45 to 54	11	10	15
55 to 64	9	10	10
65 and over	11	12	13

Tranquil America. In America, 1 woman in 5 and 1 man in 7 takes the tranquilizer Valium, the most widely prescribed medicine in the world. U.S. doctors write 60 million Valium prescriptions a year, and their patients shell out half a billion dollars for the stuff.

What health costs. A total of $863.01 was spent on the health of the average American in 1978. That's up from $22.65 in 1935.

The average American coughs up $.33 of every dollar spent on his or her health. Health insurance pays $.27, charity kicks in a penny, and the remaining $.39 is paid by the government.

Due to what is covered by health insurance and what is not, the average American spends more out of pocket for drugs than for doctors. On average, Americans pay 84 per cent of their drug bills and 76 per cent of their dentist bills, but only 35 per cent of their doctor bills and 9 per cent of their hospital bills.

The older you are, the more your health care costs. For every dollar spent on the health of an average child through age 18, two dollars are spent on the health of the average adult, age 19 through 64, and six dollars are spent on the health of the average American 65 or older.

One at a time, but often. The average person's feet hit the floor 7,000 times a day. Each.

Swelled feet. The average person's feet swell in the course of the day so that at day's end his or her feet are 5 per cent bigger than they were in the morning. On hot days, they're 10 per cent bigger.

Soft and lovely. The average American female is 28 per cent fat. The average American male is 15 per cent fat.

The average woman gains 3 pounds every 5 years.

The typical overweight man has a pot belly. The typical overweight woman packs it onto her hips and thighs.

Listen to the decibel. Decibels indicate the intensity of sound. The least perceptible sound registers 1 decibel. A whisper 15 feet away produces 30 decibels. Leaves rustle at 20 decibels. Freeway traffic registers 80 decibels at 50 feet.

According to the Better Hearing Institute of Washington, D.C., the noise level in the average home is about 70 decibels. In the average factory, it is about 85 decibels—the level at which prolonged exposure can damage hearing. That's about the level of noise an electric shaver emits into the shaver's ears, too.

A conversation in a normal tone emits 60 decibels. A passenger in a car is exposed to 70. A screaming child gives off 90 decibels, on average, and would cause hearing damage if he or she kept it up for 8 hours.

The Led Zeppelin, in full concert, pound out 123 decibels. The average discotheque blasts away at 110, and exposure there for more than 30 consecutive minutes would be harmful, according to the Occupational Safety and Health Administration. The threshold of pain for the average person is 140 decibels.

In a survey of more than 4,000 freshmen at the University of Tennessee's Noise Study Lab, 60 per cent were shown to be suffering from some hearing impediment.

Here are some noises and the duration of safe exposure for the average person, according to the Better Hearing Institute:

	Decibels	Safe Exposure
Riding in a car	70	no limit
Standing in a factory	85	16 hours
Being passed by a motorcycle	90	8 hours
Riding a subway	100	2 hours
Riding a helicopter	105	1 hour
Using a power mower	105	1 hour
Sandblasting	110	30 minutes
Standing next to an air-raid siren	130	3¾ minutes
Firing guns	140	dangerous for any time
Standing beside a jet engine	140	dangerous for any time
Standing nearby a rocket launching	180	dangerous for any time

What with food processors, garbage disposals, dishwashers, and blenders, the kitchen is the noisiest room in the average home.

Here are the average noise levels of some machines used in and around the house, as heard by someone close to the appliance:

	Decibels
Stereo	up to 120
Chainsaw	100
Riding mower	90 to 95
Power mower	87 to 92
Home shop tools	85
Electric lawn edger	81
Garbage disposal	67 to 93
Sewing machine	64 to 74
Vacuum cleaner	62 to 85
Hair dryer	59 to 80
Clothes dryer	55
Dishwasher	54 to 85
Washing machine	47 to 78
Refrigerator	40
Floor fan	38 to 70

Delicate machinery. Three of every 10 important diseases suffered by women are in the reproductive organs.

I can't make it today, boss. The average American is sick in bed 7 days a year, missing 5 days of work.

Squish. The average man takes in and gets rid of about three quarts of water a day—mostly by drinking and urinating. But not all.

According to Charles Kleeman, in *Clinical Disorders of Fluid and Electrolyte Metabolism,* the average man drinks nearly 2 quarts of water a day and gets the third quart through other means. He gets four fifths of a quart directly from his food (the moisture in a nice slice of chocolate cake, for a good example) and another three tenths of a quart when the body breaks down foodstuffs into their elements (when the carbohydrates in the chocolate cake are ultimately broken down into water and carbon dioxide, for instance).

To operate properly—so that his kidneys can dissolve and

excrete salt, for example—the average man is obliged to take in 2 quarts of water per day. The third quart is extracurricular.

Two of the quarts exit as urine; half a quart is sweated away; four tenths of a quart is exhaled; a seventh of a quart is in the excrement.

Miscarriages. Of every 100 conceptions, 55 abort spontaneously —40 of them before the first menstrual period is missed and before the woman even suspects she is pregnant, according to Dr. Dwight Cruikshank, assistant professor of obstetrics and gynecology at the University of Iowa. He says that after standard tests confirm pregnancy, at about 6 weeks, a woman still has a 15 per cent to 20 per cent chance of aborting spontaneously.

What's on the average American's mind. About 100,000 hairs grow at any one time atop the typical human head. Each grows about 5 inches a year, and lasts up to 6 years before falling out. About 100 come loose on the average day. If people didn't patronize barbers, the average person with straight hair would have it reaching to his or her hips.

Say again? The average person hears better at age 10 than he or she ever will again.

The epileptic. On average, a woman is more likely to have an epileptic child if she is a teen-ager, a drug addict, or an alcoholic.

According to the Epilepsy Foundation of America, the average epileptic makes $148.53 a week, $36.47 less than the average American.

The average epileptic spends $213 a year on drugs to help control seizures.

Old folks in hospitals. Of every 100 Americans 65 or over, 35 a year are hospitalized. Their average stay is 12 days.

This list will make you sick. But don't blame us. The chart was worked up by Dr. Thomas H. Holmes and Richard Rahe of the

University of Washington. Their research concludes that change, whether good or bad, produces stress, and hence illness.

If any of these things have happened to you in the past 12 months, fill in the value. Then add them all up. If your score tops 300, chances are 4 to 1 that you've been sick, or soon will be. If your score is 150 to 299, you've got a 50-50 chance of escaping illness. Under 150, the odds are 7 to 3 in your favor.

Item value	Life event	Your score
100	Death of spouse	
73	Divorce	
65	Marital separation	
63	Jail term	
63	Death of close family member	
53	Personal injury or illness	
50	Marriage	
47	Loss of job	
45	Marital reconciliation	
45	Retirement	
44	Change in health of family member	
40	Pregnancy	
39	Sex difficulties	
39	Addition of new family member	
39	Business readjustment	
38	Change in financial state	
37	Death of close friend	
36	Change to different line of work	
35	Change in number of arguments with spouse	
31	Mortgage over $10,000	
30	Foreclosure of mortgage or loan	
29	Change in responsibilities at work	
29	Son or daughter leaving home	
29	Trouble with in-laws	
28	Outstanding personal achievement	
26	Wife begins or stops work	
26	Begin or end school	
25	Change in living conditions	

Item value	Life event	Your score
24	Revision of personal habits	
23	Trouble with boss	
20	Change in work hours or conditions	
20	Change in residence	
20	Change in schools	
19	Change in recreation pattern	
19	Change in church activities	
18	Change in social activities	
17	Mortgage or loan less than $10,000	
16	Change in sleeping habits	
15	Change in number of family get-togethers	
15	Change in eating habits	
13	Vacation	
12	Christmas	
11	Minor violations of the law	

Ulcers. On average, 1 man in 10 gets ulcers.

Blindness. You have 1 chance in 470 of losing your sight.
  One American in 5 wears bifocals.

Long-lived babies. Babies born in the year 2000 will live to be 74, on average, the Census Bureau estimates, as opposed to the 72 years, 10 months, that babies born in 1977 can expect to live. The average baby born in 2050 will live 76 years, 5 months. Some people may think that women won't outlive men then, because so many women will be working, and work is supposed to create stress. But the government predicts that the average woman of the twenty-first century will outlive the typical man by just as many years as she does today.

What Kills Us

Your turn will come. Of every 1,000 people in America today, 9 won't be around a year from now.

It's a matter of life or death. Here are the odds against your dying within a year, based on your age and sex:

Age	Male	Female
Under 1 year	57 to 1	70 to 1
1 to 4	1,282 to 1	1,639 to 1
5 to 9	2,439 to 1	3,571 to 1
10 to 14	2,273 to 1	4,000 to 1
15 to 19	714 to 1	1,887 to 1
20 to 24	505 to 1	1,563 to 1
25 to 29	535 to 1	1,389 to 1
30 to 34	508 to 1	1,053 to 1
35 to 39	382 to 1	719 to 1
40 to 44	246 to 1	444 to 1
45 to 49	154 to 1	281 to 1
50 to 54	98 to 1	186 to 1
55 to 59	63 to 1	124 to 1
60 to 64	40 to 1	81 to 1
65 to 69	28 to 1	58 to 1
70 to 74	18 to 1	35 to 1
75 to 79	12 to 1	21 to 1
80 to 84	9 to 1	13 to 1
85 or older	6 to 1	7 to 1

Look out for weekends, Mondays, and most holidays. You're more likely to die on those days. Christmas, New Year's, and the Fourth of July are the worst.

You're twice as likely to be murdered on Christmas or New Year's as on an average day. On the other hand, Memorial Day and Labor Day are nice; fewer people die then than on an average day.

As you might expect, Monday is a big day for suicide. And, on average, you're more likely to die on Monday than on any other day of the week from a heart attack, a stroke, or—tied with Sunday—pneumonia or the flu.

Cancer. Your chances of eventually getting cancer are 1 in 4, according to the American Cancer Society.

In 1900, 65 of 100,000 Americans died of cancer. By

1960, that proportion had more than doubled, to 150 in 100,000. But don't worry too much. The difference is due in large part to the dramatic increase in life expectancy in this century: The longer you live the more likely that you will die of cancer rather than of something else.

The chances of someone in your family getting cancer are 2 in 3.

If you get cancer this year, chances are 2 in 3 that you will be dead within 5 years.

Of every 4 people who die of cancer, 1 might have lived if the disease had been diagnosed and treated earlier.

Cancer's favorite countries. A Scot has 1 chance in 488 of dying from cancer this year. That's the worst odds anywhere in the world, according to the American Cancer Society.

The United States ranks twenty-second. Cancer has 1 chance in 636 of getting the average American this year.

If that scares you, move to Thailand. The average Thai has a cancer death risk this year of 1 in 3,401.

Beating the reaper. If heart disease were eliminated, the average newborn American could expect to live an additional 6 years.

Another 6 years would be added to average life expectancy if we eliminated diseases of the kidney, blood vessels, and other ducts—what doctors call vascular-renal diseases.

If we won the war against cancer, we would add 2½ years to the life of an average newborn. Three quarters of a year would be added to the average baby's life if we eliminated fatal auto accidents, and another three quarters of a year would be added if all other lethal accidents were eradicated.

Average life expectancy would increase by a half year if there were no more suicide or homicide.

Sunstroke. Hot weather kills 450 Americans in an average year, snowstorms kill 97, and floods kill 83.

Suicide. Suicide is consistently among the 10 leading causes of death in America. In the average year, 25,000 people in this country kill themselves, and another 200,000 try to.

Men commit suicide 3 to 4 times more often than women, and three quarters of the men who end their lives had been fired or had suffered a sharp loss of income. In the United States, women are 50 per cent more likely to kill themselves than to be murdered. But women are only a quarter as likely as men to be murder victims, and only a third as likely to kill themselves.

One survey found that 53 per cent of people asked said they knew someone who had committed suicide, and for 21 per cent a suicide or attempted suicide had involved someone close.

Researchers say two thirds of those who commit suicide give warnings—direct or indirect—of their intention. Those who are talked out of it are usually grateful.

The average college student is half again as likely to commit suicide as the typical nonstudent of the same age.

In the past couple of decades, suicides among the young have tripled. Three out of 4 young suicide attempts are girls. Suicide is the second or third major killer of the young in every industrialized society. In the United States, auto wrecks rank first, other accidents second, and suicides third.

The yellow killer. In an average year in this country, school-bus accidents kill 98 students, 7 bus drivers, and 80 other people. Only 13 of the 98 students are killed inside the bus. The other 85 are pedestrians; half of them are hit by the school bus, half by another car. About another 6,100 students are injured in school-bus accidents in an average year, 5,673 of whom are in the bus.

Per mile driven, a school bus faces about the same accident risk as a car.

How to get a heart attack. According to the Framingham Heart Study, which kept track of 2,200 men for 8 years, the man with a blood cholesterol level of 300 or more has triple the risk of heart attack as does someone with a cholesterol level below 175.

That's averaging everyone. It's worse for younger men. The

cholesterol level for the average American male is about 225. A man in his 30s with a level about 240 has triple the risk of heart attack as a man with the same age with a cholesterol level below 220.

If you're over 50, breathe easy. According to the study, cholesterol levels don't seem to mean much after that.

But high blood pressure can get you at any age. If your diastolic blood pressure (that's the bottom figure) is 95 to 105, you have mild hypertension—and double the heart-attack risk of someone with normal blood pressure (from 75 to 85). If your blood pressure is above 105, your risk is triple that of the person with normal pressure.

A man who smokes a pack of cigarettes a day doubles his risk of heart attack. If he smokes more than a pack a day, his heart-attack risk is triple that of an average nonsmoker.

The average pipe smoker or cigar smoker is about tied with the ex-cigarette smoker. They both have just a little higher risk of heart attack than does a nonsmoker.

That's for men. The average woman smoker doesn't have as much to worry about, as far as her heart goes.

But diabetes works the other way. A woman diabetic in her 30s has about 5 times the heart-attack risk of a woman the same age without diabetes. For men that age, diabetes doesn't quite double the risk of heart attack.

You also increase your risk of heart attack if you are fat, old, sedentary, aggressive, or have a family history of premature heart disease.

All these causes aside, the average man is more likely to have a heart attack than the average woman.

Cancertown, U.S.A. In an average American city of 50,000, 75 will die this year from cancer. The disease will eventually kill another 7,500, says the American Cancer Society, if present death rates continue.

Where accidents kill you. You are much more likely to be killed in a car wreck in the West than in any other part of the country.

Driving the same distance in each state, you are twice as

likely to die in your car in New Mexico, which has the highest
death rate, as in Massachusetts, which has the lowest.

After New Mexico, you are most likely to die in an auto accident in Nevada, Wyoming, Arizona, Idaho, Mississippi,
Alaska, and Louisiana, in that order.

Among cities of 350,000 people or more, you are 5 times
as likely to be killed in a car wreck in Atlanta, which ranks
No. 1, as in Boston or Buffalo, which tie for the safety award.
After Atlanta come Nashville, Houston, Phoenix, and Dallas,
in that order. After Boston and Buffalo, the safest cities to
drive in are Washington, Indianapolis, and Milwaukee.

If you're going to die in a collision, odds are 6 to 1 that
it will be a collision with another car, not with a fixed object
like a tree or a bridge abutment.

An American is 11 times more likely than an Egyptian to
die in an auto accident. But Portugal has the worst ratio of
auto deaths to population, followed by Venezuela, Canada,
Australia, Belgium, West Germany, France, and the United
States, in that order.

Murder, here and there. On average, an American's risk of
being murdered is several times that of a person in Australia,
Austria, Belgium, Canada, Denmark, Finland, France, West
Germany, Ireland, Italy, Japan, Holland, Norway, Sweden,
Switzerland, or Britain.

Men are accident prone. A man is almost 3 times as likely
as a woman to be killed in a car wreck, and more than 5
times as likely to drown or be accidentally shot to death.

In fact, most any kind of accident you can think of kills
more males than females. A man is twice as likely to be fatally
poisoned and 3 times as likely to be asphyxiated. He is half
again as likely as a woman to die in a fire or choke to death
on something, and a tiny bit more likely to die in a fall.

Gunpoint politics. There was a political assassination or attempted assassination an average of once every 7.3 years between 1865 and 1975 in the United States.

Killers. On average, heart disease is much more likely to kill you than anything else, followed in order by cancer, stroke, accident, flu or pneumonia, diabetes, cirrhosis of the liver, arteriosclerosis, suicide, murder, and emphysema.

Take care of your ticker. Of every 100 Americans who die, 35 die from heart disease, 21 from cancer, and 44 from something else.

The older you get, the more likely it becomes that your death will be caused by heart failure of one kind or another.

Together, heart disease and cancer account for more than half of the deaths of people 45 to 54 years old, and two thirds of the deaths of people between 55 and 64.

Through age 34, accidents are the biggest killers. Then disease takes over.

If you are going to die between 25 and 44, cancer is a bit more likely to get you than heart disease. After that, the averages tilt in favor of heart disease.

To avoid violent death, live longer. Among Americans who die after their seventy-fifth birthday, only 1 in 50 is murdered, commits suicide, or is killed in an accident. Among Americans who die between the ages of 15 and 24, 3 of every 4 are murdered, commit suicide, or are killed in an accident.

Dead, anyway. Of every 100 murder victims in the United States:

  64 are shot to death
  18 are stabbed
   5 are done in with a club, hammer, or other blunt instrument
   8 are strangled or beaten
   1 is burned to death
   4 are poisoned, drowned, killed by bombs, or victimized by other means.

War. Figures from the Veterans Administration show that some wars are vastly more unsafe than others. One American participant in 143 in the War of 1812 (which lasted until

1815) died in service. By contrast, 1 of every 6 Union soldiers in the Civil War and 1 in 6 American soldiers in the Mexican War died in service. Proportionately, those were America's most deadly wars.

All told, 1,215,000 Americans have died and 42,287,000 have served in America's wars, so the average war has consumed 1 of every 35 of its American participants.

	American Deaths	Death Ratios
War of 1812 (1812–15)	2,000	1 in 143
Korean Conflict (1950–55)	55,000	1 in 124
Indian Wars (1817–98)	1,000	1 in 106
Vietnam (1964–75)	109,000	1 in 90
American Revolution (1775–83)	4,000	1 in 73
World War I (1917–8)	116,000	1 in 40
World War II (1940–45)	406,000	1 in 40
Spanish-American War (1898–1902)	11,000	1 in 35
Civil War (1861–65)		
Confederates	134,000	1 in 8
Union	364,000	1 in 6
Mexican War (1846–48)	13,000	1 in 6

Crib death. One baby in 750 dies from sudden infant death syndrome, or "crib death."

For a white baby girl, chances are only 1 in 910. A nonwhite baby boy faces the greatest risk: 1 in 365.

When accidents kill. You are more likely to die in a car wreck during August than in any other month. February is the safest month to drive.

You are most likely to burn, strangle, or fall to your death during January, most likely to drown in July, most likely to be accidentally shot to death in November, and most likely to be fatally poisoned in March.

The hazards of youth. In 1925, an average teen-ager had 1 chance in 2,222 of dying in some kind of accident. Fifty years later, the odds had become worse: 1 in 1,750.

Teen-age suicide rates doubled in the same half century, and the percentage of murdered teens almost doubled.

The average teen-ager is 1.6 times as likely to be murdered as to die from cancer.

Car wrecks have been the biggest single killer of teen-agers since 1940.

Waiting too long. The National Heart and Lung Institute says 350,000 people a year die from heart attacks before getting to a hospital.

On average, these victims wait 3 hours before deciding to get help.

Death around the clock. One American dies in an accident every 5½ minutes, and one is injured in an accident every 20 seconds.

But cashing in is awkward. The minerals and trace elements in the average person's body were worth $7.28 in 1980. That's a 643 per cent increase in only 10 years.

Thunderbolts. Each year between 1970 and 1976, the United States averaged

   25 deaths from hurricanes
 115 deaths from tornadoes
 167 deaths from flash floods
 200 deaths from lightning and its aftereffects.

The gas within. According to a study published in the *New England Journal of Medicine,* the average person releases about 6.1 cubic inches of rectal gas an hour. But this can be expected to increase by 68 per cent if he or she eats a diet in which 51 per cent of the calories are provided by baked beans.

The average person breaks wind 14 times a day.

Rectal gas is composed primarily of hydrogen and carbon dioxide, with traces of nitrogen, pure oxygen, and carbohydrates.

Elimination, one way or the other. While most people sweat more on hot days, they urinate more on cold days.

Lab tests. The average American undergoes 25 medical lab tests in a year.

The stuff we take. Each of us spent $17.46 in 1976 for nonprescription pills, tonics, balms, and the like. So says the Proprietary Association, whose members make the stuff.

In that year, the average American spent $2.21 for vitamins, $3.76 for cough and cold medicines, $1.20 for laxatives, $3.63 for aspirin and other analgesics, $.61 for tonics and such, $.68 for stomach settlers, $.50 for suntan oils, and $.06 for athlete's-foot medications.

Life in the womb. An average fetus 12 weeks old weighs only half an ounce and is only 3 inches long. In the next 4 weeks, it grows to nearly 4 ounces in weight and a little over 6 inches in length.

At 24 weeks—roughly two thirds of the way—it weighs 1 pound, 6½ ounces, and is 11%10 inches long.

After the full pregnancy term of 266 days, the average fetus weighs 7 pounds, 5 ounces, and is 1 foot, 8 inches long.

What a time to diet! The average baby loses 7 ounces in his or her first 2 days of life, and gains back 6 ounces during the next 4 days. Most of it is fluid; babies start out pretty wet, and a lot of it evaporates the first couple of days. Although they suck a lot, babies don't really take in much milk until their third day of life.

Let's weigh baby. The average newborn baby boy weighs 7 pounds, 11 ounces. The typical newborn baby girl weighs 7 pounds, 2 ounces.

Breast-fed babies gain weight a little faster, on average, than bottle-fed babies.

Let's assume our baby boy and baby girl are breast fed. At eight weeks, he weighs 11 pounds, 3 ounces; she weighs 10 pounds, 1 ounce. At 20 weeks, he's up to 15 pounds, 12 ounces, she to 14 pounds, 6 ounces.

At 40 weeks, he tops 20 pounds by 5 ounces. She weighs in at 18 pounds, 8 ounces.

Happy birthday! He weighs 22 pounds, 9 ounces. She weighs 21 pounds, 5 ounces.

Boys and girls. For every 100 girls who are born, 105 boys are born. But girls are sturdier, so by the adolescent years they outnumber boys. The older they get, the more disproportionate, too. By age 65, there are 100 women for every 72 men.

Son-rise and Daughter-rise. The average American 2-year-old stands 32.2 inches tall, whether a boy or a girl. The boy weighs 27.2 pounds; the girl weighs 26 pounds even.

At 5, the boy is 3 feet, 7.3 inches tall and weighs 41.2 pounds. The girl is .6 inch shorter and 2.2 pounds lighter.

Girls catch up at age 9 and quickly edge ahead. The average 10-year-old girl is 4 feet, 6.4 inches tall and weighs 71.76 pounds. The typical boy that age is .3 inch shorter and weighs 2.4 pounds less.

Twelve is the age at which girls stand the tallest, relatively speaking; the average girl is .7 inch taller, and 4 pounds heavier, than the average boy her age. She stands 4 feet, 11.6 inches tall and weighs 91.6 pounds.

Boys edge ahead again at 14. At 15, the average boy is 5 feet, 6.5 inches tall, and weighs 125 pounds. The typical girl is 5 feet, 3.7 inches tall, and weighs 118.3 pounds.

At 18, the average boy stands 5 feet, 9.6 inches tall, and weighs 151.8 pounds. The average girl is 5 feet, 4.4 inches tall, and weighs 124.8 pounds.

Sweat. The average body has 2,300,000 sweat glands.

The envelope we're in. The average person has about 2 square yards of skin weighing about 7 pounds.

Who's hospitalized? On average, a woman is 12 per cent more likely to be hospitalized than a man, even if you don't count pregnancy-related problems or childbirth. But once in the hospital, the man stays a day longer. The average hospital patient is there for 8 days, at a cost (in 1978) of $109.05 per day.

So why does it take so long to buzz a nurse? In an average American hospital, there are 3 to 4 employees for every patient. Thirty years ago, the average hospital had 1.7 employees for every patient.

The odds on disease. Not counting cancer or heart ailments, the serious disease you are most likely—by far—to get is

gonorrhea.

But there is about only 1 chance in 200 that you will catch it this year.

For any given year, there is only about 1 chance in 3,000 that you will get the mumps, 1 in 6,000 that you will get tuberculosis, and 1 in 10,000 that you will get the measles.

You are less likely to get polio than leprosy or tularemia (sometimes called "rabbit fever"). But don't worry. Your chances of getting either disease are less than 1 in a million.

Your chances of catching the chicken pox this year are about 7 in 10,000.

Pinworms. One American in 10 has pinworms in any given year. Kids between 4 and 12 have them most. Pinworms do not discriminate. "Members of the most fastidious of households can become infected," according to the New York *Times*.

Yawn oh ouch ump puff. One of every 6 Americans finds it hard to get up in the morning, and 1 in 11 has trouble getting to sleep at night. One of every 9 has back pains, and 1 of every 59 feels dizzy. One of every 11 is fidgety, 1 of every 33 has sweaty hands, and 1 of every 19 gets tired quickly. One of every 27 hasn't much appetite. One of every 11 is smoking more, and 1 of every 45 is drinking more.

Whoops. Four out of 10 hospital patients in this country have operations. Six out of 10 malpractice claims are for alleged surgical boo-boos.

Better get the next plane home. On an average day, 19 Americans die abroad.

Who has health insurance. Of every 100 Americans, 80 have private health insurance or Medicare, 6 are on Medicaid, 2 come under some other program, and 11 have no health coverage. That adds up to 99 because we rounded the numbers.

About 93 per cent of professional and technical workers —doctors, lawyers, engineers, and the like—have health insurance, but only 54 per cent of farm workers do.

The poorer you are and the younger you are, the more likely you don't have health coverage.

Americans with a family income under $10,000 are twice as likely to lack health insurance as persons with a family income of $10,000 to $15,000. The former are 3 times as likely to be without it as are Americans with an income above $15,000.

One of every 100 Americans 65 or older lacks health insurance. One of 5 Americans 19 to 24 years old doesn't have any.

On average, the worst combination is to be between 19 and 24 and have family income below $5,000. One of every 3 such persons has no health insurance.

Warning: The Surgeon General Has Determined That Cigarette Smoking Is Dangerous to Your Health.

Smoking kills. A cigarette smoker is 10 times more likely to get lung cancer than a nonsmoker, and twice as likely to die prematurely from coronary heart disease.

In an average year, according to the U. S. Public Health Service, 1 of every 677 people in America dies from cigarette smoking.

Cigarette smoking causes 9 of every 10 lung cancer cases, 8 of every 10 emphysema cases, 3 of every 10 cases of arteriosclerosis, and 7½ of every 10 bronchitis cases.

About 10 years after kicking the habit, the death risk to an ex-smoker is nearly the same as that of someone who never smoked.

One of every 4 Americans smokes cigarettes. Men with high incomes smoke less than men with low incomes. But women with high incomes are *more* likely to smoke than women with low incomes.

More men than women smoke, but teen-age boys and girls puff away at an equal rate.

The U. S. Public Health Service says that among teen-age girls, a cigarette smoker is much more likely than a non-smoker to use marijuana, get drunk, engage in sex, and hate school.

Quitting betters the odds. The average person 30 to 64 years old doubles his or her risk of death by smoking 2 packs of cigarettes a day. When he or she quits, the mortality ratio declines from 2 to 1 to

1.7 to 1 the first four years
1.6 to 1 the next five years
1.4 to 1 the next five years
1.1 to 1 after 15 years.

The smoke-filled room. Two thirds of the smoke from a burning cigarette enters the air around the smoker, not her or his lungs. The smoker inhales an average of 24 seconds per cigarette, but the cigarette burns for about 12 minutes, according to the American Lung Association. As a result, nonsmokers around smokers inhale lots of smoke.

In a smoky room, a nonsmoker could inhale enough nicotine and carbon monoxide in an hour to have the same effect as having smoked a whole cigarette. A study in Erie County, Pennsylvania, revealed that, on the average, the nonsmoking wives of smokers die four years younger than the nonsmoking wives of nonsmokers.

The clean-air premium. Among American men 30 years old, nonsmokers can expect to live

4.6 years longer than smokers of less than 10 cigarettes a day
5.5 years longer than smokers of 10 to 19 cigarettes a day
6.1 years longer than smokers of 20 to 39 cigarettes a day, and
8.1 years longer than smokers of 40 or more cigarettes a day.

The relative risks of cigars, cigarettes, and pipes. Compared with nonsmokers, a man increases his risk of death 19 per cent by smoking a pipe, 25 per cent by smoking cigars, and 85 per cent by smoking cigarettes.

Women, smoke, cancer. In an average year, more than 20,000 women get lung cancer. Nearly all are smokers; nearly all will die of their cancers. Women who smoke more than a pack a day are 10 times more likely to die of lung cancer than nonsmoking women. Women who are light smokers, but keep it up for 30 years, are also 10 times more likely to die of lung cancer. Since 1964, lung cancer has moved from the fifth to the third leading cause of death in women.

Women smokers are more likely than nonsmokers to suffer heart attacks and hemorrhages under the skull, to develop ulcers and cancers of the larynx and bladder, chronic lung diseases, and other respiratory diseases.

Women who smoke more than two packs a day, and inhale, die at twice the rate of women their age who don't smoke. Pregnant smokers have more spontaneous abortions. The babies of smokers are smaller at birth and, throughout life, never grow to the size of children born of nonsmokers. If they survive. The babies of smokers are more likely to die in infancy. These children score lower in psychological tests. They are more hyperactive. Children whose mothers smoked 10 cigarettes a day or more during pregnancy were shorter, and were three to five months behind the children of nonsmokers in reading, mathematics, and general ability.

The fetus gets less oxygen and more carbon dioxide when Mom smokes. Research indicates that a two-pack-a-day pregnant woman reduces her baby's oxygen supply by 40 per cent.

Cigarettes tax. Health economists at the University of California calculate that people who smoke cost us an average of

$459 each. We spend $8 billion a year treating smoke-related diseases, according to the National Commission on Smoking and Public Policy.

They quit. When the surgeon general's smoking report came out in 1964, more than half the men and a third of the women in America smoked. Now it's down to 39 per cent of the men and 29 per cent of the women. In the 11 years following the report, 29 million have quit—95 per cent by themselves, with no help from formal how-to-quit programs. Most quit cold turkey.

Two thirds of the physicians and 60 per cent of the dentists who used to smoke have quit. Four people in 5 in the health professions don't smoke.

Seventy per cent of heavy smokers say they'd quit if ordered to by the doctor. Only 5 per cent say they've talked to the doctor about their smoking.

Over half of divorced and separated people smoke.

I don't feel good, Mommy. The average American child gets sick three times a year.

Nursing homes. There is 1 nursing-home bed for every 16 senior citizens in America. More than a quarter of American women 85 or older live in nursing homes. For men, the figure is 17 per cent.

That's partly because the average man 65 or older is twice as likely still to be married as a woman the same age. Of every 2 American women 65 or older, 1 is a widow.

Popping health pills. According to the U. S. Department of Health and Human Services, 1 in 6 of us takes unprescribed nutritional supplements, such as vitamin pills, on the general theory that they'll do us some good.

Is my room ready? There are about 7 hospital beds for every 1,000 Americans.

Who is diabetic. A woman is half again as likely to get diabetes as a man, a black is more likely to get it than a white, and a poor person is more likely to get it than a rich person.

One of every 10 nonwhites 65 or older has diabetes.

A really fat man is 20 times more likely to get diabetes than a thin man is.

Bland Christmases. One American man in 10 suffers from hereditary blindness to shades of red and green.

Say, "Ahhh. . . ." The average American goes to the doctor 5 times a year. Rich people used to go more often than poor people, but now poor people go more often. The average American with an annual family income under $3,000 goes to the doctor 6.4 times a year. The average American with an annual family income of $25,000 or more goes 4.9 times a year.

Women go more than men. The older you get, the more often you see the doctor.

The unkindest cut. When 1,500 patients who were advised to undergo surgery sought a second medical opinion, 1 in 4 were spared from the knife, according to a study by Blue Cross-Blue Shield of Greater New York.

The Rx backlash. In the average year, adverse reactions to prescribed drugs kill 13,000 hospital patients, according to *The Handbook of Prescription Drugs*. Adverse reactions force another 1.5 million people into the hospital, and lengthen the stay of 18 to 30 of every 100 hospitalized patients.

Including Clark Kent. Eyeglasses are worn by 431 of every 1,000 boys and men, and 509 of every 1,000 girls and women, in America. Contact lenses are worn by 7 boys and men of every 1,000, and 18 girls and women of every 1,000.

By the time they're 45 years old, 883 of every 1,000 Americans wear glasses or contacts.

Keeps the backbone moist and supple. The average person has about a half cup of spinal fluid.

Doc

The doctor at work. According to an AMA poll of 5,288 physicians, the average doctor in America works 51 hours, 48 minutes a week, 47.2 weeks a year. He (or, 16 per cent of the time, she) sees 126 patients a week. Specialists in internal medicine tend to work the most, 55 hours, 12 minutes a week on average. Psychiatrists, on the other hand, leave for the golf course after 46 hours, 42 minutes a week. Country doctors work about 3.5 hours a week longer than big-city doctors. The average physician spends about 28 hours a week in his office, 10 hours on hospital rounds, 6.5 hours in the operating, delivery, or labor room, 54 minutes a week on house calls, and 3.5 hours a week running his or her office.

The cost of being a doctor. According to an AMA survey in 1976, the average doctor's professional expenses came to $42,443. That included $4,714 for malpractice insurance.

Doctors' roots. Four families in 10 earn over $15,000 a year, but they produce 65 per cent of all medical students.

Where the doctor is. For every 10,000 Americans, there were 14 doctors in 1960 and 18 in 1976. By 1990 there will be 24. One in 4 American doctors works in New York or California. There are 137 doctors actually engaged in caring for patients for every 100,000 Americans. Washington, D.C., ranks first, with 359 practicing doctors for every 100,000 residents, followed by New York (198 per 100,000), Massachusetts (186), Connecticut (178), and Maryland (169). At the bottom of the list are Mississippi (82), Alaska (79), Idaho (90), Arkansas (88), and Alabama (89).

In small-town and rural America, there are only 80 doctors for every 100,000 residents.

¿Que pasa, doc? One in 4 doctors practicing in the United States attended medical school abroad. Half of the foreign medical graduates in the United States went to med school in

1 of 8 countries: the Philippines, India, South Korea, Italy, West Germany, Cuba, Britain, or Mexico.

Hurrah for the docs. Asked to express their degree of confidence in 13 important institutions, Americans rated them in this order:

Medicine
Scientific community
Education
Military
Banks and other financial institutions
Organized religion
U. S. Supreme Court
Major companies
Press
Television
Executive branch of federal government
Congress
Organized labor

Cutting up. The average surgeon performs 211 operations a year and makes $69,910—a 1976 figure that has surely climbed since.

There is nearly 1 chance in 10 that you will undergo surgery this year. In 1965, chances were only 1 in 13. Patients eligible for Medicaid have twice as many operations as people who are not.

On average, surgeons charged $350 for an appendectomy in 1976, $543 to remove your gall bladder, $335 to fix a hernia, $694 for a prostate job, $629 for a hysterectomy, and $645 for a cataract operation.

The money in medicine. In 1976, the average American doctor netted $59,544 before taxes. So reports the American Medical Association. The income of self-employed doctors averaged $73,000 and was growing by 9.3 per cent a year.

The average obstetrician-gynecologist made $65,800. The average was $60,459 for internists, $60,059 for anesthesiologists, $47,565 for psychiatrists, $47,438 for general practitioners, and $46,962 for pediatricians.

By age, the doctors who averaged the highest income were those between 46 and 50, at $64,797, followed by those between 41 and 45, at $64,535. Old and young doctors averaged the least: $42,847 for doctors 61 and older, $43,746 for doctors 35 and younger.

For an average doctor, the optimum earning combination of specialty and age was to be a surgeon between 46 and 50 years old. Those fellows cleared $80,209 on average—and remember, that was back in 1976.

Not very sick. Half the time you go to the doctor, he thinks your ailment isn't at all serious, whether he tells you so or not, a government report says. Another third of the time he considers your condition only slightly serious.

As you get older, more of your complaints are serious, at least to the doctor.

The doctor's age. The average doctor in the United States is 46 years old.

Physician, heal thy image. In a survey of 1,759 patients by *Medical Economics* magazine, 1 in 2 thought his or her doctor "sees medicine chiefly as a business" and 9 in 10 thought his or her doctor should have to pass periodic tests to keep his or her license.

See you again, doc. On average, your doctor will prescribe a drug every other time you see him or her. Six out of every 10 times, he or she will schedule you for another appointment.

Madame Doctor. Sixteen out of 100 medical school graduates these days are women.

Next! An AMA survey shows that the average general practitioner sees 3.5 patients an hour. Country doctors see slightly more—3.85 per hour. Patients with appointments wait an average of 26 minutes to see a GP, 21.3 minutes to see a pediatrician, but only 5.5 minutes to see a psychiatrist.

The human juice factory. Every day the average person produces

1 to 2 quarts of saliva
2 quarts to a gallon of gastric juice
1½ pints of pancreatic juice
four fifths of a cup of intestinal juice
1½ to 2½ pints of bile.

The checkup breakdown. Three Americans in 4 consider themselves healthy as long as nothing is bothering them. One in 4 wants a checkup to be sure.

One American in 7 agrees with this statement: "Going for checkups when nothing bothers you is looking for trouble."

Two in 5 agree with this one: "There is something very frightening about going for checkups because you never know what you will find out."

To grow old cold. According to University of Michigan researchers, people would live to an average age of 200 if they could get their body temperatures down to 86 degrees.

Stand in the moonlight, on one foot, whistling. Sooner or later, almost everybody has warts. Right now, 7 to 10 per cent of the population have them. Viruses cause them.

Do you get sick much? Twice a year, on average. That's counting injuries, but not chronic conditions like diabetes or a bad heart. Actually, the average is 2.19 times, so don't feel bad if you were sick 3 times.

The average American is sick in bed 6½ days a year, and feels bad enough to take it easy on another 12 days.

The average kid is home sick from school 5 days a year. The average worker is off the job 5 days a year—4 days for white-collar workers, 6 days for blue-collar workers. Women are home sick a bit more than men, and people who get paid when they're sick miss more work days than those who don't. The champs are government office workers, who miss 7 days a year. The average farm worker misses fewer than 4 days a year.

Of every 100 Americans:
Fifteen say they've never had a headache.

Eight or 9 will at some time be hospitalized for mental illness.

Ten are allergic enough to something to require medical attention. Another 20 to 50 have a constitutional allergic tendency.

One stutters.

Fourteen have their activities limited as a result of a chronic disease or impairment.

Forty-five of 100 men and 47 of 100 women have at least 1 cold per year.

At birth, 6 whites in 100 and 13 blacks in 100 weigh 5 pounds, 8 ounces or less.

Eighteen have high blood pressure.

Twenty will have to go to a hospital emergency room this year.

Twenty-five will go a whole year without seeing a doctor.

One has epilepsy.

Two have diabetes.

One will get kidney stones.

Eleven of 100 men and 9 of 100 women will suffer a fracture, dislocation, sprain, or strain in a given year.

Sixteen a year are hospitalized. Ten undergo surgery.

Twenty of 100 teen-agers think they are too fat, and 13 think they are too skinny.

Eight of 100 men and 3 of 100 women donate blood.

Five of 100 men are 6 feet, 1.6 inches or taller.

Twenty-five of 100 women weigh less than 123 pounds.

Eighty-two of 100 little girls and 68 of 100 little boys will live beyond age 64.

Must be something in the water. Hawaiians outlive their fellow Americans. The average Hawaiian man doesn't die until he's 71, and the average Hawaiian woman lives until she's nearly 77. South Carolinians, on the other hand, die hastily—men before they're 64 and women at 72.

Here are the long-living states, in descending order:

	Average man	*Average woman*
Hawaii	71 yrs.	76 yrs., 10 mos.
Utah	69 yrs., 6 mos.	76 yrs., 6 mos.
Minnesota	69 yrs., 5 mos.	76 yrs., 10 mos.
North Dakota	69 yrs., 3 mos.	77 yrs.
Nebraska	68 yrs., 10 mos.	76 yrs., 7 mos.

Here are the short-living states, beginning with the shortest:

	Average man	*Average woman*
South Carolina	63 yrs., 10 mos.	72 yrs., 4 mos.
Mississippi	64 yrs.	72 yrs., 5 mos.
Georgia	64 yrs., 3 mos.	73 yrs.
Louisiana	64 yrs., 10 mos.	72 yrs., 5 mos.
Nevada	65 yrs., 7 mos.	73 yrs., 4 mos.

In terms of longevity, the residents of Ohio and Missouri are the most typical in the country. In Ohio, the average man dies at 67 years, 3 months, and the average woman at 74 years, 6 months. In Missouri, the average ages at death are 66 years, 11 months, for men, and 74 years, 7 months, for women.

The Red-blooded American

Pumping blood. One American in 3 has high blood pressure.

According to a federal government study, the blood pressure of the average American 55 or older is a little higher than it should be.

On average, your chances of having high blood pressure, sometimes called hypertension, increase if you are

old
black
poor or
uneducated.

Lord help you if you are all of the above.

The average Southerner has higher blood pressure than the average Yankee or Westerner.

Of every 2 Americans with high blood pressure, 1 is unaware of the condition.

Here is the blood pressure of the average American by age:

	Male	Female
1	96:66	95:65
10	103:69	103:70
15	112:75	112:76
18 to 24	123:76	115:71
25 to 34	125:81	117:75
35 to 44	128:85	124:80
45 to 54	135:88	133:84
55 to 64	140:87	144:87
65 to 74	147:85	152:86
80 to 84	145:82	157:83
90 to 94	145:78	150:79
95 to 106	145:78	149:81

Passing up the butter. Since the 1960s, the average American has cut the level of cholesterol in his or her bloodstream by 10 per cent.

Bloodletting. A service veteran is more likely to donate blood than someone who has never served. A veteran of peacetime service is more likely to donate than a wartime veteran. So says a government study.

You are more likely to donate blood if you work, have a good income, live in a metropolitan area, and consider yourself in good health.

Of all the blood donated in 1978, 5 per cent came from people who were paid for it and 95 per cent from donors who gave it away.

The busy heart. Every minute, the human heart beats 70 times, and pumps 5 quarts of blood.

That's more than 100,000 beats a day and more than 2.5 billion times in 70 years, pumping 1,800 gallons a day and 46 billion gallons in the course of a lifetime.

That's the equivalent of lifting 70 pounds every minute, enough in a lifetime to lift a 10-ton load 10 miles into the air.

The heart of a long-distance runner beats more strongly, but less often—only about 30 or 35 times a minute—than a nonrunner's ticker.

The human body has 62,000 miles of blood vessels, enough to stretch from New York to Los Angeles 22 times.

Flu is more common. You've got a little better than a 50-50 chance of getting through the whole year without catching cold.

The headache. Headaches account for half of all visits to doctors. Nine in 10 of us get headaches. Half a billion dollars are spent each year on over-the-counter headache remedies.

Dr. Arthur S. Freese, a headache expert, says that 9 in 10 are "tension headaches."

Migraine headaches strike 1 American in 8, including children. Two thirds of the victims are women. If both parents suffer migraine headaches, three quarters of their children will; if 1 parent does, half the children will.

A third type is the "terrible cluster headache," so called because they tend to occur one after the other. Here 9 victims in 10 are men, most of them in their 30s or 40s.

Pillish Americans. One in 4 American adults takes aspirin at least once a week. One in 18 takes sleeping pills that often.

Dog bites man. About 1,500,000 Americans a year are bitten by dogs.

Hand me a towel. An average newborn baby is three quarters water, by weight.

The older you get, the less of you is water, but it's still a lot.

The average man 23 to 54 years old is 54 per cent water. The average woman that age is 49 per cent water.

Old folks are sometimes spoken of as "dried up," and they are. The average man 71 to 84 years old is down to 51 per cent water, and the average woman 61 to 74 years old is only 43 per cent water.

This attack of hypochondria is making me sick. The National Institute of Mental Health says that 15 per cent of the people who visit doctors are suffering only from hypochondria.

Since they go to the doctor more often than other people, they may account for 30 per cent of all doctors' visits.

Work and backaches. In an average year, 700,000 U.S. workers suffer back injuries severe enough to lose time on the job.

A survey of kids. In a government survey of 7,514 youngsters between the ages of 12 and 17, half had acne; 16 per cent said they never worried about pimples.

Half had never been a hospital patient, 1 in 10 had never seen a doctor, and 1 in 6 had never visited a dentist. Five per cent walked in their sleep. Nearly half had nightmares, at least occasionally.

Seven per cent said they were "very fussy" about what they ate. More than a third wished they were taller, but only 7 per cent wished they were shorter.

Bumps on the road of life. Chances are 1 in 20 that you'll get a bad back before you're 45. By the time you're 65, odds are 1 in 5 that you'll get arthritis, and 1 in 8 that you'll have hypertension. After that age, chances are 4 in 10 that you'll have arthritis, 3 in 10 that your hearing won't be so good, and 1 in 5 for a bad heart or impaired vision.

Physicians heal themselves. Of every 1,000 males in the United States, 15 die in an average year. But of every 1,000 male doctors, only 11 die.

Long life for short people. The average American man is 5 feet, 9 inches tall. The average woman is 5 feet, 3.6 inches.

Only 1 man in 1,000 is shorter than 5 feet. Three women in 1,000 are 5 feet, 11 inches or taller.

In a study of 750 successful men, the short ones—5 feet, 8 inches or shorter—lived longer, on average, than those standing over 6 feet tall. Five U.S. Presidents (Madison, Van Buren, Harrison, and both Adams) were shorter than 5-8, and averaged 80.2 years of life. Not including Lincoln, 5 Presidents (Washington, Arthur, Franklin Roosevelt, Lyndon Johnson, and Jefferson) were taller than 6-1, and lived an average of 66.6 years. The same kind of difference favoring short men was found among baseball players, football players, and boxers.

The average basketball player is taller than the average track-and-field athlete, and dies 9 years sooner.

The things that keep us idle. Four out of 5 Americans say they're not getting enough exercise. Of every 100 such folks, 43 don't have the time and 16 don't have the willpower. Twelve plain don't feel like it, 9 have a medical reason, 8 lack the energy, and 12 have some other excuse.

Age and concrete. People who live in the city are, on average, 18 months older than people living in the suburbs.

Upward bound. The average young man in America is 2½ inches taller than the typical old man in America, and weighs a pound more.

The average young woman is 2 inches taller than the average old woman, and weighs 14 pounds *less*.

Every generation of Americans is taller than its parents by about an inch.

The average woman in the early 1960s was 5 feet, 3 inches tall and weighed 140 pounds. A decade later she was an inch taller and 3 pounds heavier.

The average man, standing 5-9 and weighing 172 pounds, was an inch taller and 4 per cent heavier in the early 1970s than he was in the early 1960s.

Tall people have gained the most. Men 6 feet tall and aged 35 to 44 weighed an average of 164 in the 1970s, a full 10 pounds over their 1960s counterparts. Women that age who were 5-8 weighed 167, a sizable 13 pounds more.

The only group weighing less in the 1970s than they did in the 1960s were women aged 55 to 64. They trimmed off 2 pounds.

The big boss. A survey of chief executives of large American industrial firms found that more than half were at least 6 feet tall. Only 3 per cent were 5 feet 7 or less.

The average boss was 57 years old and weighted 184 pounds.

Specialists. The average city person goes to a specialist twice as often as to a general family doctor. The average country or small-town person goes to a family doctor twice as often as to a specialist.

Toothed and Toothless

Calling all dentists! Americans have an average of 4.6 cavities (filled and unfilled combined) each.

The mouth in need. One in 5 Americans need to have his or her teeth cleaned, 2 in 5 need some drilling and filling, and 1 in 20 needs a tooth pulled.

Going to the dentist. The average American sees the dentist once or twice a year—1.6 times, to be exact.

People between 15 and 64 years old go most, and people 65 or older go least.

According to the U. S. Bureau of Prisons, the average federal inmate sees the dentist 4.7 times a year.

The family dentist. Most families in America—66 in 100, according to the American Dental Association—have a single dentist who takes care of the entire family's dental needs.

So much for the tooth fairy. At age 2, 1 child in 2 has cavities. Between the ages of 6 and 11, the average kid has 3 teeth that are decayed or filled, or have been pulled.

Tooth decay, black and white. According to a U. S. Public Health survey, the average black kid has fewer cavities than the average white kid. But the white kid is much more likely to have his filled.

Tooth truth. The average American teen-ager has 4 fillings and 2 unfilled cavities.

Cheaper than Crest. One American in 2 drinks fluoridated water. In Kansas, Illinois, and Colorado, more than 4 in 5 do. In Utah and Nevada, fewer than 3 in 100 do.

Look, Ma. Kids who have drunk fluoridated water since birth have 65 per cent fewer cavities than kids living in communities that don't fluoridate.

Bright teeth. Six college graduates in 10 have all their own teeth.

Choppers. One American in 6 wears a full set of false teeth.
Fewer Americans wear false teeth now than used to. In 1960, 35 in 100 Americans 30 or older wore full sets of either upper or lower dentures. By the late 1970s, only 25 in 100 wore them.

Toothlessness. One 20-year-old in 100 has no teeth. One 70-year-old in 2 has none.

Zap! The average American is exposed to 100 to 200 millirems of radiation a year, about half of it from Mother Nature.

Intact colonials. Modern Americans suffer 4 times as many fractured bones as their colonial predecessors. Automobiles, household accidents, and "interpersonal conflicts" account for the increase, the experts say.

Pill vs. no pill. A study in 21 countries shows that women using the pill for birth control are 5 times more likely to die of heart disease or hypertension than nonusers. But a Harvard Medical School study says that pregnancy is 5 times as likely to kill a woman as is the pill.

How much we breathe. A sleeping newborn baby breathes 43 times a minute, on average. An average adult breathes 12 times a minute while resting. While doing heavy work, an average man breathes 21 times a minute, and an average woman breathes 30 times. His lungs hold 1½ gallons of air; hers hold 1⅛ gallons.

The young heal fast. Say you're hospitalized with a broken bone. On average, you will go home in 5.4 days if you are under age 16, in 6.8 days if you are between 15 and 44, in 9.4 days if you are between 45 and 64, and in 14.4 days if you are 65 or older.

The chemicals we take. The average American has 6.4 prescriptions filled a year at a cost, in 1977, of $5.98 each. People over 65 spend an average of $80 a year on prescription drugs, according to the Pharmaceutical Manufacturers Association.

Why some Harvard graduates live longer than others. A study of nearly 17,000 Harvard alumni establishes that people who expend 2,000 calories a week in vigorous physical activity have a 64 per cent lower heart-attack risk than sedentary people. Two thousand calories can be burned off by running 20 miles a week.

What we're made of. By weight, the average adult is 43 per cent muscle, 26 per cent skin, 17.5 per cent bone, 7 per cent blood, 2.7 per cent liver, 2.2 per cent brain, 2.2 per cent intestines, 1.5 per cent lungs, .5 per cent kidneys, .5 per cent heart, .2 per cent spleen, and .1 per cent pancreas.

That adds up to a trifle over 100 per cent, but don't blame us. It's from an impressive medical book.

3 Habits, Tics, Rituals, and Other Routines

How much do you sleep? Of every 100 adults:

6 sleep or nap less than 5 hours a day
16 sleep 6 hours
26 sleep 7 hours
37 sleep 8 hours
9 sleep 9 hours
6 sleep 10 hours or more.

Half of us have trouble sleeping at least 1 night a week. Among people who don't exercise much, nearly 1 in 3 has trouble sleeping on 3 nights a week. Only 1 in 6 active people has that much trouble sleeping.

That soft, young look. Three out of 4 American women put moisturizer on their faces. Three out of 5 put it on their hands, and a little over half moisten up their elbows.

Teen-agers and young women prefer Noxzema, but as she gets to be about 25, the average American woman switches to Oil of Olay or Avon.

As for lotion, two thirds of American women use it on the

body, and four fifths use it on their hands. Vaseline Intensive Care is the favorite brand, although lots of older women prefer Rose Milk.

The wardrobe of the working woman. In 1977, the average working woman spent $960 on clothes. The average career woman spent $1,460.

Those figures are from *Retail Week* (formerly *Clothes, Etc.*), a leading trade publication. It defines "career women" as the 15 per cent of working women classified by the U. S. Labor Department as professional and technical workers. Nearly two thirds of these career women are teachers, nurses, writers, artists, and entertainers.

Our average working woman, career class or not, is no patsy for the fashion industry. When asked to name their three favorite designers, only 21 per cent of the working women named even one. The average career woman spends less on clothes than the average nonworking wife of a professional or top executive. Working women buy 44 per cent to 63 per cent of their ready-to-wear clothes, and 28 per cent to 43 per cent of their intimate apparel, accessories, and shoes, at reduced or discount prices.

Here's another blow for freedom. Know how the stores stock up on fall and winter clothes in July, and on spring clothes in January and February? The average working woman buys only 1 per cent of her fall wardrobe in July. She buys 48 per cent of it in September and October, and 18 per cent in November. As for her spring and summer wardrobe, she buys only 3 per cent of it in January and February, and 50 per cent of it in April and May.

All the married career women in the survey had family incomes above $25,000, and all the single ones had an income above $15,000. But only 11 per cent paid $35 or more for a blouse, only 22 per cent paid $40 or more for slacks, and only 18 per cent paid $40 or more for a skirt. Only 15 per cent paid $100 or more for a suit, 30 per cent paid $60 or more for a dress, and 33 per cent paid $125 or more for a coat or jacket.

The average working woman spent $.44 of her clothing dollar at department stores, $.16 at specialty stores, and $.16 at clothing chains. Two out of every 5 wore junior sizes, and 70 per cent wore size 12 or smaller.

Here's how the average working woman in general, and the average career woman in two different areas of the country, spent her income in 1977:

	Working women	Career women	
		NEW YORK	MIDWEST
Rent and living expenses, including food, insurance, and medical care	42%	45%	41%
Her clothes	9%	12%	6%
Cosmetics	2%	3%	2%
Car	14%	5%	10%
Entertainment and vacations	11%	15%	12%
Hobbies, books, records, sports	5%	5%	6%
Liquor, cigarettes, drugs	3%	2%	3%
Savings, charity, baby-sitting, education, other things	14%	13%	20%

The career women were asked their taste in daytime skirt and dress lengths. Of the New Yorkers, 6 per cent picked knee grazers, 53 per cent went for below the knee, and 41 per cent chose midcalf or longer. Of the Midwesterners, none selected knee grazers, 85 per cent came down for below the knee, and 15 per cent picked midcalf or longer.

Talking dirty. At leisure, 1 of every 8 words spoken by the average adult is a cuss word. At work, he or she tones it down to 1 in 29.

The average college student throws in a dirty word for every 11 clean ones. The average college woman has just as foul a mouth as the average college man, except she says "shit" more than he does, and he says "fuck" more than she does.

That's what sociologist Paul Cameron found some years ago when he sent out 47 field workers to eavesdrop on people's conversations. To get a good cross section, the spies were told to spend no more than 10 minutes listening to one conversation and to listen to conversations between members of the same sex two thirds of the time. They collected 66,767 words (2,740 not counting repetitions).

Among vulgar words spoken, the sexual outnumbered the sacred marginally and surpassed the excretory by a 3-to-2 ratio.

The most common in each category were: "fuck," "bastard," and "bitch"; "damn," "hell," and "Jesus"; and "shit," "bull," and "piss."

Cameron concluded that "damn" is the most popular vulgarism and is "possibly among the 15 most frequent words in spoken English."

Male vanity. By the region, here are the percentages of American college men who

	Use cologne or after-shave	Blow-dry their hair
Northeast	74%	52%
Southeast	92%	80%
Midwest	82%	72%

Giving up drink. At an average meeting of Alcoholics Anonymous, 35 per cent to 40 per cent of those present have been sober for less than a year, 35 per cent to 40 per cent have been sober 1 to 5 years, and 20 per cent to 30 per cent have been sober over 5 years.

Just over half are between ages 31 and 50. Eleven per cent are under 30, and 35 per cent are over 50.

Of those who attend, 41 per cent say that another AA member helped get them there, 38 per cent walked in on their own, 24 per cent came through counseling, 10 per cent came at the urging of a member of their family, and 10 per cent through the family doctor. (Many listed more than one factor, so the percentages total over 100.)

One in 3 is a woman.

Among the men, 26 per cent are professionals and 29 per cent are businessmen or salesmen. Among the women, 40 per cent are homemakers, 21 per cent are professionals, and 14 per cent are in sales or business.

Who stutters. For every girl who stutters, there are 3 or 4 boy stutterers. On average, twins stutter more than other people. Among identical twins, if one stutters the other most likely will too.

Altogether, 649,000 American males and 261,000 American females stutter.

Blink. The average person blinks 25 times a minute.

Nail biters. According to a study conducted in 1948 and still cited in the social-science literature, 25 to 36 of every 100 college students bite their fingernails.

Why people who stay in motels often look wrinkled. The motel industry says only 1 guest in 5 unpacks.

The bookish American. The average American reads at least 2 books a year, and 10 per cent claim that they read more than 50.

A survey of 1,450 adults in 1978 found that 55 per cent were book readers—someone who finished a book within the past 6 months.

Women read somewhat more than men. Really heavy readers generally are women.

Six per cent said they don't read anything—books, magazines, or newspapers.

These findings are in line with earlier surveys. In 1971, Gallup found that 26 per cent of people asked had read a book the previous month. And a 1965 study said that on any given day, 17 per cent of Americans spent some time with a book.

The average American goes to the library at least once every 2 years. One person in 3 goes every other month.

The jeans generation. The average American college man owns 5 pairs of jeans. The average American college woman owns 6 pairs.

Not all hourglasses are alike. Half of all women—OK, 49 per cent—wear the same size tops and bottoms. But 38 per cent wear larger tops than bottoms, and 13 per cent wear larger bottoms than tops.

Four out of every 5 college women wear size 7 to size 12. For every college woman who prefers loose clothing, 2½ prefer figure-revealing clothes.

Let's go to the mall. In a typical metropolitan area, only 1 family in 5 shops downtown.

Good citizens. In the 1976 presidential election, 1 working American of every 7 not only voted, but also attended a rally, gave some money, or was otherwise involved.

Insomnia and pills. According to Daniel Kaufman, coauthor of *Natural Sleep (How to Get Your Share)* (Rodale Press, 1978), between 1 person in 4 and 1 in 10 in the United States is an insomniac. He says 15,000 Americans die in the average year of sleeping-pill overdoses—and only 1 per cent are intentional suicides.

Cosmetics go to college. In 1978, 26 per cent of American college woman preferred Revlon blush, with Estée Lauder a distant second at 10 per cent. Cover Girl and Maybelline tied for the lead among foundations, with 15 per cent of the market apiece; Estée Lauder was close behind with 13 per cent. For other face and cheek stuff—cover sticks, gels, powders—Love led Clinique, 21 per cent to 15 per cent.

Moving to the lips, it was Bonne Bell over Revlon in lip gloss, 20 per cent to 15 per cent; Vaseline in a romp as a lip moisturizer with 65 per cent, and Revlon and Cover Girl tied for first among lipsticks with 21 per cent each.

Up around the eyes, it was Revlon eye shadow (27 per cent) 2 to 1 over second-place Aziza (13 per cent), and Maybelline mascara (26 per cent) by a wide margin over Revlon (14 per cent).

The average college woman bought 7 bottles of shampoo in 1977, preferring Revlon, followed by Fabergé, Johnson's, and Clairol. She bought six bottles of creme rinse or instant conditioner, with Revlon again in front.

She bought five bottles of nail polish—Revlon, Cutex, and Sally Hansen were preferred, in that order. For her skin, she bought three bottles of moisturizer. Vaseline Intensive Care was the favorite brand, followed by Oil of Olay and Aloe. Skin cleansers? Three jars were enough, and Noxzema was the top brand. Bonne Bell was second; Neutrogena and Clinique tied for third.

Just a trim this time. The average American man gets his hair cut every 4 to 6 weeks, according to Gerald R. St. Onge, national president of the Associated Master Barbers and Beauticians of America.

The average haircut costs $4.50, but many men go for a hairstyle job. That includes shampoo, conditioner, haircut, and blow dry, and costs $8.00, on average. "The average American man is not tipping today like he used to," St. Onge says. "I would say that probably 1 of 5 customers tips. Probably 10 or 20 years ago it was 4 out of 5 customers."

A woman's shampoo and set cost $7.00 to $9.00, on average, and the average woman adds a tip.

He's got to start somewhere. In the Southeast, 4 out of 5 college men buy their own socks and underwear. Three out of 4 buy their own in the Northeast, but only 2 out of 3 in the Midwest. Mom and Dad do the shopping for the others.

The drugs that kill. The drug most likely to kill you, on average, is alcohol taken with some other drug. So reports the National Institute on Drug Abuse.

The second-biggest killer is heroin, followed by Darvon, Valium, Seconal, Elavil, Nembutal, and in a tie, Luminal and Tuinal.

Most of those are commonly prescribed drugs. The folks who die from them have taken too much, and some of them have taken the drug in combination with another drug.

As a killer, marijuana is twenty-sixth on the list of 26 drugs. By comparison, aspirin is tied for tenth.

If you are going to go the emergency room as a result of abusing some drug, it's most likely to be Valium, followed by alcohol, aspirin, heroin, Dalmane, Darvon, Librium, and Luminal, in that order.

The Devout American

Who believes and who doesn't. Here are the results of a survey:

Denomination		Percentage believing in			
	GOD	VIRGIN BIRTH	JESUS WALKED ON WATER	SECOND COMING	THE DEVIL
Congregational	41	21	19	13	6
Methodist	60	34	26	21	13
Episcopal	63	39	30	24	17
Disciples of Christ	76	62	62	36	18
Presbyterian	75	62	62	36	18
American Lutheran	73	66	58	54	49
American Baptist	78	69	62	57	49
Missouri Lutheran	81	92	83	75	77
Southern Baptist	99	99	99	94	92
Total Protestant	71	51	50	44	38
Roman Catholic	81	81	71	47	66

Faith in Congress. If there were an average politician in America, he would be a Protestant.

Protestants and Jews are proportionally overrepresented in high public office, especially in the Senate.

In 1977, for example, 77 of the 100 senators were Protestants, while only 61 per cent of the public was.

Only 13 per cent of the senators were Catholic, while 27 per cent of the public was. While 2 per cent of the public is Jewish, five Jews (5 per cent) sat in the Senate. People expressing no religious preference constitute 6 per cent of the population, but only 1 per cent of Congress.

Among Protestants, Methodists are highly overrepresented in Congress—7 per cent of the population, but 20 per cent of the Senate and 14 per cent of the House. Also overrepresented are Episcopalians, Unitarian-Universalists, and members of the United Church of Christ.

Among denominations that are underrepresented are Lutherans, Baptists, and evangelical and Pentecostal Christians.

What the Bible means. Thirty-eight per cent of adult Americans believe that the Bible is the literal word of God, while 45 per cent consider it the "inspired" word of God.

Thirteen per cent would rather categorize it as an ancient book written by men.

How America prays. Ninety-four in 100 of us believe in God. That's down a bit from a quarter of a century ago, when 98 in 100 Americans professed religious belief.

Of the 94 faithful, 61 are Protestants, 27 are Catholics, 2 are Jews, and 4 are adherents of some other religion.

For more than 20 years, a majority of Americans have said "no" when asked whether they had attended church or synagogue within the past 7 days.

Catholics are the most likely to attend church: 58 per cent of them say "yes." Thirty-eight per cent of the Protestants and 20 per cent of the Jews had been in a house of worship within the week.

Here's some more on America's religious proclivities:

Of every 100 of us, 7 have dabbled in faith healing, 4 in Transcendental Meditation, 3 in charismatic Yoga, 2 in mysticism, and 1 in an Eastern religion such as Zen.

One American in 3 says he has been "born again"—that is, went through a turning point in life when he or she committed or recommitted to Christ. There are 50 million "born again" Christians over 18 years old among us.

Sixty-eight in 100 Americans say they believe that God observes peoples' actions and rewards or punishes them for the way they behave.

Sixty-nine in 100 believe in life after death, and another 11 are undecided.

Sixty-eight in 100 see Heaven the way it is traditionally pictured, as a place where those who led good lives are eternally rewarded. Fifty-four see Hell as a place where the unrepentant are eternally damned.

But when questioned in a survey, only 11 per cent saw any real possibility that they personally might go to Hell.

Eighty in 100 people believe Jesus was God or the Son of

God. Thirteen believe he was "another leader like Muhammad." One in 100 believes that Jesus never existed.

Of 100 people, 91 pray to God, 83 had religious training as a child, 53 call religion "very important" in their own lives, but 81 say you can be a good Christian or Jew without attending a house of worship.

In 1978, a cross section of Americans was surveyed to find how churchgoers differ from the "unchurched"—those who don't belong to one and haven't set foot in a church or synagogue for 6 months except for a funeral, wedding, or religious holiday.

The survey estimates that 41 per cent of American adults are "unchurched"—that's 61 million people.

There was little difference between the two groups in at least one regard. Asked if they had prayed privately during the past month, 89 per cent of the churchgoers and 84 per cent of the church avoiders had.

But God loves us all. The average American woman is more likely to go to church than is the average American man. Widows are particularly likely to go, followed by single and divorced women, married women without children, and married mothers.

America, the religious. Nearly 9 out of 10 Americans polled by Gallup in 1976 said their religious beliefs were important to them. Among 10 countries or groups of countries where people were asked the same question, only Italy, with about 8 out of 10, came close to the United States. Third in religious beliefs was Australia, followed, in order, by the Benelux countries of Belgium, Luxembourg, and the Netherlands; Canada; France; West Germany; Japan; the Scandinavian countries of Denmark, Finland, Norway, and Sweden; and Britain.

I get carried away. The average person tends to profess belief in a higher standard of morality than he or she practices.

Passing the plate. A survey of 45 Christian denominations totaling 42 million members shows that the average church member in the United States gave $159.33 to his or her church in 1977. In Canada, members of 27 denominations gave an average of $90.39 each.

The survey was made by the National Council of the Churches of Christ in the U.S.A., which says that, in constant dollars, U.S. per-capita giving has increased by 14 per cent since 1960.

Here's a sampling:

African Methodist Episcopal Zion	$ 43.69
American Lutheran	$161.41
Christian Church (Disciples of Christ)	$213.60
Church of the Nazarene	$359.07
Episcopal	$190.01
Friends United Meeting	$168.07
Lutheran Church in America	$142.87
Lutheran Church—Missouri Synod	$179.84
Mennonite Church	$326.27
Methodist	$118.83
Presbyterian Church in the United States	$263.96
Seventh-day Adventists	$602.45
Southern Baptist	$137.33
United Church of Christ	$143.03
The United Presbyterian Church in the U.S.A.	$208.44

Here are some Canadian church groups:

Baptist Convention of Ontario and Quebec	$318.36
Baptist Union of Western Canada	$278.61
Church of the Foursquare Gospel of Western Canada	$723.49
The Evangelical Lutheran Church of Canada	$153.14
Canadian Conference of Mennonite Brethren Churches of North America	$491.04
The Presbyterian Church in Canada	$168.29
Seventh-day Adventist Church in Canada	$663.26
The United Church of Canada	$149.07

Catholics. Catholics polled in 1974 reported giving an average of $184 per family to the Church.

Religion and the life cycle. The average American is pretty religious through about age 11, after which intellectual doubts begin to creep in. By about age 16, he or she usually resolves these doubts by deciding either to accept or to reject the religion of her or his childhood. Of those who accept, about 1 in 5 experiences a sudden conversion; the others drift in gradually.

Religious activity begins declining at about age 18, and plummets to its lowest point between the ages of 30 and 35. Then it begins rising, and peaks in old age, with solid belief in God and life after death.

Our daily bread. Three families in 10 start their meals with grace.

The Good Book is everywhere. According to a survey by the Christian Bible Society, 98 per cent of American homes have a Bible.

The Thursday yawn. A study of 1,667 households in the Washington, D.C., area suggests that the average person is most likely to turn in early on Thursday night and to sleep late on Sunday morning.

Participants were awake an average of 16.3 hours on Monday, Tuesday, and Wednesday, but only 15.4 hours on Thursday. They were awake 16.8 hours on Friday, 15.6 hours on Saturday and 14.5 hours on Sunday.

Thursday is also the day, the study found, that people are likely to spend the most time in quiet diversions—reading and watching TV, mostly.

His wardrobe. The average American man owns 15 dress shirts, 6 pairs of slacks, 6 sport shirts, 5 knit shirts, and 3 sweaters.

During the past 2 years, he bought 3 dress shirts, 3 pairs of slacks, 3 sport shirts, 2 knit shirts, and 2 pairs of jeans.

How does it fit in the back, dear? Half the men in America bring their wives along when they buy their clothes, according to a study reported in *Daily News Record,* a menswear industry publication.

Women buy about as many men's pajamas, neckties, and sportswear as men do.

The noose. The average man, if he wears one, spends 4 hours a year tying his tie.

This year's man in last year's clothes. The average young man gets 2 to 3 times as much wear out of his clothes as the average young woman does. He wears jeans 2 to 3 years, jackets and coats 2 to 3 years, sweaters 2 to 4 years, and slacks 1 to 2½ years. Knit shirts last him a year, on average. A pair of shoes lasts 6 months to a year. So does underwear, much of which he loses, perhaps in the laundry.

Dog-eared, and no wonder. According to the Magazine Publishers Association, the average magazine is read by 4 people for a total of 6 hours, 3 minutes, and it sits around the house for 29 weeks before someone throws it out.

The average magazine reader is 35, married, a suburbanite who owns his or her own house and has an income 24 per cent above the national average.

The average American reads the most magazines in October and November, and the fewest in July, August, and September.

The magazine reader, when compared with the average American, is 6 per cent more likely to vote, 39 per cent more likely to contribute to a political party, 21 per cent more likely to give to the United Fund, 29 per cent more likely to have written something that was published, and 44 per cent more likely to have taken adult education courses.

Whatever happened to the natural look? Nineteen out of 20 American college women wear makeup, and 7 out of 10 make up differently for dates than they do for classes.

From the Ankles Down

Sweat socks. The average college man buys two pairs of athletic socks for every pair of dress socks.

Fast and casual. The average American college man wears sneakers or running shoes at least half the time.

Shoes. The average American man wears size 10½ D shoes.

The plastic we wear. Americans use 3 pounds of manmade fibers for every pound of cotton and wool.

Decisions, decisions. Thirty years ago, a retailer could satisfy 88 per cent of his customers if he stocked 5 brands of cigarettes. Today, to satisfy the same percentage, he must carry 58 different lengths, packs, and filters, mentholated and not. So reports *Esquire* magazine.

Here's an expert's look at an average night's sleep. Dr. J. Allan Hobson, renowned dream researcher, is director of the Laboratory of Neurophysiology, Department of Psychiatry, Harvard Medical School. Here's his rundown of a typical night's sleep, from the Dreamstage Exhibit Scientific Catalog, copyright 1977 by J. Allan Hobson and Hoffman-LaRoche, Inc.

"At regular intervals during sleep, the eyes of a person move rapidly back and forth beneath the eyelids. Brain electrical activity is strikingly similar to that of a person awake. If awakened during a period of rapid eye movements, which we call REM episodes, a person frequently reports that he or she has been dreaming, and often gives long, clear, detailed accounts of the dream. REM sleep is the sleep during which most dreaming takes place.

"The other kind of sleep that alternates with REM is called

nonREM or NREM. Stage I of NREM begins the night. Brain waves are small and fast. The muscles begin to relax and the eyes drift slowly beneath the eyelids. Stage I does not last long, and sleepers may be easily awakened.

"During the next half hour or so, sleep becomes deeper as stages II, III, and IV of NREM progress. In Stage II, bursts of brain waves resemble spindles on the electroencephalogram, or EEG. The eyes continue to roll and the muscles continue to relax. Arousal is more difficult.

"Stage II sleep gives way to an even deeper sleep, Stage III, in which the brain waves are larger and slower. The sleeper cannot be easily awakened; heart rate and respiration become slow and very regular.

"The last stage of NREM is Stage IV, the deepest sleep. Brain waves are large, slow, and regular. The body muscles are so relaxed that few movements are likely to be observed. After several minutes of this, a sleeper usually reverts for a while to one of the lighter stages of NREM sleep.

"When roughly 90 minutes have elapsed, the first installment of REM appears. The sleeper dreams. This first REM period is brief; the sleeper drifts back into one of the NREM stages. This pattern of alternating REM and NREM sleep repeats itself 4 to 6 times a night, depending on the length of the sleep period.

"Later in the night, REM periods become longer and NREM periods become shorter. The first 90-minute cycle might include 85 minutes of NREM and 5 minutes of REM; the fourth 90-minute cycle might have 60 minutes of NREM and 30 minutes of REM. As a result, the likelihood of waking up during a dream increases toward morning. That's why we tend to remember those dreams that occur close to the time of awakening.

"Dreaming is not limited to REM sleep. People awakened from NREM sleep often report having mental activity of a thoughtlike nature. For example, one might say, 'I was thinking about getting my car fixed tomorrow.'

"But this is quite different from REM dreams, which are rapidly shifting, intense, and visual in nature. Some scientists think that the eye movements represent the dreamer scanning the visual imagery of his or her dream. The strangeness of dreams may simply be a reflection of the brain's cerebral cortex putting together the most coherent story possible from a series of evoked, but not necessarily related, memories.

"People are generally unaware of their changes of posture during sleep. Statements such as, 'I tossed and turned all night,' or, 'I never moved from the moment my head hit the pillow' are rarely accurate. The average sleeper rolls over or otherwise changes posture between 10 and 20 times a night, and rarely goes more than an hour and a half without movement."

Cats, incidentally, have sleep cycles much like those of people, and are excellent for studies of sleep and dream phenomena.

Preferably with a vest. The average American college man much prefers a traditional suit to a sport coat or leisure suit. When college men suit up, half of them invariably wear a tie.

Ah, sew. Sewing is done in 6 homes out of 10. According to an estimate by the Simplicity Pattern people, 1 in every 4 women's and children's garments is made at home. The Agriculture Department estimates that 41 million women do some home sewing.

The average home sewer makes 3.4 garments a year. Nearly 6 in 10 make a dress in a typical year, and a third make women's sportswear. Children's clothing is next in popularity.

Eighty-two per cent of the people who sew learned how before they were 19. Most learn in school, but 38 per cent are self-taught. Among people who sew, 40 per cent also crochet or do embroidery or crewel work, 36 per cent knit, 13 per cent do needlepoint, 9 per cent appliqué, 7 per cent do découpage, and 3 per cent make collages.

Sewers are not procrastinators. Sixty-one per cent sew a garment within a week of buying the pattern.

The printed word. Three Americans in 4 buy magazines at least occasionally. A fifth of us buy 60 per cent of all magazines sold.

Asleep afloat. According to *Money* magazine, 1 U.S. household in 10 is equipped with a water bed.

The Coed Adorned

What she buys. In 1977, the average American college woman bought 3 or 4 pairs of jeans, 5 pairs of pants, 3 skirts, 7 sweaters, 7 blouses, 6 T-shirts, 3 dresses, 2 coats or jackets, 2 swimsuits, and 2 outfits for special occasions or evening wear.

She paid $19.09 a pair for jeans, $17.70 for pants, $17.21 for skirts, $17.65 for sweaters, $13.21 for blouses, $6.14 for T-shirts, $27.14 for dresses, $63.27 for coats and jackets, $19.87 for swimsuits, and $46.06 for those special outfits.

What she wears on campus. In 1977, the average American college woman wore jeans 4 to 7 days a week, pants 3 times a week, and a skirt and a dress once a week each.

Underneath. The average American college woman owns 6 bras and 17 pairs of panties.

Body art. Minneapolis tattoo artist Dave Yurkew, president of the North American Tattoo Club, says 3 adults in 10 are tattooed.

Ha! The average person laughs 15 times a day.

The cost of excess. According to the Alcohol, Drug Abuse, and Mental Health Administration, alcoholism and problem drinking cost the U.S. economy over $71 million a day—$27 million in lost work, $23 million in health and medical costs, $18 million in motor accidents, $2 million in research and prevention programs, $1.4 million in criminal-justice costs, and $400,000 in welfare payments.

Abuse of other drugs costs another $27.6 million a day—$17 million in property loss through crimes, $5 million in lost work, $4 million in health programs, and $1.6 million in criminal-justice costs.

The Tobacco Habit

Got a smoke? The average American smoker smokes 31 cigarettes a day. That's 11 cigarettes a day for every adult in the country.

Reach for a Lucky instead of a gun. Kids start smoking because they're rebellious, right? Right, on the average. A study of 160 adults who had been given batteries of psychological tests as youngsters showed that those who later smoked were more rebellious, less controlled, and more resistant to authority between the ages of 5 and 15, especially when they were 12 and 13. As adults, the smokers remained more rebellious than nonsmokers. This was true of men and women alike.

Nonsmoking men tended to show a stronger drive for achievement, and to be more effective, in tighter control of themselves, less self-indulgent, and more self-satisfied than the smokers. On average, nonsmokers and moderate smokers did better in their careers than heavy smokers.

Among women, abstainers tended to be more conformist, fearful, and guilt-ridden than smokers.

Nonsmoking women had been rated, when they were adolescents, as conventional, unassuming, calm, serious, self-sufficient, and well-adjusted—though less popular than the girls who later took up the habit. Boys who did not later become smokers had been rated creative, well-adjusted, eager to succeed, popular, and prestigious.

Can't quit. Nine out of 10 smokers have already quit at least once, or would like to quit.

It makes you look grown up. Among children 12 to 14 years old, 1 of every 8 smokes.

There's nothing like a deep drag. Of every 5 cigar smokers, 2 inhale—1 a lot, the other moderately. Only 1 of every 13 pipe smokers inhales a lot, and another 1 in 13 inhales a fair amount. When it comes to cigarette smokers, only 1 of 4 *doesn't* inhale much.

Smoking it up with the gang. On average, the more extroverted you are the more cigarettes you will smoke, provided that you already have the habit.

Smoke before birth. Babies born to women who smoke in pregnancy weigh, on average, 7 ounces less than babies born to nonsmoking women.

A long way, baby. Since the surgeon general's first report on smoking and health in 1964:

The number of adult male smokers has fallen by 8.5 per cent.

But the number of adult women smokers has increased by 11.1 per cent.

Still, more men than women smoke. Of every 99 men in America, 37 smoke, 27 used to, and 35 never took up the habit. Of every 99 women, 30 smoke, 14 used to, and 55 never have.

Among heavy smokers, women outnumber men. Among people holding managerial or administrative jobs, a greater proportion of women than men smoke.

Among smokers who have quit, 38 per cent more women than men pick up the habit again.

Women tend to smoke more while talking on the phone than at any other time. Men tend to smoke less during phone conversations than at other times.

America's favorite cigarette, through the years. Let's go back to 1925, before the age of filters, with John C. Maxwell, Jr., a securities analyst who specializes in the tobacco industry.

In 1925, Camels were the most popular brand in America, with Chesterfields second and Lucky Strikes third. Luckies pulled ahead in 1930; by then Old Gold was a respectable fourth.

It took Camels almost a decade to regain the lead, but they

pulled ahead again in 1939, by a nose. Luckies were second, Chesterfield third, Philip Morris fourth, and Raleigh fifth.

Luckies, boosted by "Your Hit Parade," edged back ahead in 1941. But Camels trotted ahead in 1949 and widened their lead through the 1950s.

By then, longs and filters were coming on strong. In 1956, Pall Mall pulled ahead of Lucky Strikes to take second place, and Winston pulled ahead of Chesterfield for third. By 1960, the old order had toppled. Pall Mall was the leading brand, with Camels second, Winston third, Luckies fourth, Kent fifth, Salem sixth, L&M seventh, and Marlboro eighth.

Winston became America's favorite in 1966. And it still was in 1976, although Marlboro was a close second. Kools were third, Salem fourth, and Pall Mall fifth.

In 1976, for every American who smoked unfiltered, regular-size Camels or Luckies, three smoked Winstons.

Puff, puff, puff. In an average year, a pack-a-day cigarette smoker takes 50,000 to 70,000 puffs.

These smokers are fiends! Eighteen women smokers in 100 go through a pack a day when they're smoking heavily; 29 men smokers in 100 go through a pack on those heavy days.

Here's your typical smoker. On average, the Americans most likely to smoke are men 18 to 49 years old who live in the Midwest and have graduated from high school but not college.

That's from a 1977 Gallup Poll that asked, "Have you smoked in the past week?" Among men, 41 per cent had; among women, 36 per cent said "yes."

That's why it tastes so good. On average, a Winston gives you 40 times as much "tar" as a Carlton. More than twice as much nicotine, too.

What's in a puff? When the average American woman puffs a cigarette, each drag lasts 1.49 seconds. She puffs every 25 seconds, and gets 11½ puffs per cigarette. Altogether, her cigarette lasts 4 minutes, 29 seconds.

The average man's puff lasts a little longer—1.7 seconds. And he waits 26 seconds between puffs. He gets only 10.9 drags from a cigarette, but it lasts him 4 minutes, 34 seconds.

Some like it hot. According to a 20-year study conducted by Tufts University, the average smoker likes more spices and salt on his or her food than the average nonsmoker. The typical nonsmoker has a sweeter tooth.

Moreover, the average smoker is more energetic, self-reliant, restless, and impulsive. He or she changes jobs more often. The average nonsmoker works harder, and is a less colorful character.

Remember those delicious Camels? In 1954, the average cigarette smoker smoked a nonfiltered brand containing 36 milligrams of "tar" and more than 2 mg's of nicotine. In 1977, the average smoker was smoking a filtered brand with 17 mg's of "tar" and 1.1 mg's of nicotine.

This is real smoking. Counting cigar smokers and nonsmokers alike, the average American man smokes 63 cigars a year, and smokes up twice as much tobacco in cigars as he does in his pipe.

Dip and Chaw. Snuff is taken by 2.5 per cent of American men and by 1.3 per cent of American women. Chewing tobacco is used by 4.9 per cent of American men and by 0.6 per cent of American women.

A wad in the cheek. The average American is cutting down on cigarettes, cigars, pipe-smoking, and even snuff. But he's chawing a little more than he used to.

In 1978, 1¼ pounds of tobacco was chawed for every man in America. That's up 2½ ounces from 10 years before, and the increase has been pretty steady.

Them that chaw. According to *The Wall Street Journal*, the average tobacco chewer keeps a wad going about 2 hours. A 3-ounce package lasts him or her a week or so.

Don't you have any willpower? More than 3 Americans in 4 view smoking as a sign of weakness.

Can't beat corn silk. On average, unmarried Americans smoke less than married Americans, who in turn smoke less than widowed or divorced Americans.

As far as occupations go, a farmer is the least likely to smoke.

And I look awful at the beach. Three out of 10 American college women say they have trouble getting clothes that fit. Of those facing that agony, 1 out of 4 is too tall and 1 out of 4 is too short. One out of 10 is too fat, 1 out of 20 is too skinny, and 1 out of 3 just lacks standard measurements.

Good as new. The U. S. Agriculture Department says that moderate-income families get a fifth of their clothes from places other than retail stores—from secondhand shops, hand-me-downs, or home sewing.

Shirt story. According to the merchandise consulting firm of April-Marcus, Inc., the average man has 15 dress shirts—5 striped, 3 blue, 4 white, and 3 of some other color. Ten years ago, he owned 10 shirts, all white.

Hello. The average American makes 1,029 telephone calls a year. Together we make more than 1 billion every 2 days, 221 billion in the course of a year. We make 11 billion long-distance calls, plus 253 million overseas calls.

Fifty-three per cent of the calls are made from home phones, 46 per cent from business phones, and 1 per cent from public phones.

One phone call in 13 is long-distance. The average long-distance call connects people 543 miles apart. It lasts 8 minutes, 15 seconds, and costs $2.35. Overseas calls cost an average of $8.33 each.

Telephones are found in 96 per cent of U.S. homes. The average phone is used to make about 6 calls a day. Bell Laboratories says we answer the phone, on average, 7.1 seconds after it rings.

Where we get the news. On an average day, two thirds of us read a newspaper.

Half of us watch the news on television.

Half catch a radio newscast.

One in 4 of us gets news from a magazine.

This news comes from John P. Robinson of Cleveland State University, an expert on how people use time.

For a third of the time we're getting the news, either from the paper or from the tube, we're also doing something else—eating, dusting, chatting with the family, reading the paper while watching television, or some such.

On average, we spend 15 minutes a day reading a paper—less if we're young, more if we're old.

Older people are more likely to rely on both TV and newspapers. Young people are more likely to rely on neither, though half of young adults read a paper on an average day and a third of them catch the news on television.

The tailor will be out to fit you. Suppose the average American college man were given an unlimited clothing budget, and asked what he wanted to buy, in what order. Well, he would say, first a suit. Then more jeans, followed by sport shirts, then slacks.

Forget the unlimited budget, and ask him whether he would buy another pair of jeans before another pair of slacks, or vice versa. Three of 5 of our average college men would pick jeans.

The American in bed. The average pregnant woman sleeps 2 hours more than she did before becoming pregnant.

A woman is twice as likely as a man to have insomnia.

In one study at a sleep clinic, insomniacs estimated it took them an hour to fall asleep. Actually, the average was only 15 minutes, compared with 7 minutes for people who didn't have trouble sleeping.

Even if you go several days without sleep, you need only 11 to 13 hours to catch up.

The average person 60 or older takes naps.

On the run. The average career woman buys 22 pairs of pantyhose a year. The average college woman buys 9.

Here's his size, in case you lost it. The average American college man wears jeans size 32 waist, 32 inseam.

The book reader. The average person who reads books reads 16 of them a year and spends $36 to get them.

One reader in 5 belongs to a book club and gets a book a month.

Two readers in 5 buy books that they don't read right away, but intend to. Sometime.

The let-George-do-it approach to saving energy. In a survey, three quarters of those asked said they would be willing to carpool to save energy, but only 1 in 10 actually did it.

Half the respondents said they set their winter thermostats at 68 degrees, but only 1 in 6 cut it back to 60 degrees at night.

Forty-two per cent didn't know where the controls were on their water heater, even though it is one of the chief energy users in the average home.

Only 13 per cent thought their home had enough insulation.

Alcohol's fallout. According to the U. S. Department of Health and Human Services, alcohol plays a role in

37 of every 100 suicides
50 of every 100 highway accidents
70 of every 100 murders
40 to 50 of every 100 arrests
205,000 deaths a year
more mental-hospital admissions than any other cause.

Young drunks. Alcoholics Anonymous says more than 11 per cent of its members are under 30—that's up 50 per cent since 1974.

On your own. After the time taken up by work and other obligations, the average American has about 35 hours per week—20 per cent of his time—to himself. Housewives have about 40 hours of free time, and women with outside jobs about 30.

For racing for the bus. One pair of shoes in 4 worn by Americans these days are athletic shoes or sneakers.

Here's your average American nudist. He or she is 32 to 38 years old, according to The American Sunbathing Association, Inc., a nationwide club of 25,000 nudists. Two thirds of the club's members are married. Among single nudists, men outnumber women 7 to 3.

The average nudist is no sex bomb. According to the Sunbathing Association, "About 1 figure in 20 seen at a nudist park will be exemplary." One in 3 has surgical scars.

The average man visiting a nudist park doesn't get turned on sexually, so he does not, as the Sunbathing Association delicately puts it, "become visibly embarrassed."

Lots of Americans go out nude without joining a club. "On a given weekend," says the Association, "you might find 50,000 unaffiliated nudists at the more popular free beaches."

Why it's called high school. Of every 100 American high-school seniors, 30 smoke tobacco every day, 9 smoke marijuana every day, and 6 drink every day.

4 Sex: With Ourselves, Spouses, Friends, and Strangers

The first time. The average male has intercourse with his first sex partner 1 to 3 times before trying it with someone else. The average female has sex with her first partner 10 times before moving on.

Even the Puritans. Premarital sex was not unknown in Puritan times, according to Richard Lingeman's book *Small Town America* (G. Putnam's Sons, 1980). In Bristol, Rhode Island, for example, 49 per cent of married couples had a child within 8 months of their wedding. In Concord, Massachusetts, a third of all births in the 20 years before the Revolution were the result of out-of-wedlock couplings. Sometimes couples whose folks opposed their proposed marriages forced the issue through a pregnancy. Lingeman reports that the Puritans punished mothers who gave birth on Sundays because the Puritans believed that a child was born on the same day, 9 months later, as it was conceived. "Sexual relations on the Lord's day were of course sinful," he notes.

The gradual approach. In *Intimate Behaviour,* published by Random House in 1971, author Desmond Morris says that the average courtship works through 12 stages of contact, in this order:

1. Eye to body
2. Eye to eye
3. Voice to voice
4. Hand to hand
5. Arm around shoulder
6. Arm around waist
7. Mouth to mouth
8. Hand to head (caressing)
9. Hand to body
10. Mouth to breast
11. Hand to genitals
12. Genitals to genitals

Another dull evening with Mr. and Mrs. Swinger. Most swingers are white, middle-class, and highly educated. Betty Fang, an educator who studied the subject, says swingers also tend to be "dull homebodies with few interests, excluding watching television and reading the newspaper." One scholar gave a bunch of swingers a test called the Minnesota Multiphasic Personality Inventory. They were graded "uninterestingly normal," on average.

Inside the testicle. The average testicle is 1½ inches long, three quarters of an inch in diameter, and weighs half an ounce. It contains a third of a mile of tubes, in which it produces 50 million sperm cells in an average day—enough to populate the entire United States in 4 or 5 days.

Something usually gets in the way. The average young man ejaculates with enough force to squirt his semen 12 to 24 inches. The average old man's squirting force is a mere 3 to 12 inches.

Can't you see I'm busy now? Ask your mother. A study by the Project on Human Sexual Development—in which 1,400 parents in Cuyahoga County, Ohio, were interviewed—established that only 1 mother in 7 and 1 father in 14 got around to telling their kids about um, uhh, well, uhh, about sexual, you know, intercourse.

The wages of sin. The average prostitute makes $36,000 a year, tax-free.

She entered her line of work at the age of 17½. Before starting their careers, 4 of every 5 prostitutes were victims of incest, rape, sexual abuse, or physical abuse.

Two prostitutes in 3 were runaways. Two of 5 didn't finish high school. Four of 5 support a pimp. One of 3 has children. Only 1 of 8 has any money saved.

All that is from a study of 60 San Francisco streetwalkers, sponsored by the Unitarian Universalist Service Committee.

Get out your ruler. Erect, the average penis is 6 inches long.

The American bosom. The average American woman takes a size 34B brassiere. Next most common are 34C and 36C.

"Statistically," reports Maidenform, Inc., "our figures indicate that approximately 37 per cent of women wear B cups, 30 to 31 per cent wear C cups, 12 to 13 per cent wear D or larger cups, 16 per cent wear A cups and under A represents 3 per cent."

Molesters. According to experts in the field, the average child molester has a *subnormal* sex drive, and knows the child he or she is molesting.

Women

The Hite Report. Sociologist Shere Hite surveyed 3,000 women between the ages of 14 and 78 to find out all about their sex lives—what they do, how often, and how much they like it.

Here are some of the results, reprinted with permission of Macmillan Publishing Company, Inc., copyright © 1976 by Shere Hite:

What do women think of their genitals? Here are the results of two such questions asked by Ms. Hite:

"Do you think your vagina and genital area are ugly or beautiful?"

Beautiful; I like them	33%
Neither; neutral	26%
Ugly	16%

The rest of the answers fell somewhere in between.
"Do they smell good or bad?"

Good	28%
Good if clean	19%
Bad	15%
Sometimes good, sometimes bad	8%

The remaining 30 per cent were divided among various descriptions. One half of 1 per cent answered, "Yummy."

I want it now. Asked how often they desired sex, 21 per cent of the women queried by Ms. Hite said they wanted it daily, and another 12 per cent said they wanted it more than once a day. Eighteen per cent opted for 3 to 5 times per week, 14 per cent for 2 to 3 times a week, and another 14 per cent for 1 to 2 times per week. Eight per cent simply replied, "Often."

A list every man should read. When asked, "What is it about sex that gives you the greatest pleasure?" women replied this way:

Emotional intimacy, tenderness, a closeness, sharing deep feelings with a loved one	20%
Orgasm	16%
Touching, sensuality, body contact	14%
Pleasing him/giving	9%
The excitement just before orgasm—the passion and losing control	4%
Intercourse	4%
His orgasm	4%

Tied at 3 per cent each were "A partner I like"; "Giving and receiving pleasure"; "Foreplay"; "The sexiness of it"; "Release and relaxation"; "The 'entry,' penetration"; and "Being together after, the feeling after."

"Good cunnilingus" was picked by 2 per cent, and fellatio by 1 per cent.

Intercourse, oral sex, orgasms, and whatnot. Among women, intercourse ranks a poor fourth as a source of orgasm.

Masturbation is the hands-down winner. Eighty-two per cent of women masturbate, and of those, 95 per cent orgasm regularly.

Foreplay is second. Forty-four per cent orgasm regularly during foreplay, when the man stimulates their clitoris with his hand.

Cunnilingus is close behind, with 42 per cent of women reaching orgasm regularly from it.

As for plain old intercourse, only 30 per cent of women orgasm regularly from *that*. But another 19 per cent orgasm during intercourse with the help of clitoral stimulation by hand. Twenty-two per cent orgasm rarely from intercourse, and 29 per cent never.

Men don't know much. When women were asked, "Does your partner realize you are having an orgasm when you do?" these were the replies:

My regular partner, yes; others, almost never	47%
Yes, because I tell them	11%
Yes, if the partner is experienced	10%
Usually	9%
Yes, because I cry out, and utter moans and sighs	9%
I don't know	3%
I think so	2%
I hope so	1%

Hollywood orgasms. Ms. Hite asked women whether they faked orgasms, and 34 per cent reported they did. Another 19 per cent said they used to, but 47 per cent said they did no such play-acting.

I like it. Nearly all women say that they enjoy sex, and women who never orgasm during intercourse are just as likely to say they enjoy intercourse as women who do orgasm.

More specifically, Ms. Hite asked: "Do you like vaginal-penetration intercourse?" Of 617 respondents, 87 per cent said they liked it, 4.4 per cent said they did not, 3.4 per cent said they liked it sometimes, 3 per cent said it depends on the man, and 2 per cent said intercourse was only OK.

How women masturbate. Seventy-three per cent stimulate their clitoral-vulval area with their hand while lying on their back. Otherwise,

- 5.5 per cent do the same thing, but lying on their stomach
- 4 per cent press and thrust their clitoral-vulval area against a soft object, like a pillow
- 3 per cent press their thighs together rhythmically
- 2 per cent water-massage their clitoral-vulval area
- 1.5 per cent use vaginal entry with fingers, a vibrator, or some other object
- 11 per cent use various methods.

It's time they learned. Ms. Hite asked 587 women this question: "Are men uninformed about your sexual desires and your body?" The results:

Yes	57%
No	15%
In general most men are uninformed, but my partner is informed	12%
It varies	8%
I inform them	6%
Men are not uninformed, they just don't care	2%

Timing. Asked whether their sexual desire increased at certain times of the month, 56 per cent of the women queried by Ms. Hite said that it did before and during menstruation.

The lesbian side of things. One question Ms. Hite asked was "Do you prefer sex with men, women, yourself, or not at all?" The results:

72 per cent preferred men
 9 per cent had experience both ways, and expressed no preference
 8 per cent preferred women
 3 per cent preferred to do it alone
 3 per cent said they were too inexperienced to answer
 1 per cent preferred no sex at all.

Sexual Behavior in the 1970s

That's the title of a book by Morton Hunt, who conducted a survey of American sexual customs in 1972 and compared his findings with those of the late Dr. Alfred C. Kinsey, whose landmark surveys were conducted in the 1940s. The following items are distilled from Hunt's book.

Wow! Singles of the 1970s were at least twice as likely to vary the old missionary position by having intercourse sitting, standing, female above, on the side, and such. Hunt found that 37 per cent of single women sometimes used rear-entry vaginal intercourse, 6 times the rate in Kinsey's day. One sixth of the young, sexually active singles surveyed by Hunt had tried anal intercourse, an act on which Kinsey didn't even publish any data.

Oral sex has really taken off. Among white men up to age 25, Kinsey found that one third had experienced fellatio and 14 per cent had engaged in cunnilingus. Among Hunt's young men, the participation figures were 72 per cent and 69 per cent, respectively.

Initiation. The average young person today is most likely to have his first experience at home or at his partner's home; that includes college dorms. Compared with the average young person of past generations, he's much less likely to have it in a car, a motel, or outdoors.

Four of 10 young single men rated their first intercourse "very pleasurable," another 4 found it "mostly pleasurable," and the last 2 said it was neutral to unpleasant. The young women were less enthusiastic. Two of 10 said their first intercourse was "very pleasurable," about another 2 others rated it "mostly pleasurable," and the remainder—nearly 6—found it neutral to unpleasant.

More than a third of the males and nearly two thirds of the females said they felt regret afterward. Fear of pregnancy was the biggest reason, followed by moral conflict.

Bed census. The average single man under 25 made love with 2 women during the past year, and the average single woman that age matched him exactly. The average single man 25 to 34 years old had sex with 4 women during the year; the average single woman that age made it with 3 men.

Prolonging the pleasure. The average young, unmarried couple spends about 15 minutes in foreplay. Most of them spend at least half this time fondling their partner's genitals, but a quarter of them spend at least half the time in oral sex. Singles a little older—25 to 34—spend 5 minutes more in foreplay.

As for intercourse itself, the younger men said it averaged 12 minutes, while the younger women said it averaged 15 minutes. The older single men estimated 15 minutes, and the older single women pegged it at 17 minutes.

That foreplay time is about the same as in Kinsey's day, but intercourse seems to be lasting a lot longer. According to Kinsey, about three fourths of the men reached orgasm within 2 minutes.

Anal sex. More than half of men and women under 35 have experienced manual-anal foreplay, and more than a quarter have experienced oral-anal foreplay. Among married couples under 35, nearly a quarter use anal intercourse, at least occasionally.

The orgasmic wife. According to Hunt's research, 53 per cent of married women reach orgasm in intercourse always or almost always, 21 per cent do so about three fourths of the time, 11 per cent about half the time, 8 per cent about a quarter of the time, and 7 per cent never, or almost never.

But who watches the clock? For the average married couple, foreplay lasts 15 minutes and intercourse lasts 10 minutes.

Married folks are sexier, too. Married couples are making love more often than they used to.

Kinsey found in his research from 1939 to 1949 that couples 16 to 25 years old averaged sex 2.45 times a week, those 26 to 35 averaged 1.95 times a week, those 36 to 45 1.4 times a week, those 46 to 55 0.85 time a week, and those 56 to 60 1 time every 2 weeks.

But in 1972 Hunt found that those under 25 averaged 3.25 times a week, those 26 to 35 averaged 2.55, 36 to 44 averaged 2 times, and from 45 up 1 time a week.

Is that enough? Fewer than 5 per cent of the wives and fewer than 1 per cent of the husbands want less sex. About 1 out of 3 wives and 2 out of 5 husbands want more.

The average husband is much more likely than the average wife to want more variation in their sex life.

Divorce can be fun. A generation ago, Kinsey found that 4 per cent to 18 per cent of widowers and divorced men under 55, and nearly one third of widows and divorced women that age, had no sex life at all. In 1972, Hunt found no celibate men at all in that age range; only one tenth of the women were sexually inactive.

Hunt's divorced men and women were having sex about twice a week, the same as married couples. But the men averaged 8 different sex partners in the past year, and the women averaged 4. Also within the past year, nine tenths of the divorced men and eight tenths of the divorced women had had oral sex, and half of the group had had anal intercourse. Those rates beat every other group. The average divorced man and woman also were way ahead of the pack in diversity of intercourse positions.

Swapping and swinging. There's less of this than the tabloids would have us believe. Among married couples, Hunt found that only 2 per cent of the men and less than 2 per cent of the women had ever swapped partners; most of these women had done it only once. As for group sex, 18 per cent of the married men and 6 per cent of the married women had had sex while others were doing the same thing in the same room; 13 per cent of the married men and under 2 per cent of the married women had had real group sex, meaning three or more people in bed together. But most of them did it before marriage, and even then only once.

Among young singles, 15 per cent of the men and 4 per cent of the women had tried partner swapping; 17 per cent of the men and 5 per cent of the women had tried real group sex.

Fidelity. Here's a surprise for you: The average husband and wife today are no more likely to cheat than were their counterparts of a generation ago.

Of course, a generation ago, Kinsey found a good deal of it, with about a quarter of American wives cheating on their husbands by age 40, and even more husbands cheating.

Hunt concluded that about half of married men had cheated. Among married women, only 17 per cent of those still married had cheated, whereas 52 per cent of the divorcees had cheated while married.

Nice people don't do it. About 1 out of every 25 men has had intercourse with a cousin, and about 1 of every 67 with a sister. On average, an incestuous mating costs the offspring about 20 IQ points.

Masturbation and religion. Hunt found that 93 per cent of nonchurchgoing men masturbate. But going to church doesn't make a whole lot of difference: Ninety-two per cent of men who regularly attend worship services masturbate, too.

Among women, however, 75 per cent of nonchurchgoers, 69 per cent of irregular churchgoers, and only 51 per cent of regular churchgoers reported masturbating.

More than Kinsey, but less than Portnoy. The average man between 18 and 24 who masturbates does it once a week—three times a year more than in Kinsey's day.

At age 30, more than 90 per cent of those who masturbated when young still masturbate, and they do it more often than before, averaging 60 times a year.

The average woman between 18 and 24 who masturbates does it 37 times a year—16 more times than in Kinsey's day.

Among single women, 60 per cent of those 18 to 24 masturbate, and more than 80 per cent of those in their late 20s and early 30s do.

About 2 out of 3 married men and women in their 20s masturbate. The husbands average 24 times a year, the wives 10.

The sexual revolution is real. Proportionally, about twice as many single men in their late teens and early 20s are sexually active today than were a generation ago. They're having it a third again as frequently, too.

That's nothing compared to feminine progress. A single woman in her late teens or early 20s is 2 to 3 times as likely to be having sex as her more demure predecessor. And she's having it at least three times as often.

By age 17, half the boys who later went to college, and nearly three fourths of those who did not, had had intercourse.

Nearly one fifth of the white married women said they had had intercourse before their seventeenth birthday. Among white women who did not later marry, one third had done it before age 17.

By their twenty-fourth birthday, 70 per cent of white women who remained single and 80 per cent of white women who later married had had premarital intercourse. Just over half of the nonvirgin brides had made love with one man only— their future husband.

Who did men have sex with in the old days? Married men and women ranging from teen-agers to old folks were asked whether they had had sexual intercourse before marriage. Among men, the "yes" answers were pretty high at all ages— ranging from 95 per cent of those between 18 and 24 to 84 per cent of those over age 54.

But while 81 per cent of young married women said they had engaged in premarital sex, only 36 per cent of those over 45 and 31 per cent of those over 54 said they had.

Whip-and-chain stuff. Sado-masochism ain't the average couple's cup of tea. Hunt found that only 4.8 per cent of men and 2.1 per cent of women get sexual pleasure from inflicting pain. Interestingly, 2.5 per cent of men and 4.6 per cent of women get sexual pleasure from receiving pain.

A real trend. Nearly three fourths of men 25 or younger have been fellated before marriage, up from less than a third in Kinsey's day.

Who patronizes prostitutes? Most men used to, at least occasionally, but no more. Among married men surveyed by Hunt in 1972, a majority of those 35 and older had patronized prostitutes. But of those men under 35, less than a third had done so. The average college man is less likely to go to a prostitute than is the average noncollege man; that's always been true.

Now, there's a young mother! One of every 500 babies in America is born to a girl under 15 years old.

Babies or books. On average, for every year a high-school girl puts off having a baby she'll finish another year of school.

Late pregnancies. Almost 1 baby in 20 in the United States is born to a woman who is over 35.

Prostitutes again. The average call girl turns 15 to 20 tricks a night. At least three quarters of her clients choose fellatio.

So writes David Reuben, M.D., in *Everything You Always Wanted to Know About Sex—but were afraid to ask,* published by David McKay Co., Inc., in 1969.

Sex and the thermometer. The average person's sexual vitality seems to increase when the weather is nice. Women are more fertile in May and June, when the temperature is around 65 degrees, than in the dead of winter or the height of summer.

It's seductive. The average American woman, regardless of age, anoints herself with cologne or perfume. So does the average American man.

To be exact, 97 per cent of American women and 81 per cent of American men wear scents.

Among women, 92 per cent use cologne and 48 per cent use perfume, with, apparently, a lot using both. Among men, 2 out of 3 use aftershave, half use cologne, and 3 out of 10 use both.

Younger women go for colognes with a spicy floral scent, like Charlie, which outsells the rest. Older women prefer the oriental or semioriental smell of brands like Youth Dew. But that could change; 3 women out of 4 have switched brands sometime or another. At the time of the survey, the average cologne user had been faithful to her brand for 1.91 years.

One perfume user of every 11 uses Chanel No. 5. One in 20 uses Charlie perfume (as opposed to Charlie cologne). L'Air du Temps ranks third, but it slipped between 1976 and 1978. So did Youth Dew.

Among men, cologne is gaining at the expense of aftershave. In 1978, Brut and Old Spice were head-to-head leaders in the cologne business, with 13 per cent of the market apiece. Old Spice had 22 per cent of the aftershave market, twice as much as the second brand, Mennen Skin Bracer.

In and out of wedlock. Nine per cent of kids today are born before their mothers marry. Another 24 per cent are born less than 9 months after the wedding. Thus a third of all first births in the United States are conceived before marriage.

Eighty-five per cent of women who bear children out of wedlock eventually marry.

Eleven per cent of the children born to women who divorce and remarry are born between marriages.

Women who remarry tend to have three fifths of their children by husband No. 1.

You never know when. Pregnancy results from 1 of every 288 acts of intercourse (taking birth control into account).

The pregnancy bulge. An average woman increases her weight by 24 per cent during pregnancy. She loses about 9 per cent of her weight just before and during childbirth, and another 4 per cent during the next 10 days. From there on, weight loss comes slow and hard.

A practical note about intercourse positions. A woman is most likely to get pregnant if the couple has intercourse in the "male superior" position, with the woman on her back.

It also helps to put a pillow under her buttocks, because that tends to keep the semen in.

What Kinsey learned about homosexuality. When Kinsey asked 5,300 white males and 5,940 white females, he discovered:

Among the males:

37 per cent had at least one overt homosexual experience between the onset of adolescence and old age.

10 per cent were predominantly homosexual for at least 3 years between the ages of 16 and 55.

4 per cent were solely homosexual after the onset of adolescence.

The highest incidence of homosexual activities occurred among unskilled and semiskilled workers and the lower white-collar class; among those with high-school education and urban backgrounds; among the least active church members. The lowest incidence occurred among professional, white-collar, and college-educated men.

Among the females:

13 per cent had at least one overt homosexual experience between adolescence and old age.

28 per cent had either a covert or an overt experience.

In any age group, there were likely to be more male than female homosexuals. In some age groups, there were twice as many male homosexuals.

The incidence of female homosexuality was highest among those with college and postgraduate education. The better educated they were, the more likely women were to engage in homosexual activity.

Who's homosexual? Nearly 1 American in 10, says the Institute of Sex Research—13 per cent of the country's males and 5 per cent of the females. The Institute defines a homosexual as any adult who has had more than 6 sexual experiences with someone of the same gender.

Alcoholism runs 20 per cent to 30 per cent heavier among homosexuals than among the population as a whole.

Pregnant so soon? According to the Alan Guttmacher Institute, 1 in 10 teen-age girls in the United States gets pregnant in an average year. That's 1 million girls. About 300,000 of them are married when their baby is born; another 100,000 marry after giving birth; 300,000 have abortions; and 200,000 miscarry. Thirty thousand have not reached their 15th birthday at the time of conception.

We could watch the late news. . . . . After intercourse, the average man must wait a half hour before he can get another erection. But it's a strain for him to ejaculate more than once a session.

Turned on by porn. Some of Kinsey's findings indicated that women don't get as aroused by pornography as men do. To test this, Professor Marvin Zuckerman of the University of Delaware showed two sexy movies to a group of men and women. One was more wholesome; it had intercourse and all that, but between a loving couple, with no oral sex. The other was pure porn—a motel orgy with one man, two women, and all sorts of sex acts.

Zuckerman found that the women, on average, got a bit more aroused *anticipating* the movies than the men did. Most everyone, male and female, got turned on by both movies. The professor concluded that the average man and woman respond equally to pornography.

Surprise packages. According to the Census Bureau, 40 per cent of the infants born in the United States are unwanted or ill timed.

In a study by the National Survey of Family Growth several years ago, 13 per cent of mothers said their last child was unplanned and unwanted at the time of conception.

The Census Bureau, reporting that result, cautions that it may be "a substantial understatement of the reality," since women might not recall or might not want to recall how they felt about a baby they have since come to love.

A flash of flesh. According to research by home economists at Stanford University and the University of Tennessee, women are well aware of sexy clothes and their effect on men, but don't wear them often.

The Tennessee scholars asked coeds to rate items of feminine clothing according to sex appeal.

The results indicate that the average woman considers her bosom sexier than her legs. The women rated halters highest in sex appeal, followed in order by plunging necklines and midriff tops. Then came short dresses and skirts, clingy knits, hot pants, bare shoulders, knit shirts, buttons partially unfastened, and sheer garments.

The women seemed to have a high opinion of the brassiere. Going braless came out sexy, but just barely.

Problems in bed. William H. Masters and Virginia E. Johnson, the renowned sex researchers and clinicians, estimate that every other married couple suffers from a sexual "dysfunction."

They used the term broadly. One common dysfunction is one spouse wanting to make love a lot more often than the other one.

Here's some stuff about sex therapy. The average couple taking sex therapy goes for 3 to 12 hourly sessions at $35 to $100 a crack. Of every 10 patients, 8 are married and are between 25 and 55 years old.

These are the estimates of Patricia Schiller, M.A., J.D., executive director of the American Association of Sex Educators, Counselors, and Therapists. She lists the most common problems, in order, as:

Nonorgastic female

Vaginismus (painful intercourse)

Premature ejaculation

Secondary impotence (Inability to have intercourse, after having had it successfully before)

Ejaculatory incompetence (Inability to ejaculate during intercourse)

Sex and the aging

Aversion to sex

Sex and the physically handicapped

We asked Ms. Schiller how long the average couple had gone without treatment. "Longer than you think," she replied.

Ugh. One married woman in 100 is absolutely repelled by intercourse.

Not tonight, honey. When 227 husbands and 233 wives were asked to list their favorite recreational activities, more men listed sex than anything else. More women said they would rather read a book.

As couples get older, the study concluded, both husband and wife tend to prefer other kinds of recreation to sex. Among couples married fewer than 5 years, 55 per cent of the husbands and 27 per cent of the wives named sex as their favorite leisure activity. Among those married 36 to 50 years, only 14 per cent of the husbands and none of the wives listed sex as No. 1.

Here it comes, ready or not. For 2 to 4 seconds just before he ejaculates, the average man knows that he's about to ejaculate, and couldn't stop if he tried.

What little angels learn from each other. In Kinsey's day, the average little boy learned about sex considerably before the average little girl did. Now the average little girl learns at just as young an age—in fact, a trace younger.

Grown-ups always tell each other that kids shouldn't learn about sex on the street, but most of them still do. They're told by other kids. But mothers and the media are gaining fast as sources of initial sex knowledge. Fathers aren't much good at it. A little boy is almost twice as likely to have been told about sex by his mother than by his father. As for little girls, fathers rate a 0 on the list of sources of sex knowledge.

College women catch up. When Alfred Kinsey did his studies in the 1940s, he found that 42 per cent of college men and 18 per cent of college women had had premarital sexual intercourse. When Professor Marvin Zuckerman of the University of Delaware surveyed students at his university in 1973, he found that 66 per cent of the men and 63 per cent of the women had had premarital intercourse.

Zuckerman found what seemed to be a contradiction between attitudes and behavior. When he asked University of Delaware students whether they *approved* of various sexual joys before marriage, the females, on average, disapproved more strongly than the males. But on the same questionnaire, he also asked the students whether they had *done* these things. To screen out youngsters who might have gotten carried away once or twice, he asked them to answer "yes" only if they had engaged in the act 10 times or more. Here are the percentages of those who had done these things or had them done to him or her.

	Male	Female
Feeling nude breasts	73%	75%
Manipulation of penis	55%	62%
Manipulation of female genitals	63%	65%
Fellatio	34%	40%
Cunnilingus	33%	39%
Intercourse		
Male on top	34%	40%
Female on top	36%	39%
Sideways	20%	19%
Rear entry	22%	13%

Does that mean the girls were hypocrites? Nope, Zuckerman decided, merely that the girls felt pretty free about sex with someone they cared for, but disapproved of casual sex, while the boys were more on the casual side. Zuckerman pinned that down by asking how many sex partners each student had had in the past year. The results:

Numbers of partners	Male	Female
None	16%	27%
1	14%	35%
2	10%	15%
3	16%	5%
4 or more	43%	17%

Rape. One woman is raped in the United States every 9 minutes.

Man versus machine. According to research by Masters and Johnson, the average woman using an electric vibrator can keep it up for an hour or more, and have as many as 50 orgasms.

During sex with a partner, only about 1 woman in 6 has multiple orgasms.

Should you cheat on your spouse? Never, said two thirds of the respondents in a 1978 Gallup Poll.

The proportion who believed that cheating is "always wrong" was 52 per cent among people 18 to 29 years old, 61 per cent among those 30 to 49, and 77 per cent among folks 50 or older. It was 53 per cent among people with a college background, 66 per cent among those who went to high school, and 80 per cent among those who went no farther than grade school. It was 71 per cent for Protestants and 64 per cent for Catholics, 74 per cent among people who go to church, and 53 per cent among people who don't.

Altogether, 60 per cent of men and 69 per cent of women said that it was always wrong to cheat on your spouse.

Four Americans in 5 disapprove of mate swapping, even when it is agreed to by both partners in a marriage.

What the unfaithful's spouse would do about it. Sixteen per cent of the husbands and 9 per cent of the wives in a survey say they'd demand a divorce if they found their mate were unfaithful.

Fifty-two per cent of the couples would talk it over. Twelve per cent of the husbands and 11 per cent of the wives say they'd try to forgive cheating, but none of the husbands and only 2 per cent of the wives say they'd ignore it.

Twenty-eight per cent say they don't know what they'd do.

The majority of those surveyed felt that, among their friends, unfaithfulness by husband or wife would cause a divorce.

The double standard. For every American wife who cheats on her husband, 2 American husbands cheat on their wives.

By the numbers, now. An average ejaculation lasts 10 seconds and squirts one quarter fluid ounce of semen in about 6 bursts. That's about two thirds of a teaspoon.

The average man squirts out about 18 quarts of semen in a lifetime, containing nearly 1.5 trillion sperm.

Replacing what's lost. It takes the average man 30 to 40 hours to replace all the sperm and semen from an ejaculation.

Living Together

What roommates also do. A study at Cornell University indicates that living together doesn't hurt grades. Students who shared their beds got grades as high as or higher than those who didn't.

Who cohabits. One bachelor in 5 lives with a woman before he's 30.

How often does living together lead to marriage? About 1 time in 3, according to two sociologists who surveyed 2,510 males aged 20 to 30.

"Living together" was defined as cohabitating for six months or more. Most men who do it do it only once. One third said they had lived with more than one woman.

High-school dropouts, the survey showed, are more likely than college students to live together; blacks are more likely than whites; and men in big cities are twice as likely as those in small towns.

In a survey of college students who had cohabitated, 57 per cent said they had neglected to tell their parents about their new living arrangement. Ninety-one per cent of the women and 75 per cent of the men said their parents would disapprove.

Incidentally, here's how a sociologist phrases the question:

"Are you now living, or have you ever lived, with someone in a cohabitant relationship?"

How it works in Florida. The average unmarried man and woman living together have had more sexual partners than the typical married couple. On average, unmarried men and women who live together also are less satisfied with their sex experiences than are married couples, and the former are more likely to have engaged in group sex. Also, the unmarried women tended to have their first sex experience at a younger age than did the married women, and the unmarried men were less satisfied with their first sex experience than were the married men.

All that came from a study of 50 married couples and 50 cohabiting couples, all in Florida.

Your place or mine? Of every 5 cohabiting couples, 3 live at his place and 2 live at hers.

Three in 4 are under 45. One in 10 includes a person 65 or older. One in 12 divorced men under the age of 35 lives with a woman.

This comes from the U. S. Census Bureau, which reports that 3.6 per cent of all unmarried adults in America live together as couples. In 1977, the Census counted 2 million such households.

Roommates whose clothes you can't borrow. By graduation, 30 per cent to 40 per cent of all college students have lived with someone of the opposite sex. In surveys, 80 per cent said they would have if they'd had the chance.

At the University of Texas, 36 per cent cohabit. Even at a commuter college like City College of New York, 1 in 5 shares quarters with a member of the opposite sex.

Gay at an early age. One third of male homosexuals know it by their thirteenth birthday, and 9 out of 10 by their seventeenth birthday. For 85 per cent of them, the first sex experience is homosexual.

Lesbians. The average young lesbian has had at least as much sex with *men* as has the typical heterosexual woman of the same age. The average young lesbian also masturbates more.

When the average lesbian passes her early 20s, she tends to stick to women more.

Artificial insemination. In an average year in America, 10,000 children are conceived through artificial insemination. In 10 per cent to 20 per cent of the instances, sperm that has been frozen, stored, then thawed, is used. But, according to Dr. Armand M.

Karow, Jr., a consultant to the sperm bank at the Medical College of Georgia, only 1 man in 7 has sperm capable of surviving the freezing process in sufficient numbers to result in a pregnancy.

The use of artificial insemination, whether the sperm is fresh or frozen, results in the birth of six boys to every four girls, Karow says.

In a University of Arkansas study of more than 1,000 children conceived through artificial insemination using thawed sperm, fewer than 1 per cent suffered from birth defects, compared with 6 per cent in the population at large. Moreover, there were fewer than 6 per cent miscarriages, half the normal number.

Sex in infancy. Sex differences show up in human beings at a very young age. Researchers have found, for example, that the average 3-week-old boy puts something in his mouth (a rattle or his fist) an average of 36.8 times every 8 hours, while a girl does it 30.6 times. At 3 months, however, girls are doing it 116.2 times per 8 hour period and boys 61.2 times.

Never too young. According to Kinsey, 1 boy in 3 has partial orgasms before his first birthday. More than half do between the ages of 2 and 5, and 4 out of 5 do between the ages of 10 to 13.

Of course, the little boys don't ejaculate.

As for little girls, Kinsey says that 1 of 333 has a partial orgasm by her third birthday, and 1 of 25 by her seventh.

Not enough to show. The left breast of the average woman is a little bigger than the right breast.

They average 6 ounces.

Practicing. According to the American Medical Association, men and women who have masturbated regularly tend to have better sex lives.

Just playing. Through about age 5, the average child picks playmates without paying attention to whether they're boys or girls. From 5 to 6 until puberty, he or she generally plays with children of the same gender, and becomes downright hostile to members of the opposite sex.

At puberty, that hostility melts into shyness.

1,500 homosexuals. Sexual preference aside, the average homosexual leads a pretty ordinary life. Psychologically, he or she appears to be well adjusted. He or she has more good, close friends than do heterosexuals, and many of the friends are straight. He or she is neither more nor less sexually active than heterosexuals. Homosexual men change jobs no more often than other men do.

That portrait comes from a government-funded investigation by the Institute for Sex Research, the outfit did the original Kinsey report. Fifteen hundred male and female homosexuals in the San Francisco area were interviewed. The results were published in *Homosexuality: A Study of Human Diversity* by Alan P. Bell and Martin S. Weinberg (Simon, 1978).

More than a third of the women and nearly a fifth of the men reported that they had been married at some time to a member of the opposite sex. Most of the once-married men said they had had pretty active sex lives with their wives; half said they engaged in intercourse 2 to 4 times a week during the first year of marriage.

Almost half the white men and a third of the black men said they had had at least 200 sexual partners during their homosexual careers.

Sexy nutrition. Among other things, semen contains a little cholesterol, protein, and vitamin C.

Going steady in the 1960s. Compare these statistics to current campus practices:

For 75 per cent of young people who went steady, the term meant a commitment not to date others and a willingness to publicly declare that they were "in love." For 50 per cent it meant a commitment to see each other whenever either one wanted. For 80 per cent of those going steady, there had been talk of getting married. Half thought they would marry each other, and 40 per cent had informally committed themselves to it.

Seventy-five to 80 per cent of young people said it was all right for couples who are in love to pet. Sixty per cent had petted. Between 70 per cent and 85 per cent of couples going steady had petted.

About one fifth had had sexual intercourse.

Not surprisingly, the longer a couple went steady the more likely they were to have decided the marriage question. In the first two months, one study said, 44 per cent of the couples hadn't decided whether to marry. After six months, only 21 per cent hadn't decided.

If their best friends were informally engaged, a steady couple were 10 times more likely to commit themselves to marriage than otherwise.

About menopause. The average American woman starts menopause at age 50, 10 years later than her grandmother did.

Childless couples. On average, 1 couple in 10 is physically unable to have a baby.

This is straight from Masters and Johnson. When a woman gets sexually excited, her vaginal barrel lengthens from about 3¼ inches to about 4½ inches, on average. At cervix level, it widens from about 1¼ inches to about 2¾ inches.

As the woman moves into the plateau phase, the outer part of her vagina actually shrinks, or tightens up, to grip the man's penis. Incidentally, that's why the experts say that the size of the penis isn't important.

Unsexy sex differences. Everybody knows that the average man is taller than the average woman. But did you know that:

The average man has a bigger mouth.

The fingers of the average woman are more tapered.

The average man has a heavier brain and heart, and more blood cells.

The average woman is more inclined to be knockkneed, and, because she has less water in her body, doesn't hold her alcohol as well.

The average girl is more likely to obey her parents than is the

average boy, and she is less likely to worry about what her
friends think.

The average boy is better at math. The average girl has
higher verbal ability.

The average baby girl smiles more than the average baby boy.

Does circumcision make a penis more or less sensitive? No
difference either way, according to Masters and Johnson.

Nurses, propositions and such. In separate studies, academic
researchers tested two theories that they considered sexual stere-
otypes.

1. Are nurses permissive about sex? The researchers compared the attitudes of nurses with the attitudes of an equal number of college women, and found no difference.

2. Does a woman turn a man off when she propositions him,
rather than playing hard-to-get? Professor Clinton J. Esser of
Northern Illinois University questioned a number of women and
men about this. The women told him, on average, they had no
better or worse luck propositioning men than trying to lure them
into bed. The men said that they generally complied with propositions and, for that matter, with indirect advances, too.

About sperm. Nine of 10 sperm are the normal oval shape. The
others are abnormally tapered, round, or big.

Keeping up the pace. The average man who is very active sexually when young continues to be very active when old.

Getting ready. Within a half minute of beginning any kind of
sexual stimulation, the average young woman's vagina is well lu-
bricated. The average woman past menopause takes a little
longer—a minute or so.

The average young woman has longer orgasms than does the
typical older woman. The former average 8 to 12 vaginal con-
tractions per orgasm; the latter average 4 or 5.

Full to bursting. As the average man approaches ejaculation,
his testicles rise in the scrotum, and swell by about 50 per cent.

Sex for Fun, Not Babies

How they do it. Of every 100 married women in America

22 use the pill
10 are sterilized
10 have sterilized husbands
 7 have husbands who use condoms
 6 use an IUD
 3 use a diaphragm
10 use the douche, withdrawal, or some other method
32 don't practice birth control.

Boycotting birth. In 1976, there were twice as many women of childbearing age in the United States as there were in 1921. But in 1976, they had only 4 per cent more babies.

Abortions. For every 10 babies born in the United States, there are 4 legal abortions. Three out of 4 abortions are performed on unmarried women. One in 3 is performed on a woman under age 20. Nine in 10 occur within the first 12 weeks of pregnancy.

Who uses birth control. The government says that white wives are more likely than black wives to use contraceptives. Women with 2 or more children are more likely to use them than those with fewer kids, or none. Catholic women are only 4 per cent less likely to use contraceptives than Protestant women. Today, fewer than 3 per cent of women use the rhythm method, the only means of birth control officially sanctioned by the Catholic Church. In 1965, a survey found that 7.5 per cent of American women were using rhythm.

Look, Ma, no . . . Thirty-seven per cent of sexually experienced teen-agers say they used no birth-control method the last time they had intercourse. Twenty-five per cent say they never touch the stuff.

Tying the tubes. In terms of unanticipated pregnancies, surgical sterilizations are, on average, 100 times more effective than the next-most-efficient method of birth control, the pill. The Association for Voluntary Sterilization says that vasectomies work 998 times out of 1,000.

About 1 million Americans undergo sterilization each year. Slightly more than half of them are women.

A quarter to a half of the women say their sexual activity and satisfaction increased following sterilization. A quarter to a half say it remained the same. A small fraction say their sexual satisfaction deteriorated following the operation.

Some sterilizations are surgically reversible, but no more than 25 per cent of the women who have had their tubes reconnected have conceived.

Which came first, the knowledge or the attitude? On average, the more a college student knows about contraceptives, the more sexually permissive he or she is. So report 3 academics who surveyed 392 college students.

Ain't nature grand? When erect, the average penis points upward at an angle of 20 to 40 degrees. So does the average vagina.

VD and condoms. On average, a kid not yet 15 is more likely to get gonorrhea than a man or woman 50 or older. But the older person is more likely to get syphilis.

You are 3 times more likely to get venereal disease this year than you were 8 or 10 years ago.

Counting every man, woman, and child, the average American buys 2 condoms a year.

Have a pleasant journey. Once ejaculated, sperm swim at an average speed of 7 inches an hour.

It's sex, sex, sex everywhere you turn. American parents think that the high rate of teen-age pregnancy results mostly from peer pressure, movies, and other outside influences, not from permissive parenting.

Their teen-age children think so, too.

Pant, pant. During orgasm, the average person's respiration increases to 40 breaths or more a minute, and the heart rate thumps up to between 110 and 180.

The blood pressure of the average man rises by 40 to 100 systolic, 20 to 50 diastolic. In the average woman, it rises by 30 to 80 systolic, 20 to 40 diastolic.

Among people who had suffered heart attacks, it was found that the heart averaged 117 beats at the highest point during intercourse, and stayed that high only 10 to 15 seconds. That uses up about the same amount of oxygen needed to climb a flight of stairs.

The pregnancy habit. Of every 20 unmarried teen-age girls who get pregnant, 19 will get pregnant again within 5 years, and 18 still won't be married. Twelve will be on welfare.

Boys first. Although the average girl matures physically before the average boy, the boy starts masturbating earlier.

Good news for some men. The average small penis grows more when getting erect than the average large penis does, so the two come out pretty close to the same size.

Rebelling with your body. Teen-age girls who don't get along with their parents in general, and adolescent boys who don't get along with their mothers in particular, tend to start their sex lives earlier than teen-agers who do get along with their parents.

Wet dreams. A man is twice as likely as a woman to have a dream that results in an orgasm.

What's your daughter been doing? The average freshman college woman who chooses a coed dorm already has more sexual experience than the typical freshman woman who chooses an all-female dorm.

For male college freshmen, there's no such difference.

And that's not all. The average person's toes curl when he or she is sexually aroused.

5 The Mind: Its Thoughts, Moods, and Memories

The spark of youth. Most creative work is done at a pretty early age. Here, from a widely accepted study by Harvey C. Lehman, are the age ranges for the "maximum average rate of creative production."

Before 30	30 to 34	35 to 39	40 and older
Chemistry	Mathematics	Astronomy	Novels
Poetry	Physics	Physiology	Architecture
	Botany	Opera	
	Symphonies	Philosophy	

Hitting the books, softly. Paul Copperman, president of the Institute of Reading Development, in California, says the average kid today learns less in school than her or his parents did.

In testimony before the U. S. Senate Subcommittee on Education, Arts, and the Humanities, Copperman said: "The average high-school student today takes 25 per cent less English, 35 per cent less world history, 35 per cent less government and civics, 30 per cent less geography, and 20 per cent less science and math than students a generation ago. He is assigned less homework, and the textbooks he is given have been rewritten with a reading level two years lower than the grade he is in."

What kids study. Of every 100 kids in grades 7 through 12 in public schools, virtually all study English, health, and social sciences, and take gym each year. Seventy-one study math, 67 study sciences, 33 study music, 34 take business courses, 31 take shop, 25 take home economics, 24 study foreign languages, 27 study art, 2 take courses in agriculture, and 3 take vocational and industrial training.

¿Que pasa en la escuela? Of that quarter of the kids in public high schools who take foreign languages, here's what they study:

Spanish	54%
French	31%
German	13%
Italian	1.3%
Russian	.4%
Other modern languages	.7%
Latin	5.4%

The sugar-pill cure. If you think a lot of reported sickness is all in the head, here's valuable evidence to support your view. Twenty per cent to 40 per cent of all prescriptions written are for placebos—harmless, unmedicated preparations given merely to humor patients.

Ten studies on the effects of placebos show that in 35 per cent of the cases patients reported satisfactory pain relief after taking them. These patients had complained of pain from surgery, cancer, headaches, and angina pectoris.

Placebos have also been known to relieve anxiety, headaches, motor sickness, warts, bleeding, ulcers, arthritic stiffness, gastric hyperacidity, coughing, the common cold, and vomiting.

A breakdown on nervous breakdowns. A woman in America is twice as likely as a man to have a nervous breakdown.

When a woman feels that she is on the edge, she will pull through without a breakdown 3 times out of 4. So will a man.

The most likely time of life for a nervous breakdown is between ages 55 and 64. Not counting childhood, the least likely period is between 25 and 34.

So Much for Reason

We're all sheep. Sociologists say that the average person picks up the opinions and attitudes that are important to him from his parents and peers, not from analyzing information and ideas. The average independent voter is less interested in politics and less informed about it than the average Democrat or Republican.

They really are stuck up. The average person's opinion of himself has a lot to do with her or his social class. Upper-class people really do tend to feel superior, and lower-class people tend to feel inferior, according to a number of studies.

Now, I'm not prejudiced myself. Social researchers have found that the typical American is more prejudiced than he or she thinks, and the average person who is prejudiced against one ethnic group tends to be biased against others as well.

The class of '82. In the fall of 1978, the American Council of Education surveyed 187,603 students entering 383 colleges and universities. Here is a portrait of the average college freshman.

He or she is 18 years old (75 per cent), white (89 per cent), and politically middle of the road (58 per cent, with 2 per cent far left and 1 per cent far right). Fifty-two of 100 are men.

He or she had a B average in high school (59 per cent) and ranked in the top quarter (46 per cent) or second quarter (34 per cent) of his or her graduating class. In high school, he or she took a college preparatory program (88 per cent) but now feels that it did not prepare him or her very well for college work, particularly in foreign languages (only 17 per cent felt well prepared) and study habits (only 19 per cent). On the other hand, he or she feels no need for remedial work.

Among these freshmen, 16 per cent came from families with an annual income of less than $10,000. Another 18 per cent came from families with an income of $10,000 to $15,000. The biggest group, 33 per cent, came from families with an income of $15,000 to $25,000, and another 17 per cent had a family income of $25,000 to $35,000. Nine per cent came from families earning $35,000 to $50,000, and 7 per cent had a family income over $50,000.

He or she has siblings (only 5 per cent are only children), but, to the parents' relief, he or she is the only family member now in college (in 67 per cent of the cases).

He or she decided to go to college to learn more (74 per cent), make more money (60 per cent), get a better job (75 per cent), get a general education (68 per cent), and to meet new and interesting people (57 per cent).

The college he or she attends was his or her first choice (76 per cent), and he or she picked it because of its academic reputation (51 per cent) and certainly not because of anything relatives said (6 per cent).

If he or she applied anywhere else (37 per cent didn't), it was to 3 or more other colleges (27 per cent). He or she was accepted by at least 1 other school.

He or she is single (99 per cent). Eight per cent of his or her classmates have no religious affiliation, and 30 per cent call themselves reborn Christians.

Of his or her classmates, 11 per cent don't know what they want to do for a living, but 9 per cent want to be engineers (including 2 per cent of the women), 9 per cent want to be business executives, 6 per cent want to be accountants or actuaries, 4 per cent want to be doctors, 4 per cent nurses, 4 per cent lawyers, and 4 per cent computer experts. Six per cent want to teach. Of the women, only 3 in 1,000 want to be full-time homemakers.

Dad is a businessman (30 per cent), skilled worker (11 per cent), or engineer (9 per cent). He lacks a college degree (64 per cent). Mom is a full-time homemaker (31 per cent), a clerk (10 per cent), or a businesswoman (8 per cent). She also lacks a college degree (77 per cent).

In the past year, our freshman has gone to a house of worship (86 per cent), attended a recital or a concert (82 per cent), drunk beer (73 per cent), stayed up all night (67 per cent), and taken vitamins (59 per cent). He or she has not played a musical instrument (44 per cent), jogged (25 per cent), participated in a demonstration (17 per cent), smoked cigarettes (14 per cent), worked in a political campaign (9 per cent), or taken a tranquilizer (5 per cent), or sleeping pills (3 per cent).

Most likely, he or she is not on a scholarship, and is therefore concerned about paying the tuition bills (65 per cent). Mom and Dad help out with the college bills (72 per cent). Parents provide over $2,000 in 23 per cent of the cases, and most families (64 per cent) contribute at least $600 per year.

Our freshman didn't save anything from a summer job (53 per cent), has no other savings (80 per cent), and doesn't have a job at school (73 per cent)—at least not yet.

He or she lives in a dormitory (56 per cent). Home is less than 100 miles away (64 per cent).

Our average freshman wants to be an authority in his or her field (73 per cent), to help people in difficulty (66 per cent), to raise a family (62 per cent), to get rich (60 per cent), and to develop a philosophy of life (57 per cent). Among his or her classmates, only 15 per cent want to influence the political structure, 28 per cent want to get involved in environmental cleanup, and 34 per cent want to promote racial understanding.

Smiling on Main Street. A Gallup poll reported that the happiest Americans live in towns with populations of 2,500 to 50,000. The largest proportion of sad people live in big cities, but even there the great majority are happy.

Happy Yankee Doodle. According to Gallup polls, the average American is twice as happy as the average West German, and more than 5 times as happy as the average resident of the Far East.

Who's happy, who's not. On average, married Americans are happier than single Americans, and working wives are happier than housewives. Old people are no less happy than younger people and happy teen-agers aren't much more likely to be happy as adults than unhappy teen-agers.

On average, the occupations that seem to make people the happiest are entertainer, psychologist, and clergyman. The average lawyer and doctor are on the unhappy side, and the unhappiest occupations of all are clerk, secretary, and blue-collar worker.

These conclusions come from a survey of 100,000 Americans conducted by Jonathan L. Freedman, a psychology professor at Columbia University.

Upbeat and downbeat. Nine of every 10 Americans say that their life is satisfying.

In a poll conducted for the U. S. Department of Labor by the University of Michigan Survey Research Center, Americans were asked to grade their own satisfaction with life as it is. There were 7 shades, from best to worst, for each of 8 categories. Here are the percentages of people who, in describing their own lives, picked either of the 2 extremes:

Interesting	30%	Boring	1%
Enjoyable	31%	Miserable	1%
Worthwhile	41%	Useless	2%
Friendly	43%	Lonely	2%
Full	37%	Empty	1%
Hopeful	37%	Discouraging	2%
Rewarding	30%	Disappointing	2%
Brings out the best in me	23%	Doesn't give me a chance	2%

Never play Scrabble with that kid. According to behaviorists, the average person is at her or his cleverest in the teens or early 20s, and at her or his most understanding in old age.

The illiterate American. The average American can read and write.

Official statistics from the Department of Education say that only 1.2 per cent of the public is totally illiterate.

Illiteracy is highest in Louisiana, where 28 in 1,000 are illiterate. It's lowest—5 people in 1,000—in Iowa, Nevada, and South Dakota.

A 1971 study by the Lou Harris organization concluded that 15 per cent of the public are "functionally illiterate"—unable to comprehend such things as want ads, job applications, directions for long-distance dialing, and Social Security forms.

A University of Texas study in 1975 reported that as many as 1 person in 5 has such trouble reading that he or she functions only with difficulty.

Educator Ernest Boyer makes this point: "On the frontier two centuries ago, a man who could read his name and also several books and messages was looked upon as 'educated.' Today with new technology and more complicated functions to perform, a person with limited language skills is considered ignorant."

Early development. A person's IQ is fairly constant from age 6 or 7 on.

IQ. By definition, the average person has an IQ of 100. Sixty per cent of us have IQ's between 85 and 115.

Here's how psychologists interpret the numbers:

IQ of 145 or above	Brilliant
130	Very superior
115	Superior
105	High average
95	Average
85	Low average
70	Inferior
55	Very inferior
below 55	Severely subnormal

Fifteen per cent of the population fall in the superior range, and 5 per cent in the very superior or brilliant categories. Fifteen per cent are in the inferior, very inferior, or severely subnormal categories.

What a bright average baby! The average little baby knows more than it lets on.

Newborn babies can distinguish colors. They tend to prefer red and blue. Annoy a newborn with an obnoxious light or rattle and baby will shut you out by going to sleep.

A newborn baby can tell where a sound is coming from, and often turns his or her head in that direction.

Here's some bad news for parents who plan to keep their child from developing a sweet tooth: Babies are *born* with a sweet tooth. Give the average newborn a choice between sugar water and mother's milk, and he or she will take sugar water every time.

Little kids learn fast. The average child learns as much in the year between his or her third and fourth birthdays as in the 3 years between his or her ninth and twelfth birthdays.

Empty desks. The average American grade school has a decreasing enrollment, and will keep on losing students at least until 1985, when the trend is expected to reverse again.

The average American high school will lose enrollment steadily until at least the early 1990s.

So will the average American college. According to *Changing Times,* the Kiplinger magazine, between now and 1990 the number of 18-year-olds who might enter college will dwindle by about 20 per cent.

Highway deference. Does the average person defer to those he or she sees as social superiors? Yes. To prove it, psychology researchers arranged this experiment:

Two cars—a high-status, highly polished, 2-year-old Chrysler Imperial and a low-status, rusty, 14-year-old Ford station wagon —were driven, one at a time, to an intersection. The drivers were told to wait at the stop light at least 12 seconds after it turned green, or until the driver behind them honked twice.

The results: Eighty-four per cent honked at the Ford, but only 50 per cent honked at the Chrysler. Two behind the Ford got so impatient they bumped it. Nobody bumped the Chrysler.

Satisfactions. When sociologist John Robinson asked people to rank 18 aspects of living according to how much satisfaction each produced, home life came out way on top. Men got the least satisfaction from shopping, and women from clubs they belong to.

Here is how each activity scored (with 5 standing for "great" and 1 for "none"), on the 1-to-5 scale, and the percentage who reported that their satisfaction from it was "great":

Activity	Per cent saying "great"	Average score (out of 5)	
		MEN	WOMEN
Your children	79%	4.6	4.8
Your marriage	75%	4.7	4.6
Your house or apartment	40%	4.1	4.1
Religion	34%	3.5	4.0
Helping others	33%	3.9	4.2
Being with friends	34%	4.0	4.2
Reading	32%	3.6	3.8
Being with relatives	27%	3.6	4.0
Making or fixing things	27%	3.5	3.7
Sports or games	26%	4.0	2.8
Your work (or housework)	25%	3.7	3.6
Your car	25%	3.6	3.5
Relaxing, sitting around	24%	3.7	3.4
Cooking	23%	2.5	3.7
Watching TV	17%	3.5	3.4
Shopping, except for groceries	17%	2.5	3.7
Clubs	13%	2.7	2.6
Following politics or voting	9%	3.0	2.7

Family warmth. According to surveys by the University of Chicago's National Opinion Research Center, the average American is more satisfied with his or her

family life than friendships   health than hobbies
friendships than health   hobbies than hometown.

He or she is also more satisfied with his or her job than with his or her financial situation.

Je ne comprends pas. In 1966, 9 in 10 candidates for a B.A. degree were required to study a foreign language, but now only 53 per cent of colleges require it.

Only 19 per cent require foreign-language study in applicants for admission, compared to 33 per cent in 1966.

Between 1973 and 1978, the number of undergraduates studying foreign languages fell 15 per cent.

Uncle Sam didn't want them. Back in 1972, when we still had the military draft, 35 of every 1,000 young men failed to meet the mental or emotional requirements for induction.

Here are the states where the rejection rates were the lowest and the highest. The figures are the number rejected per 1,000.

The lowest		*The highest*	
Oregon	0	Puerto Rico and the Virgin Islands	489
Montana	3	Mississippi	171
South Dakota	3	South Carolina	143
Minnesota	5	Louisiana	123
North Dakota	5	Georgia	116
Oklahoma	5	District of Columbia	111

Gone fishin'. On an average day, 200,000 school kids in New York City are not in school. That's 1 in 5.

Is your kid on schedule? In the 1920s, the renowned child-development expert Arnold Gesell studied the development of little children, step by step. His findings are still considered valid; those things don't change much. Here's a summary of Gesell's list for the average child:

1 month   Baby makes crawling motions, turns her head and even lifts it, although unsteadily.

2 months   When you hold baby to your shoulder or horizontally on his back, he can raise his head briefly. He can also lift his chest a little when lying down, and while lying on his back he can move his arms up and down.

3 months	Now baby holds her head erect and steady when you hold her to your shoulder. She rolls over from her back to her side, and pushes herself up with her arms.
4 months	Baby's head is steady even when he's being carried or rocked. Lying on his back, he tries to sit up.
5 months	Baby rolls from her back to her stomach, sits nicely (when propped up), and even picks up a block from the table.
6 months	If you place baby in a well-balanced position, he can sit momentarily without support. He now can briefly hold a block in each hand simultaneously.
7 months	Baby rotates her wrist, and uses a scooping or raking motion to get hold of a small object.
8 months	Baby sits up, and stays up momentarily without support.
9 months	Baby sits all by herself. And she crawls, or at least tries to.
10 months	Upsy-daisy! Baby pulls himself to his feet. He's now quite deft at picking up objects.
1 year	She stands with support, walks with help, reaches with one hand, and can scribble with a crayon if you show her how.
15 months	He stands and walks alone.
18 months	She climbs the stairs, or onto a chair. She can scribble by herself, and she throws a ball into a box.
21 months	Baby goes for walks with Mom or Dad. He can walk backwards, too.
2 years	Look out! She's running now. She can play a simple game of catch, and can pile blocks 6 high with good coordination.
30 months	Up and down the stairs he goes, by himself. He piles up 7 or 8 blocks, copies a vertical line, and tries to stand on 1 foot.
3 years	Now we're into nursery-school stuff. She copies a circle, neatly creases a piece of paper, and aligns a card to the edge of a table. The sky's the limit!

Listen! Listen! She said "Mommy"! Here's the crying, cooing, shouting, and talking schedule for the average child, from studies by Dorothea McCarthy and Elizabeth B. Hurlock:

1 to 2 weeks	He cries intensely and frequently, even when asleep and often for no apparent reason. Much of the crying is in a monotone.
2 to 4 weeks	She cries less and wakes up less at night. Crying starts to vary, depending on the reason.
2 to 3 months	Crying most often begins with a need, such as hunger, and ends with its satisfaction.
3 months	Babbles.
4 months	Shouts.
6 months	He mimics simple sounds, pronouncing most vowels and some consonants, but can't speak words.
8 months	Babbling peaks.
9 to 12 months	She imitates simple words and understands gestures.
1 year	He learns meanings through associations, and responds to simple commands accompanied by gestures.
12 to 14 months	She speaks 5 or 6 words, mostly nouns like "Mommy" and "Daddy."
18 months	He says simple phrases, using verbs, adjectives, and adverbs such as "good," "cold," "give ball."
2 years	She says simple sentences.
2 to 3 years	He learns new words rapidly, uses many descriptive adjectives, and picks up basic grammar.
4 to 5 years	She talks in whole sentences.

That's My Boy/Girl!

What kids know. The average 9-year-old can tell time but can't understand puns. The typical 13-year-old can make change but can't choose the most economical buy in a supermarket. The average 17-year-old can multiply fractions but can't convert Fahrenheit into Celsius, even with a conversion formula.

These findings come from the National Assessment of Educational Progress, which has been testing kids since 1969.

The average 9-year-old:

Knows the difference between even and odd numbers.

Knows there are more stars in the universe than have been counted.

Knows clouds are necessary for rain, and cold for snow.

Knows that penguins can't fly, fish have scales, rabbits eat no meat.

Will draw a running person's arm in a bent position.

Knows what a dictionary is used for.

Knows who is President.

But the average 9-year-old:

Can't subtract three-digit numbers.

Can't write an essay without misspelling words and including fragmented or run-on sentences.

Can't divide or multiply.

Can't grasp the principles of supply and demand.

Doesn't know that the head of a state is called a governor.

Can't follow detailed written directions.

Can't pick out the main idea in a reading passage.

The average 13-year-old:

Can read a phone bill to figure out the origin of a call and what it cost.

Knows that the earth moves around the sun once a year.

Can list at least two things he or she does well and two he or she doesn't do so well.

Takes the words of songs to be the literal truth.

Is able to distinguish facts from opinions.

Knows whether a specific musical instrument is played by blowing, striking, or plucking.

Knows who Red Riding Hood and Alice in Wonderland are.

Can write a satisfactory letter to a pencil company to complain that the wrong name had been printed on her or his personalized pencils and to suggest a solution to the problem.

Can identify by name "This Land Is My Land" and "When the Saints Go Marching In."

But the average 13-year-old:

Doesn't know that the decimal .3333 . . . is the same as the fraction ⅓.

Doesn't know what to do when a person faints.

Can't calculate a simple average (!).

Can't name famous Indians or famous black Americans.

Doesn't know that every state has two senators.

Can't identify Don Quixote.

The average 17-year-old:

Can name 3 famous blacks and 2 famous Indians, but not any famous Orientals or Spanish-speaking Americans.

Knows that a meal of milk, bread and butter, meat, and cake requires a green or yellow vegetable to be nutritionally balanced.

Knows that a frog is a vertebrate.

Can identify Samson and Moby Dick, and knows the story of the Trojan horse.

Uses words averaging 4 letters each when assigned to write an essay.

Knows that the diameter of a circle is twice the length of its radius.

But the average 17-year-old:

Can't convert Fahrenheit to Celsius, even with a conversion formula.

Hasn't read many poems or plays except those assigned in school.

Rarely listens to country and western, jazz, folk, or classical music.

Has trouble writing a good letter applying for a job.

Can't identify the biblical figure Job.

Can't figure out the difference in temperature between 31 degrees and −7 degrees.

What did you get on your SAT's? That stands for Scholastic Aptitude Tests, which have a lot to do with whether your son or daughter gets into that prestigious college. SAT's are taken during the junior or senior year of high school. There's a verbal test and a math test, and a perfect score is 800 in each.

The average 1978 high-school senior who took SAT's (that's 1 of 3 seniors) scored 429 on verbal, 468 on math. If all seniors had taken them, the averages would have been 368 verbal, 402 math. That's the estimate of the Admissions Testing Program of the College Board, which administers the SAT program.

SAT scores have been declining. In 1967, the average senior who took the tests scored 466 on verbal, 492 on math. In 1975, he or she scored 434 on verbal, 472 on math.

SAT's of students admitted to the typical state university average from about 950 to 1050. SAT's of students admitted to the most exclusive colleges average in the 1200's and 1300's.

Here are the average SAT scores of 1978 freshmen at these schools:

Harvard	1400
Duke	1276
Cornell	1230
Emory	1150
Syracuse	1100
Tulane	1100
University of Denver	1053
University of Florida	1042
University of Miami	960

What goes on inside your brain. The average brain weighs only 3 pounds, but uses a fifth of the body's oxygen and blood.

By age 35, the average person's brain is losing more than 1,000 nerve cells a day.

How we respond to advertising. These are from surveys conducted in 1977 by R. H. Bruskin Associates, a market-research firm. The first survey checked how many of us could name the product when given the advertising slogan. The second survey checked how many of us believe certain familiar advertising claims.

Slogan	Per cent correctly naming the product
"Please don't squeeze the . . ." (Charmin)	81.5%
"Plop, plop, fizz, fizz, oh what a relief it is." (Alka-Seltzer)	79.1%
"It's the real thing." (Coca-Cola)	59.4%
"When it rains, it pours." (Morton's Salt)	57.1%
"Give your cold to . . ." (Contac)	54.6%
"The Superstar in Rent-A-Car." (Hertz)	47.2%
"Tastes so good cats ask for it by name." (Meow Mix)	40.7%
"We do it all for you at . . ." (McDonald's)	37.9%
"Tan, don't burn with . . ." (Coppertone)	33.2%
"Take . . . against cavities." (Aim)	32.8%
"The last battery your car will ever need." (J. C. Penney)	19.1%
". . . adds life." (Coke)	15.5%
"The closer you look, the better we look." (Ford)	15.1%
"Can we build one for you?" (Olds)	4.0%

	Per cent who consider this claim			
	COMPLETELY TRUE	PARTLY TRUE	NOT TRUE AT ALL	NO OPINION
"When you care enough to send the very best." (Hallmark)	62%	29%	7%	2%
"Kodak makes your pictures count."	60%	32%	6%	2%
"The quality goes in before the name goes on." (Zenith)	49%	37%	11%	3%
"We're involved." (U. S. Steel)	40%	40%	14%	6%
"Just slightly ahead of our time." (Panasonic)	34%	43%	15%	8%
"The last battery your car will ever need." (J. C. Penney)	25%	39%	30%	6%
"When America needs a better idea, Ford puts it on wheels."	22%	47%	29%	2%
"You're good for more." (Beneficial Finance)	20%	40%	31%	9%

Look, Junior, you're not so bright. Compared with his or her parents, the IQ of the typical child tends to be a little closer to the national average of 100.

The average child of parents with IQ's of 120 has an IQ of 116. The average child of parents with IQ's of 80 has an IQ of 84.

Here are the average IQ's of 1,000 men in various occupations, and of their children, from a British study a while back:

	Men	*Their children*
Higher professional	140	121
Lower professional	131	115
Clerical	116	108
Skilled	108	105
Semiskilled	98	99
Unskilled	85	93

Smart kids. Roger Brown, Harvard's expert on the psychology of language, says that by the time the average kid is 3 she or he has developed a basic grammar. When a child says, "I throwed the ball," far from indicating his or her incompetence, it shows that she or he has figured out the rules for forming the past tense.

At the age of 18 months, the average child has a vocabulary of several hundred words. She or he speaks in short sentences— "Suzie sleep"—because of a limited ability to apply the rules for connecting words. A 2-year-old speaks in sentences averaging 2 words; a typical 3-year-old speaks in 5-word sentences.

"Hello, Harvard? My 1-year-old just said, 'Da-da.'" A study that followed 167 persons through the first 30 years of life found a relationship between the age at which a kid starts to talk and what type of personality she or he later develops.

Early talkers—those who said 5 recognizable words before they were 12 months old—turned out to be the most intellectual. This trait was particularly strong among the males. A government report on the study says:

"Through adolescence, at least, the early talkers were on the restrained and somber side. Their IQ's were consistently higher than those of the later talkers, but largely because of the difference in scores on the verbal factor tests. In high school, the early talkers were known as eggheads; at 30, they still valued intellectual matters, and were inclined to intellectualize about a subject, even to the point of splitting hairs. They were also at 30 more practical, prudent, and conservative. The late talkers [who first spoke after 15 months] were active, relatively uninhibited, and even rebellious. The middle group [who first spoke between 12 and 15 months] turned out to be the most conventional."

Does the average kid with a high IQ really do better in life?
You'd better believe it. Starting in about 1920, a Stanford University researcher named Lewis M. Terman located 1,500 California children with IQ's averaging about 150—the very top of the scale. He monitored their progress for almost 40 years, and published the results.

There were 857 boys and 671 girls. We hate to say it, but at least back then, boys with IQ's that high were easier to find, and on average they maintained their IQ levels better than the girls did.

These 1,500 kids were 10 times more likely than the average child to have fathers in the professions. Almost none of them were the children of laborers. Compared with the general population, the bright kids were more likely to be of Western European or Jewish extraction, and short on Latin, black, and non-Jewish Eastern European roots.

You'd think a kid so bright might be a frail little bookworm. Nope. In fact, he or she was taller, heavier, and stronger, had broader shoulders, and outperformed the average child in athletics.

They way outperformed the average person their age academically, socially, and professionally. On average, they earned a lot more money and they seemed a lot happier. They came from a generation when few married women worked, so Terman plotted the careers mostly of the men, and found their most common occupations were, in order, lawyer, engineer, college teacher, middle-level major business manager, financial executive, scientist, physician, educational administrator, top business executive, and accountant.

Lots of them are in Who's Who. Most of them married bright spouses. Their children, on average, had IQ's above 130.

Those smart city kids. The average 17-year-old in a big metropolitan area reads better than his or her peer in the country, but not by much—score 95.9 per cent for the city kid, 91.2 per cent for the country kid. The difference is greater in science, where the city kid scored 47.4 per cent to 41.2 per cent for the country kid.

A heap of schools. Used to be that youngsters generally enrolled in a college and emerged from it four years later with a degree. Now, due to the growth of junior colleges and the fact that transferring is more common, 6 out of 10 graduates get their bachelor's degrees from institutions other than those they enrolled in as freshmen.

You are falling into a deep sleep. On average, people are most susceptible to hypnosis between the ages of 7 and 8. Girls and women are easier to hypnotize, in general, than boys and men, and smart people are easier to hypnotize than dumb people.

Words, words, words. The average American adult has an active vocabulary of 10,000 to 20,000 words that she or he uses in speaking or writing, and 30,000 to 40,000 that she or he recognizes when reading or listening. The average child enters school recognizing 3,000 words.

Of the 600,000 words in English, 10,000 are slang, and another 3,500 are cant, jargon, or argot, according to Harold Wentworth, cocomplier of *The Dictionary of American Slang*.

What words are used most often?

In 1923, G. H. McKnight concluded that 25 per cent of all communication is composed of just 9 words, and another 25 per cent of all speech uses only 34 more.

In 1930, *The Bell System Technical Journal* came up with the 9 most commonly spoken words in telephone conversations.

And in 1967, researchers at Brown University analyzed 500 samples of "present-day edited American English." Each sample had about 2,000 words and was culled from sources as diverse as the sports pages, scientific journals, popular romantic fiction, and abstruse philosophical discussions. Computer analysis determined that the samples contained 50,406 *different* words.

McKnight's 9 words: *and, be, have, it, of, the, too, will, you.*

The Bell System's 9: *a, I, is, it, on, that, the, to, will.*

And the Brown University computer's 10 most common: *the, of, and, to, a, in, that, is, was, he.*

The only words common to all 3 lists are *the* and *to.*

Ah, youth and middle age. According to a survey, you are most likely to think that life in the United States is getting better if you are between 18 and 24, or between 55 and 64. You are most likely to think life is getting worse if you are between 25 and 34.

At any age, the upbeaters and the downbeaters are outnumbered by folks who think that life is just staying the same.

I have a smart accountant. Based on intelligence tests given to 18,782 white enlisted men by the Army Air Corps in 1945 (the last time they tried such a thing) here are the average IQ's for 67 occupations:

Accountant	128.1	General clerk	117.5
Lawyer	127.6	Clerk-typist	116.8
Engineer	126.6	Manager,	
Public-relations man	126	miscellaneous	116
Auditor	125.9	Telephone installer	
Chemist	124.8	and repairman	115.8
Reporter	124.5	Cashier	115.8
Chief clerk	124.2	Instrument repairman	115.5
Teacher	122.8	Radio repairman	115.3
Draftsman	122	Printer, pressman	115.1
Stenographer	121	Salesman	115.1
Pharmacist	120.5	Artist	114.9
Bookkeeper	120	Store manager	114
Sales manager	119	Laboratory assistant	113.4
Purchasing agent	118.7	Toolmaker	112.5
Production manager	118.1	Stock clerk	111.8
Photographer	117.6	Musician	110.9

Machinist	110.1	Carpenter	102.1
Foreman	109.8	Pipefitter	101.9
Watchmaker	109.8	Welder	101.8
Airplane mechanic	109.3	Auto mechanic	101.3
Sales clerk	109.2	Chauffeur	100.8
Electrician	109	Tractor driver	99.5
Lathe operator	108.5	Painter	98.3
Sheet-metal worker	107.5	Crane-hoist operator	97.9
Lineman	107.1	Cook and baker	97.2
Assembler	106.3	Weaver	97
Mechanic	106.3	Truck driver	96.2
Machine operator	104.8	Laborer	95.8
Riveter	104.1	Barber	95.3
Cabinetmaker	103.5	Lumberjack	94.7
Upholsterer	103.3	Farmer	92.7
Butcher	102.9	Farmhand	91.4
Plumber	102.7	Miner	90.6
Bartender	102.2		

Two kinds of depression. According to Dr. Frederick Goodwin of the National Institute of Mental Health, about 1 of every 50 Americans is a manic-depressive. It's a serious thing, and the average manic-depressive comes down with the condition in his or her mid-20s. It's as likely to be a he as a she.

Neurotic depression, which isn't so serious, afflicts 1 of every 27 Americans. It usually starts in your mid-40s or 50s, and a woman is 3 times as likely to get it as a man.

These folks need help. One American in 50 has an IQ between 50 and 69; 1 in 313 has an IQ of 30 through 49; and 1 in 50,000 has an IQ of 29 or below.

Retarded children. A child with an IQ of 68 or below is considered retarded; 2.27 per cent of the children in America fit that definition. The great majority of them are mildly retarded, with IQ's of 52 to 68.

Sad statistics on the retarded. Nearly 1 of every 1,000 Americans is in an institution for the mentally retarded.

The average such person spends 8½ years in the institution.

One out of 4 hasn't seen a relative in a year. Seven of 10 watch television, but only about 1 of 6 plays competitive sports.

The age of skepticism. Half the kids in kindergarten say they believe TV commercials.

Twelve per cent of third graders believe TV commercials.

Only 3 per cent of sixth graders do.

Would you vote for a Jewish, divorced woman? When the Gallup poll asks people whether they would—or would not—vote for various categories of people for President, fewer than ever are willing to say they wouldn't. Thus:

76 per cent of Americans say they would vote for a woman for president; in 1937, only 31 per cent said they would.

91 per cent say they would vote for a Catholic, up from 64 per cent in 1937; 82 per cent would vote for a Jew, up from 46 per cent.

84 per cent say they would vote for a divorced person; in 1962, only 78 per cent would.

Homestate U. About 85 per cent of all college students attend a school in their home states. The percentage would be somewhat lower if it weren't for two-year community colleges, which draw 90 per cent or more of their enrollments from their home states. Some states are traditional exporters of students, some are importers. Here are the largest in both categories for 1975:

Exporters	Number sent out of state	Importers	Number imported
New Jersey	98,884	California	167,633
Illinois	30,019	District of	
Connecticut	29,027	Columbia	43,725
Pennsylvania	27,381	Massachusetts	33,646
Ohio	13,957	Texas	31,098
		Utah	21,389
		North Carolina	20,688

Where'd ya go? One elementary schoolkid in 10 in America attends a nonpublic school.

No wonder they're so uppity! Intelligence testing has long shown that upper-class people are smarter, on average, than middle-class people, who in turn are smarter than lower-class people. Some educators suspected that the tests had a built-in bias favoring the upper classes. To counter this, supposedly "culture-free" forms of the IPAT and Binex IQ tests were devised. The results? According to Dorothy I. Marquart and Lois L. Bailey in the *Journal of Genetic Psychology,* upper-class people still scored higher, on average, than middle-class people, who in turn scored higher than lower-class people. But the differences weren't as wide.

Tongue-tied twins. On average, twins and triplets are slow to pick up language, particularly between ages 2 and 5. By their ninth birthday, they've usually caught up.

The skills we have and lack. According to a study conducted at the University of Texas in 1975, the average American adult is more proficient at writing than at any other of 9 skills tested. He or she is least proficient at consumer economics, of all things.

In between, in order of proficiency, are

Community resources
Problem solving
Occupational knowledge
Health
Government and law
Reading
Computation

The American at the library. The average American goes to the library at least once a year. There, 2 out of 3 find exactly what they're looking for.

That comes from the American Library Association, which commissioned a Gallup poll and a separate study of library use and reading. Some results:

Who reads: The typical reader of books is a college-educated mother whose children, under 18, still live at home. She most likely lives on the East Coast or the West Coast. She reads 21 books a year.

Who doesn't: The typical nonreader is a man over 35, with a high-school education or less, with no kids at home, living in the Midwest.

Who read last year: More than 3 people out of 4 have read at least 1 book in the past year. Among library visitors, 71 per cent have read a book in the past month. For more than half of those who have read a book within the year, it was a paperback.

What they read: Novels. Fiction was mentioned more frequently than any other kind of book. Half of those asked said the last book they read was a novel.

Where they got it: Thirty per cent borrowed their last book from a relative or friend, the single most popular source.

The library: The nation's 1,400 libraries and branches spend about $5.00 per person every year, and circulate about 5 books for each of us per year.

Who's schooled. Seventy-five per cent of today's young people finish high school, and 45 per cent go to college.

If present trends continue, of every 100 of today's teen-agers

     24 will get a bachelor's degree
     7 will get a master's degree
     1 will get a doctorate.

Who's schooled II. The Census Bureau says the average 20-year-old has completed 12.7 years of schooling.

The average 50-year-old has had 12.3 years.

The average 75-year-old has had 8.6 years.

The educated American. Altogether, the average American adult has completed 12.4 years of schooling. In 1950, the average was 9.3 years.

Misplaced innards. Researchers have established that the average person has trouble pointing to where his vital organs are.

58 per cent can't locate the heart.
40 per cent can't locate the bladder.
54 per cent can't locate the kidneys.
80 per cent can't locate the stomach.
49 per cent can't locate the lungs.
23 per cent can't locate the intestines.
51 per cent can't locate the liver.

Sneaky and insidious influences. When college women were asked in 1978 why they use the brands of cosmetics and beauty products that they do, advertising was rarely cited as a reason.

Many said they use Cachet perfume because "I like the way it smells on me."

Oil of Olay lotion was used because "it keeps skin younger looking."

Agree creme rinse was praised by the young ladies as "not greasy," and Fabergé Organic shampoo was, the respondents said, "recommended."

It's interesting to note that all these "objective" reasons match precisely the various advertising claims for the products.

How much we can remember. If digits are called out at an even rate—say, 1 a second—the average adult can repeat a string of 7 digits. Few people can remember more than 9.

Do girls study harder? The average boy gets higher SAT scores than the average girl, but the average girl gets better grades.

In math SAT's, the average boy has always outscored the average girl by quite a bit. In verbal SAT's, the girls used to outscore the boys, but the boys pulled ahead in 1972 and have held an edge ever since. Among 1978 high-school seniors, the average boy scored 433 verbal, 494 math; the average girl scored 425 verbal, 444 math.

But on a scale of 0 for a flunk to 4 for an A, the girls had a grade-point average of 3.15 compared with 3.03 for the boys. By subject, the girls were the winners in English, 3.30 to 3.04; languages, 3.15 to 2.84; biological sciences, 3.10 to 3.04; and social studies, 3.27 to 3.23. The boys came out ahead only in math, 2.86 to 2.83, and physical sciences, 2.96 to 2.95.

Psychoses on campus. According to the National Institute of Mental Health, college students often have emotional problems because of difficulty in leaving their parents, choosing a career, resolving conflicts between hometown and campus values, or because of an obsessive fear of failing.

Two to 5 students out of every 1,000 develop severe mental upsets in college, NIMH says, but "most people who have a psychotic reaction, especially if the onset is a stormy one, will recover with competent treatment."

A Harvard study of 35 students who had become psychotic found that 21 graduated from college within 5 years of their illness. Six of them graduated without losing any time, and 7 graduated with honors.

The computer in college. Today, 4 college students in 10 graduate with at least a basic knowledge of computers, according to John Hamblen, chairman of the computer science department at the University of Missouri at Rolla.

Dropouts. In 1942, of every 1,000 kids who entered the fifth grade, 954 entered the sixth grade the following year, 807 made it to the ninth grade, 505 received a high-school diploma, and 205 enrolled in college.

Twenty years later, of every 1,000 fifth graders, 987 entered the sixth grade the next year, 959 made it to the ninth grade, 750 received a high-school diploma, and 461 went to college.

Of every 1,000 students who were in fifth grade in 1967, 992 went into the sixth grade, 984 continued into the ninth grade, and 743 received a high-school diploma. By 1975, 45 per cent of that 1967 fifth-grade class had gone on to college.

The education industry. Three in 10 of us are somehow involved in educational institutions—64 million Americans in all.

That includes more than 60 million students, 3 million teachers, and 300,000 superintendents, principals, supervisors, and others on the instructional staff.

90 per cent of all 5-year-olds are in kindergarten.

99 per cent of all 6-to-13-year-olds are in school.

94 per cent of all 14-to-17-year-olds are in school.

30 per cent of all 18-to-24-year-olds are in institutions of higher learning.

What smart costs. The United States spends $1,700 a year for each pupil in public elementary and secondary schools.

All told, we spend about $142 billion on public and private education from kindergarten through graduate school—about 7.7 per cent of the gross national product.

That's 3 times as much money spent on his or her education as for the average student in France, Britain, or Japan, twice as much as the average West German student, and a good deal more than the average student in Canada, Holland, or Norway. Among the 9 nations that were compared, only Sweden spent more than we did to educate the average child in public school.

Born first and smart. The average firstborn child is smarter than kids with older brothers and sisters. So is the average kid from a small family.

Two researchers with the New York State Department of Social Hygiene studied the results of an intelligence test given to almost 400,000 19-year-old men in the Netherlands—almost all the males born in that country between 1944 and 1947. The U. S. National Institute of Mental Health reports on the results:

"No matter what the size of the families, it turned out, the 18-year-olds who had been firstborns got better scores on intelligence than the laterborns. Moreover, as birth position fell—from first to second, from second to third, and so on—the scores on the test almost always fell, too. Secondborns scored better than thirdborns, for example, and thirdborns better than fourth-borns.

"Family size was found to have a similar effect. Within a given birth order, scores on the tests grew worse as the number of children increased. Among the young men who had been born third, for example, those from families with three children scored better than those from families with four, and those in turn scored higher than those from families with five, and so on."

Of the first 23 American astronauts to fly into space, 21 either were firstborn sons or were born into small families.

If firstborn kids are so smart, lateborn kids are more likable. A study of 1,750 grade-school students in Riverside, California, found that lastborn children were most often selected by their contemporaries as playmates. But when kids chose other kids to achieve something, they turned to firstborns.

How to get into med school. The average med student applied to 7.8 schools in addition to the one she or he is attending. Of every 100 medical-school students, 46 had a perfect A average in their premed college work.

Mental unhealth. The National Institute of Mental Health says that 1 American in 10 suffers at some time from some form of mental or emotional illness. There are more patients in hospitals for mental disorders than for any other illness.

Your eyes and your personality. People with green or light gray eyes tend to be understanding, patient, firm but just, and good listeners. People with black eyes tend to be hot-tempered and impulsive, and people with blue eyes tend to have a lot of stamina. People with hazel eyes tend to be stable and imaginative, and persons with light brown eyes tend to be shy and individualistic. People with dark brown eyes tend to be thrifty and hardworking.

So say John Glover and A. L. Gary, behavioral scientists at the Chattanooga Institute of Human Studies.

How smart we are. "Suppose you purchased $200 worth of merchandise from a store on an installment plan. You are to make 24 monthly payments of $11.35 each. How much money in finance charges will you have paid at the end of 2 years?"

When that question was put to a cross section of adult Americans aged 26 to 35, in a written test, 66 per cent of them got the right answer ($72.40).

Right answers were given by 84 per cent of those with post-college education; 35 per cent of those with 9 grades or less of schooling; 34 per cent of those earning under $5,000, and 78 per cent of those earning over $15,000; 41 per cent of the blacks, and 70 per cent of the whites.

The participants were also tested in a number of other ways. They were asked to fill out a typical mail-order form, use a sales tax table, write a job application letter, read a measuring cup, use the dictionary and telephone book, calculate area, and use a map.

The national average of correct answers was 73 per cent.

The testing was conducted by the National Assessment of Educational Progress of Denver, a government-funded project of the Education Commission of the States. This outfit surveys periodically the knowledge, skills, and educational achievements of cross sections of the population.

Jen informo pri la norma parolanto de Esperanto, la internacia lingvo. That translates, "Here is something about the average speaker of Esperanto, the international language." Esperanto is an artificial language invented in 1887 by L. L. Zamenhof, a Russian philologist, to make international discourse easier.

William R. Harmon, president of the Esperanto League for North America (Box 1129, El Cerrito, Calif. 94530), asked to describe the average American Esperantist, replies that that is difficult. He says:

"In our group, the youngest is 9 years old, the oldest 94. The age curve does not fit the standard distribution curve at all. There are peaks in the 50-to-60 range and in the 20-to-30 and 35-to-45 ranges. I turned to the international organization, Universala Esperanto-Asocio, headquartered in Rotterdam, and checking their yearbook of delegates counted 684 different professions before giving up at the S level. Dipping at random, here's a sprinkling: agronomist, banker, bee breeder, dermatologist, ethnographer, philatelist, editor, historian, hydraulic engineer, linguist, judge, judo expert, chemist, machinist, nutritionist, policeman, programmer, pastor, chessmaster, typographer, welder, and zoologist.

"If there is a factor common to most Esperantists, it is probably a mixture of idealism and curiosity. It is difficult to speak the language badly—although a few Esperantists really try—and perhaps another common element is a predilection for travel. The last international Congress of Esperanto, held in Varna, Bulgaria, attracted over 4,000 delegates."

Women's unrecorded voice. Of the 40,000 quotations in the Oxford Book of Quotations, 99 per cent are attributed to men. Of the 117,000 quotes in Bartlett's Familiar Quotations, 99.5 per cent are attributed to men.

There's a job for everyone. The average IQ is 100. According to various studies compiled by a scholar named Lee J. Cronbach, the average IQ is

130   for Ph.D.'s

120   for college graduates

115   for college freshmen

110   for high-school graduates. If your IQ is 110, you have a 50-50 chance of making it through college.

90   for children from low-income city homes. If your IQ is 90, you can perform jobs requiring some judgment, such as operating a sewing machine or assembling parts.

75   A child with an IQ of 75 has a 50-50 chance of reaching high school. An adult with an IQ of 75 can keep a small store or perform in an orchestra.

60   If your IQ is 60, you can repair furniture, harvest vegetables, or assist an electrician.

50   If your IQ is 50, you can do simple carpentry and domestic work.

40   If your IQ is 40, you can mow lawns and do the laundry.

Extrasensory professors. In a poll of 1,188 college and university teachers, 16 per cent said they thought extrasensory perception is an established fact, and another 49 per cent said ESP is a likely possibility.

The Couch and You

Going to the psychiatrist. A person between 18 and 44 years old is almost twice as likely to see a psychiatrist as a person between 45 and 64.

Is that what the couch is for? According to numerous studies, roughly two thirds of neurotic people who undergo psychotherapy are cured or improved. So are roughly two thirds of neurotic people who don't.

However, some advocates of psychotherapy consider "cure" and "improvement" unfairly subjective yardsticks. A better measurement, some say, is whether the patient improved his or her sex life. In one study, the longer the patients were in therapy, the more often they had sex, and the more they enjoyed it.

Here's your typical shrink and typical patient. According to a survey published by the American Psychiatric Association, the average American psychiatrist is 48 years old, works 35 hours a week, sees 32 patients for 48 minutes each, and charges $36.73 an hour (in 1973).

His or her average patient is 35. Fifty-seven per cent of them are women; 96 per cent are white. The average patient in psychoanalysis goes to the couch 140 times a year, and 77 per cent of them keep going for more than 3 years. The average patient undergoing nonanalytic psychiatric treatment goes less than once a week, and only 31 per cent of them keep going for more than 2 years.

A doctor is 19 times more likely than the average American to go to a psychiatrist. A lawyer is 13 times more likely to go, a social worker 21 times, a writer, artist, entertainer, or public-relations person 7 times, and a teacher 3 times. A nurse, a manager, or an administrator is twice as likely as the average American to go to a psychiatrist. Some cynics suggest that psychiatric offices are filled with frustrated housewives, but it's not so; a housewife is no more likely to visit a psychiatrist than is the average person.

A clerk, a blue-collar worker, and a laborer are all less likely to go to a psychiatrist than is the average American.

Too much. Counting labels, signs, and everything else, the average American is exposed to 1,800 commercial messages a day.

Rise and fall. The average American scores best on the Wechsler Adult Intelligence Scale, a standard IQ test, between the ages of 25 and 29.

According to the famed intelligence tester, David Wechsler, he or she then begins a slow decline. Between the ages of 40 and 44, our average American dips below the average scores for 16- and 17-year-olds.

The decline gets a bit steeper at about age 50, and sharper still at about 70.

Remember that vacation? The average person recalls pleasant memories better than unpleasant ones.

TV commercials. The typical television viewer remembers funny commercials better than serious ones, but is more likely to remember the products from serious commercials. On average, a serious commercial does best on a comedy show, and a funny commercial on a serious show.

Foster IQ's. Here's a piece of evidence in the old environment-versus-heredity dispute, published by the National Institute of Mental Health.

On average, children reared by foster parents have IQ's more like those of their foster parents than like those of their less-educated, lower-socioeconomic-level biological parents.

What a set of genes! On the other hand, an expert concluded that the variation in intelligence test scores among schoolchildren resulted from:

75% heredity
21% environment
4% accidental factors

The national smarts. When the National Assessment of Educational Progress tested schoolkids, it found:

In science: The average 17-year-old in the Northeast outscored kids elsewhere; boys outscored girls; kids from big cities outscored kids from the suburbs, small towns, and rural areas.

In reading: Seventeen-year-olds from the Midwest outscored all others; girls outscored boys; big-city kids outscored kids from other areas.

Smart. In an average year, 1 million Americans get bachelor's degrees.

Anyone ever ask you? About half the people questioned in a survey said they had been surveyed previously within the past 4 to 5 years. Did they like it? Two thirds said they would be "somewhat" or "very" interested in being interviewed again. Sixteen per cent said no dice.

Words that live . . . and live . . . and live. The average human language retains 80 per cent of its fundamental, everyday words for an entire millennium. English does even better; if an Englishman from A.D. 950 were dropped into present-day Great Britain, he'd be able to make out about 85 per cent of these common words.

Do your studying at night. The average person remembers more if he or she sleeps right after studying than if he or she stays awake after study and then sleeps, even if the total hours of sleep are the same.

Ambitious, but nervous. Sociologists have found that the American climbing from one social class to another is more likely to be neurotic than the average person who sticks to his or her own class.

Loquacious. On average, little girls learn to talk earlier than little boys, and talk better. And, lisping aside, the boy is more likely to develop a speech defect.

Me Taurus, you Leo. Thirty-two million adult Americans—nearly 17 per cent—believe in astrology, holding that their lives are governed by the positions of the stars. As many churchgoers as nonchurchgoers believe, and twice as many women as men do.

Columbia University sociologist Amitai Etzioni says that 3 Americans in 4 know what sign they were born under. Among those 18 to 24 years old, 38 per cent believe in astrology, he says.

Mom, son, and IQ. Baby boys whose mothers are anxious, irritable, strict, and punitive tend to have below-average IQ's both in school and in later life. Not so for girls.

According to the National Institute of Mental Health, "Maternal love or lack of it seemed to have no effect on the mental test scores of girls. But mothers judged to be intrusive—forever meddling in the child's activities—had daughters whose IQ ratings through adolescence tended to be low."

What seniors say. When the government surveyed 18,000 high-school seniors in the class of 1972:

89 per cent said their schools should have provided more help for students having trouble with math and reading.

77 per cent said the school should have helped students find jobs.

71 per cent wanted more vocational and technical training.

68 per cent wanted more emphasis on practical work experience.

52 per cent thought the school could have used teaching machines or computer-assisted instruction more extensively.

As for their future plans:

50 per cent planned to go to college.

26 per cent planned to take full-time jobs.

9 per cent planned to go to trade or business schools.

3 per cent planned to join the armed services or go to military academies.

3 per cent planned to enter apprenticeship or on-the-job-training programs.

Of those who didn't plan further education, 48 per cent of the girls and 29 per cent of the boys said they were planning to get married.

Say it again. The more study time spent reciting material out loud, the more the average person can memorize.

6 The Money We Make and Spend

What we make and how we spend it. The average American's income in 1978 was $8,174.54. Taxes took $1,503.04, leaving $6,671.50; the average American spent all but $329.49 of it.

Of that income, $6,068.26 was earned at work and $1,025.13 came from the government in the form of Social Security and welfare. Interest on savings brought in $746.92, and dividends produced another $215.75. Our average American's rental income was $118.48.

These figures average together workers, children, retired people, and everyone else. Want to know how much the average full-time worker was paid in 1978? $13,275.

Here's how the average American spent his or her average dollar in 1978:

Housing	$.30
Food	.18
Transportation	.14
Medical expenses	.10
Clothes and jewelry	.08
Recreation	.07

Insurance premiums and other personal business	.05
Education, religion and charity	.03
Liquor and other alcoholic beverages	.02
Makeup, haircuts and other personal grooming	.01
Cigarettes and other tobacco	.01

That adds up to $.99 because the figures were rounded. All these figures came from the U. S. Department of Commerce.

Here's just how the average American spent his or her income.

Let's start with what we put in our mouths. The average American spent $806.13 on food at the grocery store and another $269.84 at restaurants, not counting the bar tab. He or she spent $141.53 on wine, beer, and liquor, and $81.93 on tobacco.

He or she spent $65.68 for new shoes, and $1.40 to shine shoes and get them repaired. Clothes cost $351.13, and in this case the Commerce Department tells us that the average she spent more than the average he. He (and she) spent $20.97 for cleaning and laundry, $42.34 for jewelry and watches, and $10.50 for watch repairs, tux and costume rentals, and other incidentals related to clothing.

Altogether, that's $492.42 on clothing and the like.

We doll ourselves up in other ways, too. The average American spent $57.81 on cosmetics, colognes, and toilet articles, and $27.13 on beauty-shop visits, haircuts, saunas, steam baths, and mud baths.

The house really soaks up money: $970.51 per person for mortgage or rent payments, and another $892.14 to run the joint. That includes $290.52 for heat, electricity, and water, and $106.98 in telephone bills. The average American spent $91.50 for blankets, sheets, carpets, pictures and frames, and lawn mowers and other tools; $77.15 for furniture; $61.06 for appliances; and $36.07 for china, pots and pans, tableware, and other eating equipment. Brooms, lampshades, curtains, and slipcovers took $49.64, and cleaning supplies cost $74.97. The average American spent $49.95 on stamps, household insurance, and other personal business, and $34.43 on servants—about enough to hire a maid for one day.

Medical expenses came to $599.39.

It's hard to believe, but the average American spent $25.16 on brokerage commissions and investment counseling in 1978. He or she paid $18.05 for a safe-deposit box and other banking and trust services, and $49.23 to a lawyer.

Cars—to be precise, autos, motorcycles, pickups, RV's, whatever Americans drove for their personal use—cost each of us $875.24 in 1978. Payments took $369.57 of that, and $182.70 went for repairs, parking, washes, and rentals. The average American spent $232.88 on gas and motor oil, and $4.20 on tolls. Does it make you feel better to think of your car insurance as costing only $39.32 a year for each member of the family? That was the 1978 average—again, premiums less benefits.

The average American spent $10.65 on local buses and trains and $5.59 on taxis. She or he spent $29.63 on travel tickets; $24.09 of it was by air.

Ah recreation. What a pleasant way to spend $417.40. Let's start with the sitting-down stuff. The average American spent $24.79 on books and maps, and $45.63 on newspapers, magazines, and sheet music. He or she spent $8.92 on records, musical instruments, TV's, and radios.

Moving out of the house, we each spent $19.49 on movies, $8.42 for sports events, and $5.81 for plays and operas. We lost $9.35 on parimutuel horse-race betting. Clubs and fraternal organizations cost $8.39. The rest of our fun cost $33.25—lottery losses, summer camp, the family pet, film processing, etc.

Now for the active stuff. Flowers, seeds, plants, and other supplies for the garden cost $22.99. Tennis and golf balls, balloons, bb's, and other nondurable sports equipment cost the average American $53.49. More durable things, like bikes, wagons, golf clubs, and boats—and pleasure airplanes, for that matter—cost another $66.42.

The average American spent $20.81 at pool halls, golf courses, bowling alleys, swimming pools, skating rinks, riding stables, amusement parks, and for sightseeing buses.

He or she spent $95.01 on tuition, $78.49 on church donations and charity, and $60.74 on foreign travel. As you might expect, the Commerce Department doesn't know what the average American spent on illegal things like marijuana and bookies.

Where the bucks stop. The average family in America had an income of $16,009 in 1977. (This is a median—half the families got more money, half got less.)

The Census Bureau calculates that the average family was better off in 1973. Its income was only $12,051, but four years later it took $16,433 to live as well.

Families headed by a full-time worker had an average income of $20,082. Families with a working wife had $20,268. But families headed by a woman averaged only $7,765.

Six-person families made more than a household of any other size. Two-person families averaged $12,890.

White-collar families averaged $21,619, blue-collar families $17,161, and farm families, $10,865. Families in which the head of the family was unemployed in 1977 didn't do much worse than farmers; the former had incomes averaging $10,334.

Suburban families brought home $20,110—more than inner-city residents' $14,677, or small-town folks' $13,789.

Families in the north-central states averaged the highest incomes—$16,850. They were followed by Northeasterners with $16,800, Westerners with $16,510, and Southerners with $14,570.

But that $16,009 for the average American family understates the case, according to economist Rudolph G. Penner of the American Enterprise Institute for Public Policy Research.

Penner says the figure is held down by families that work less than a full year because of unemployment or retirement, and by the great number of young adults who are just beginning their careers.

Instead, suggests Penner, let's take families in which the breadwinner works full time and is 45 to 54 years old. The average income for those families in 1978 was about $28,000.

Satisfaction. After studying 28,000 purchases made by 2,400 households in 34 cities, the Center for Study of Responsive Law reported that 77 per cent of the time people were satisfied with the products they bought.

Those finding fault with their purchases did something about it 40 per cent of the time; the rest of the time they just let it pass. Of those who did something, some only changed brands.

The family budget. For different income levels, here's the average budget for an urban family of four. The father is 38 years old and works full time. The mother doesn't have a job. Their son is 13 and their daughter is 8. These budgets were put together by the Bureau of Labor Statistics for autumn of 1978.

	Lower budget		Intermediate budget		Higher budget	
Total	$11,546		$18,622		$27,420	
Food	$ 3,574	31%	$ 4,609	25%	$ 5,806	21%
Housing	$ 2,233	19%	$ 4,182	22%	$ 6,345	23%
Transportation	$ 856	7%	$ 1,572	8%	$ 2,043	7%
Clothing	$ 847	7%	$ 1,209	6%	$ 1,768	6%
Personal care	$ 301	3%	$ 403	2%	$ 570	2%
Medical care	$ 1,065	9%	$ 1,070	5%	$ 1,116	4%
Other family consumption	$ 515	4%	$ 956	5%	$ 1,578	6%
Social security and disability	$ 719	6%	$ 1,073	6%	$ 1,091	4%
Personal income taxes	$ 935	8%	$ 2,738	15%	$ 5,739	21%
Other items	$ 502	4%	$ 810	4%	$ 1,365	5%

Where Wall Street and Elm Street meet. All over America, people with money to invest get together in investment clubs, pool their resources and efforts, and lay their money down. How do they make out?

Nicely, nicely, says Thomas E. O'Hara, chairman of the board of trustees of the National Association of Investment Clubs, headquartered in Royal Oak, Michigan. He says:

"We have gathered the earnings records of our clubs for 18 years. In 1978, the average investment club was 9.4 years old. Its compounded annual earnings rate was 10.45 per cent. If the clubs had put their money in the 425 Standard & Poor's Industrials for the same period of time, they would have earned 3.43 per cent. The average club has a portfolio of $30,916. The average member had a personal portfolio of $28,000, which is about double the national average of all investors. The average investment-club member puts $21.53 of new money in his club each month. Ninety-one point six per cent of our clubs reported having a profit."

Of the members, O'Hara says, 72 per cent are men, and of the clubs, 48 per cent are all male, 18 per cent are all female, and 34 per cent are mixed.

What it costs to raise a kid. If you live moderately well in a city in the heartland of America, it'll cost you an average of $6.22 a day to raise Junior or Missy from birth to age 18.

That comes to $40,866 over the kid's first 18 years, before he or she packs off to college.

The U. S. Agriculture Department makes this computation based on a government survey of what 20,000 families actually spent in 1972–74. The figures are adjusted into June 1978 dollars.

These things vary from year to year, but here are the average annual expenses of raising a child at a moderate level in a city in the north-central states:

Food at home	$732	(but twice as much at age 17 as at age 2)
Food away from home	$ 77	(how many french fries would this buy?)
Clothing	$270	
Housing (including fuel, light, refrigeration, water, household operations, furnishings, and equipment)	$982	
Medical care	$163	
Education	$ 46	
Transportation	$466	
Recreation, personal care, and all other	$363	

Costs for raising a child are higher in a city in the north-central states than in a small town or on a farm in that part of the country. But in the Northeast and West, the small-town kid runs up the highest costs. Food and housing cost more for the urban kid, but transportation less: He or she takes the bus.

Concluded Agriculture Department researcher Jean Pennock: "What does it cost to raise a child? The answer to this question is another question: How much can you afford to spend?"

The road to riches. The average multimillionaire, according to a study by the Brookings Institution, got his money from his folks.

The Brookings analysis finds that gifts and bequests, on the average, "account for half or more of the net worth of very wealthy men and for most of the net worth of equally wealthy women."

We have a nice pension and insurance program. The average American worker gets about $4,000 worth of fringe benefits a year.

Here's the average income tax for people like you. The government always talks about adjusted gross income, which means after all sorts of deductions, most of which you and I don't get. These figures refer to *total* personal income for 1978.

The average American

with income between	pays this much of it in federal income tax
$ 5,000 and $ 10,000	$ 431, or 5.8%
$ 10,000 to $ 15,000	$ 1,211, or 9.7%
$ 15,000 to $ 20,000	$ 2,072, or 11.9%
$ 20,000 to $ 30,000	$ 3,452, or 14.2%
$ 30,000 to $ 50,000	$ 6,725, or 18.3%
$ 50,000 to $100,000	$ 16,801, or 25.4%
$100,000 to $200,000	$ 43,913, or 32.9%
$200,000 and over	$176,179, or 37.1%

Dream on, paupers. Your "discretionary income" is what's left after paying for essentials. Harry S. Brown, director of the Consumer Credit Counseling Service of South Florida, says that the average family seeking help with debts thinks it has three times as much discretionary income as it really has.

Here's what the average taxpayer deducted in 1977. This one's based on adjusted gross income, which means total income minus tax "adjustments" such as business expenses, alimony, and untaxed disability payments.

Adjusted gross income	Contributions	Interest	Taxes	Medical	Total deductions as percentage of adjusted gross income
$4,000–$6,000	$426	$1,370	$932	$1,693	72%
$6,000–$8,000	$513	$1,607	$1,052	$1,368	57%
$8,000–$10,000	$524	$1,507	$1,147	$1,100	44%
$10,000–$12,000	$527	$1,598	$1,179	$882	38%
$12,000–$14,000	$475	$1,706	$1,242	$806	33%
$14,000–$16,000	$479	$1,868	$1,421	$669	30%
$16,000–$18,000	$559	$1,880	$1,553	$670	28%
$18,000–$20,000	$532	$2,006	$1,720	$596	26%
$20,000–$25,000	$563	$2,085	$1,954	$505	23%
$25,000–$30,000	$676	$2,271	$2,300	$520	21%
$30,000–$50,000	$893	$2,637	$3,124	$551	20%
$50,000–$100,000	$1,965	$4,230	$5,488	$748	19%
$100,000 and over	$9,673	$9,345	$13,839	$1,063	19%

Why college parents wear old clothes. The average family with a college-bound teen-ager can afford to pay only 37 per cent of the costs of sending the kid to a state university, and only 22 per cent of the costs of sending him or her to a private college.

This comes from the College Board, which calculated that our average family with a college-bound kid had an income in 1978 of $19,200. The College Board says it's no harder now to afford college than it ever was.

Plastic money. Eight married people in 10 have a credit card of one kind or another. Two in 3 say that credit cards make it all too easy to buy things on impulse.

Tax shaving. According to the IRS, the people most likely to try to cheat the government on withholding tax are barbers, migrant workers, band leaders and musicians, racetrack workers, stockbrokers, fishing crewmen, and civilian teachers at Army schools.

I'm no squealer. One of every 6 American adults knows someone who cheats on his or her taxes.

But few tattle, although the government pays squealers. In 1977, 483 informers got government rewards averaging $745.34.

The boss earns more. In 1978, *U.S. News & World Report* asked 372 big companies how much they paid their top executives in 1977.

The median pay for board chairmen was $308,190, up 11 per cent from the year before.

The median pay for company presidents was $259,785, a 15 per cent raise.

The median pay for vice presidents was $179,419, up 11 per cent.

Altogether, of 918 top officials, only 36 were paid less than $100,000, while 62 got $500,000 or more.

$.79 on the dollar. From the average dollar paid to Americans as income, $.113 goes for income taxes, $.055 for sales taxes, and $.041 for property taxes.

A buck lasts 18 months. Dollar bills weigh in at 490 to the pound.

The average dollar bill circulates for 1½ years. Fivers and larger denominations circulate much longer.

Ralph Nader lives. The average American thinks she or he gets a worse deal in the marketplace now than 10 years ago. She or he also thinks that the quality of goods and services has gotten worse, that products don't last as long as they used to, and that it's harder to get things fixed.

These findings are from a survey commissioned by Sentry Insurance and conducted by Louis Harris and Associates, Inc., and Marketing Service Institute of Harvard University in 1976.

Besides querying consumers, the pollsters asked the same questions of "leadership groups" to see who was most in touch with consumer attitudes. Consumer activists came the closest, and senior business managers were the farthest away.

The average American credits the consumer movement for improving consumer shopping skills, product information and labeling, and product safety.

And they all shop on Saturdays. In America, there are

    1,703 people for every grocery store
    1,191 people for every gas station
  27,250 people for every department store
    4,844 people for every drugstore
  11,474 people for every bank or savings and loan association.

You and the GNP. The average American's share of the gross national product is about $9,650. (GNP means the total value of all goods and services produced in the U.S. in a year. We don't get all of it as income.) Her or his share of all the cash in circulation is $525—$49 of it in change. Her or his share of the national debt is $3,572, and her or his share of the 1977 federal budget was $2,063, including $223 for the deficit.

Way back when. In 1875, the average American's share of the gross national product was $1,155, and his or her share of all federal receipts was $7.00.

(Reprinted with permission from *Nation's Business.*)

Down the Supermarket Aisle

The shopper observed. In 1975, researchers conducted what must be the most exhaustive study ever made of supermarket shoppers in the act of filling their carts. All told, 817 shoppers were observed on a Thursday, a Friday, and a Saturday in six stores in Philadelphia and Chicago. Most were later interviewed. *Progressive Grocer* published the results in October and November of 1975. Some of the findings:

The average shopper spent 27.5 minutes shopping (at $.93 a minute) and 6.5 minutes in the checkout line (the line moves a little faster than it did 10 years earlier).

Couples were more leisurely, spending 34 minutes shopping.

Thirty-five per cent of the shoppers were observed using unit pricing. Men used it more than women. Eleven per cent were "intense" users and 24 per cent were "moderate" users. Ten per cent said they never noticed it.

Thirty-nine per cent checked freshness dates—women more than men.

Twenty per cent cashed checks.

Two per cent used food stamps.

Six per cent used hand-held counters or pocket calculators to keep track of what they were spending. Those who did spent more than those who didn't.

Women spent faster than men. Women filled their baskets at the rate of $.95 a minute, men at the rate of $.83. That's because men didn't know their way around the store as well.

Forty-one per cent of the shoppers carried a list. List-carriers spent one third more money and 15 per cent more time. Three quarters of them were women. Fifteen per cent were men, and 10 per cent of the list users were couples.

Three per cent were in that particular supermarket for the first time.

The average customer bought 19 items.

Sixty-one per cent told interviewers they felt supermarkets make "a lot of money."

The average shopper traveled 1.8 miles to the store.

The typical shopper had been patronizing that store for 2 years.

Of every 3 couples shopping, 1 brought a child. So did 1 in 5 men, and 2 in 5 women.

"Jettisoning" is what the trade calls the practice of changing your mind at the checkout counter and putting back something from your cart. Women jettisoned 5 per cent of the time, men 4 per cent, couples 9 per cent.

Shoppers often pick something up, look it over, and put it back. *Progressive Grocer* calculates the frequency of this and calls it a "hesitation index." Here's how often it happens:

Item	Buy	Pick up and put down
Beef	45%	30% of customers
Luncheon meat	54%	22%
Flowers	3%	22%
Frozen vegetables	25%	17%
Fruit	55%	14%
Pork	17%	14%
Cereal	48%	13%
Soda	40%	7%
Frozen juice	36%	5%
Pet food	34%	5%

The farmer's share. Of every $1.00 you spend at the grocery store for food, here, according to the Agriculture Department, is the farmer's share, for

poultry and eggs	$.60
meat	$.55
dairy products	$.50
fats and oils	$.36
fruits and vegetables	$.25
bakery and cereal products	$.13

Checkout inflation. Food that cost $1.00 at the grocery store in 1940 sold for $6.00 in 1978.

Reality and illusion at the checkout. Here's something on how shoppers perceive themselves, versus how supermarket managers perceive them.

	Percentage of shoppers who say they're doing more of it	*Percentage of shoppers doing more of it, according to the store manager's estimate*
Cashing in cents-off coupons	59%	86%
Staying aware of exact prices	56%	77%
Visiting more than one store for weekly specials	38%	62%
Limiting purchases of nonfood items	33%	46%
Buying cheaper cuts of meat	32%	25%

More reality and illusion at the checkout. According to Dr. Stanley Solomon, of Stove and Webster Management Consultants, New York City, 97 per cent of supermarket checkers rate themselves "very high" in cleanliness, but only 15 per cent of the customers agree.

Dr. Solomon spent 168 hours observing 24 checkers. He also reports that only 1 checker in 25 thanks the customer, and only 1 in 6 checkers uses a warm tone of voice. When closing a lane, nearly 4 in 5 checkers visibly anger at least 1 customer by what he or she says, his or her tone of voice, his or her facial expression, or some gesture.

How much we spend at the supermarket. The average tab at the checkout counter was $9.85 in 1977 and $10.02 in 1978.

That may sound low, but the Food Marketing Institute explains that the average is pulled down by shoppers who pick up just 1 or 2 items.

The typical shopper spent $44.51 a week at the supermarket in 1977, according to *Supermarketing* magazine.

In December 1978, *Chain Store Age* published the results of the "most comprehensive poll ever taken of the habits and preferences of the supermarket shopper." It concluded that the average shopper buys 13.6 items, at an average price of $1.30 each.

If that average shopper bought the items that sell the most, here's what would be in his or her grocery basket. We'll allow 14 items.

2 fresh vegetables
2 kinds of beef
milk
eggs
1 kind of fresh fruit or another
white bread
cheese
soda pop
margarine or butter
canned soup or a soup mix
cold cereal
dog or cat food

Want to know what he or she buys if the list has, say, 9 more items? Here we go:

baking stuff
snacks
lunch meat
frozen fruits or vegetables
chicken
frozen dinners or pot pies
canned fruit
bananas, the best-selling fresh fruit of all
toilet paper

All those items are bought by at least 1 out of 5 shoppers. Only 1 out of 10 buys coffee, soap, oranges, hotdogs, cake, or baby food, to name a few.

How much we spend at the supermarket in a whole year. For the average household, it was $2,314.44 in 1977, according to *Supermarketing* magazine. That includes $2,085.93 for food, paper products, soaps and detergents, pet food and tobacco, all of which the supermarket counts as "grocery" items, and $228.51 for other stuff.

According to the *Progressive Grocer Marketing Guidebook* for 1979, here's what the average household spent at the supermarket in various metropolitan areas, and how much that amounts to for the average person:

	Average person	*Average household*
Detroit	$912	$2,728
Houston	$927	$2,693
New York	$955	$2,623
Philadelphia	$904	$2,590
Chicago	$850	$2,454
Los Angeles	$900	$2,428
Atlanta	$779	$2,297

The chains. One supermarket in 8 is part of a chain. Chains account for nearly half of all grocery sales, however.

Think how much you could save. Grocery manufacturers issue 62 billion cents-off coupons a year—about 1,100 per family. They're worth an average of $.15 each. Three out of 4 households use them, but only 1 of 3 does so regularly, and only 1 of every 20 coupons is redeemed.

Fewer than 1 family in 5 sends in boxtops or other package coupons for refunds, although the average refund on such offers is $1.00.

Coupon redemptions account for only $.42 out of every $100 in food-store sales.

What supermarkets sell. Once they carried mostly food. Now, of every 100 supermarkets

98 sell pet supplies
94 sell batteries
89 sell fireplace logs
88 sell flower and vegetable seeds
75 sell paperbacks
45 offer money orders
43 sell knitting yarn
33 sell sneakers
30 offer film processing
24 sell phonograph records
 9 have snack bars.

Moreover, supermarkets and other grocery stores sell

29% of all flashlight batteries
14% of all women's hosiery
15% of all newspapers and magazines sold in stores
13% of all motor oil sold in stores
 2% of all hard liquor sold in bottles
29% of all wine
23% of all chewing gum
94% of all bleach
44% of all pesticides
77% of all paper cups
91% of all household aluminum foil
42% of all light bulbs
48% of all shoe polish
53% of all bird food
41% of all cigarettes
13% of all reducing preparations
12% of all mascara
56% of all razor blades
37% of all comic books
 9% of all paperbacks
10% of all film
20% of all pantyhose
12% of all ballpoints
 6% of all sunglasses.

Jello or nothing. When chain-store shoppers are asked what they do when the brand they want is not in stock, 4 in 10 say they don't buy anything at all in that line.

I'm looking for catsup. The average supermarket stocks over 11,000 items.

Inedible groceries. The person who spends $20 at the supermarket buys an average of only $14.04 worth of edibles. The rest goes for nonfood items—cigarettes, soap, health and beauty aids, paper goods, and the like.

Shopping around. Home economists Patsy Crowell and Jean Bowers of the Ohio Agricultural Research and Development Center at Wooster, Ohio, did some scouting in 4 supermarkets in Columbus to see if it pays to shop around.

The conclusion: It does, on average, if you don't count the time it takes you.

When they priced their time at $3.00 an hour, they found it was more economical to shop in 2 supermarkets rather than 4. The cost of driving to the stores was included.

They shopped for 5 weeks with a 95-item list. By purchasing groceries at the lowest price available in each of the 4 stores, they saved 7 per cent to 15 per cent compared with shopping in any 1 of the stores.

Over the 5-week period, the cost of filling their carts ranged from a low of $60.51 (achieved by shopping around) to a high of $72.51 (by buying all the groceries at the store with the generally highest prices).

Shoppers of habit. An Agriculture Department survey finds that the average family in America

does the main food shopping once a week (60 per cent of us).
shops in only 1 store (65 per cent).

What your supermarket takes in. The average supermarket serves 8,000 customers a week and takes in $91,800. It sells enough food to feed 5,000 people a day. It charges you 20 per cent to 22 per cent more than it pays for the groceries, but after overhead it nets a profit of only 1.4 per cent.

In an average year, 1 of every 14 supermarkets in America closes and another 1 of 14 is extensively remodeled. One of every 25 supermarkets is less than a year old.

If that leads you to believe that the number of supermarkets is dwindling, you're right.

Shop by night. One in 3 Americans does most of her or his grocery shopping in the evening.

The average working woman is 3 times more likely to shop in the evening than is the average housewife.

We do 71 per cent of our grocery shopping on weekdays and 29 per cent on weekends.

Here's the list. I'll change baby. A man shopping alone is half again as likely to buy baby food as is a woman shopping alone.

Guessing at the checkout. According to Pitney Bowes' Monarch Marking Systems division, which sells a gadget for marking prices on grocery products, lots of price marking is illegible, and supermarket checkout clerks often guess the price rather than look it up.

The firm quotes an "industry consultant" who determined that checkers guess at the prices of some 22 per cent of the items you buy. When they guess, they usually *undercharge.* Yep.

A major midwestern chain, according to Pitney Bowes, found that 15.2 per cent of its price marks were illegible. The checkers *undercharged* on these items by an average of $.077 per $1.00.

That was $.49 just last week! One grocery shopper of every 14 is a real consumer activist, 1 of every 6 considers food prices absolutely outrageous, and 1 of every 3 is in a real financial squeeze.

That's outrageous! Who do you suppose calculates the "Outrageous Food Price Index," which keeps track of the percentage of Americans who consider food prices absolutely outrageous?

Why, the Food Marketing Institute, an association of supermarkets and other grocery stores.

In 1978, the Outrageous Food Price Index was 15.2 per cent. In 1979, it reached 16.8 per cent.

That's overall. When asked about hamburger prices in February 1979, the shouts of outrage rang up 47 per cent on the Outrageous Food Price Index.

Here's more, from Mary Ellen Burris, director of consumer affairs for Wegman's Food Markets of Rochester, New York. She's talking about changes in the index between 1978 and 1979.

"Other items cited by consumers as having outrageous prices? Gasoline was certainly one of them, with outrage jumping from 20 per cent to 31 per cent over the year. The cost of milk has moved up in outrage from 12 per cent to 22 per cent in one year. Outrage over sugar, fruits and vegetables, and egg prices is up slightly.

"It's not all bad news, though. Outrage over coffee prices has dropped from 56 per cent in 1978 to 25 per cent in 1979, and reaction to frozen-juice prices is down marginally."

Ms. Burris said that 39 per cent of Americans blame the government for high food prices, and another 39 per cent don't blame anyone. "The middleman" was blamed by 18 per cent. Only 3 per cent blamed supermarkets, and a similarly low percentage blamed farmers.

The psyche of the supermarket shopper. After surveying 1,174 shoppers, the U. S. Agriculture Department has concluded that there are 3 basic types of supermarket patrons:

Thirty-nine per cent are motivated by "the satisfaction appeal." They enjoy shopping for food, experiment with new products and recipes, spend more time than others in cooking, and buy favorite brands even if they cost a little more.

Thirty-two per cent are motivated by a concern over

"efficient use of time and money." They see shopping as a necessary chore, buy extra quantities when bargains are offered, and shop by price.

Eighteen per cent are "careful shoppers." They plan menus in advance, make shopping lists, take advantage of advertised specials, and are aware of nutritional labeling and food additives.

The remaining 11 per cent don't fit in any category.

Save enough and you can get an alarm clock. One supermarket in 7 offers trading stamps.

At the grocery. The average family spends $.72 of its food dollar on food that is eaten at home. The other $.28 is spent eating out.

Here's how we spend our food dollar at the store:

Beef	$.15
Pork	$.09
Bakery products	$.09
Milk and cream	$.08
Soda pop and juice	$.08
Other dairy products	$.06
Poultry	$.05
Other meats	$.04
Fresh fruits	$.04
Fresh vegetables	$.04
Fish and other seafood	$.03
Processed vegetables	$.03
Processed fruits	$.03
Cereals and cereal products	$.03
Sugar and sweets	$.03
Fats and oils	$.03
Eggs	$.02
Miscellaneous prepared foods, condiments, and seasonings	$.08

Some are yummy. In an average month, 103 new grocery products are introduced.

Moving into harder stuff. The supermarket shopper most likely to buy beer is in his or her 20s, the one most likely to buy wine is in his or her 30s, and the one most likely to buy hard liquor (in states where it's sold in markets) is in his or her 40s.

Working to eat. Working women spend 14 per cent more money in the supermarket, on average, than women without outside jobs.

Where does the money go? The last time they shopped for groceries, 55 per cent of shoppers spent about what they expected, 38 per cent spent more, 6 per cent spent less, and 1 per cent weren't sure.

Impulse buying. Although stores have greatly expanded their offerings, supermarket shoppers have cut down on their impulse buying by 6 per cent since 1965, when grocery prices were less than half what they are now.

Nonetheless, nearly half of what we buy in supermarkets we buy on impulse, without consulting shopping lists or comparing prices in ads.

The most likely impulse items: candy and gum, frozen baked goods, pastries, and snacks.

What we are least likely to buy without planning: coffee, laundry products, fresh produce, milk, and eggs.

These facts come from a study by a group with a wonderful name, the Point-of-Purchase Advertising Institute.

It's tiring. Nine of every 10 shoppers enter the supermarket in a good mood, but only 3 of 4 are in a good mood when they leave.

Brother, can you spare $1,992? That's what it would take to raise the average poor family in America out of what the government defines as poverty.

Machine vs. man. Two in 5 families run into trouble with a computer in the course of an average year.

Four times in 5 it's a computerized bill. Bank and government computers are the next most likely to cause you trouble.

Of every 100 billing errors, 30 times it's a case of being charged for something you didn't buy.

Fourteen times you're charged interest even though you paid your bill promptly. Thirteen times you're overcharged, and 4 times you're undercharged. Fifteen times you're not credited for a payment you made. Seven times you're charged for something someone else bought, and 6 times you're not credited for something you returned. These don't add up to 100, but that's computers for you.

At least 3 out of 4 people get the problem straightened out, but 8 in 100 don't even try. Of those who do try, 1 in 3 has to complain at least 4 times.

In summary, a study noted, "There appears to be some conflict between computer-using organizations and their public."

The public debt. Ever wonder whom the U. S. Government owes all that money to?

In November 1978, the public debt totaled $783 billion. Of every $100 of it, the government owed

$35.85 to itself; that included $21.38 owed to various U. S. Government agencies, and $14.47 owed to Federal Reserve banks

$8.82 to state and local governments

$11.94 to banks in the United States and its territories

$2.61 to mutual savings banks and insurance companies

$2.67 to corporations

$14.07 to individuals

$24.04 to other investors, including savings and loan associations, nonprofit organizations, corporate pension funds, brokers, and foreigners.

Deficit spending. The federal government has borrowed $8.20 of every $100 it has spent since 1955.

Indulging ourselves. The average American spent only $634 in 1929, and spent $6,395 in 1978.

Sure, you'll say, but the difference is mostly inflation.

Only partly. Let's translate both figures into 1972 dollars. The U. S. Commerce Department did that for us, and reports that:

In 1929, the average American spent the equivalent of $1,769.

In 1978, the average American spent the equivalent of $4,150.

That's for what the Commerce Department calls "personal consumption expenditures."

So we really are spending a lot more money on ourselves these days.

The all-American U.S. savings bond. One of every 3 American households owns U.S. savings bonds. Among those bond-owning households, the average has $3,500 worth.

More than 1 of every 10 American workers buys savings bonds regularly through the payroll savings plan. The average payroll saver buys $504 worth a year. (That's the purchase price.)

Asked why they buy savings bonds, 31 per cent cited safety, 18 per cent mentioned the interest rate, or the fact that income tax on the interest could be deferred, and 17 per cent said they were moved by patriotism. The average bondholder waits 5½ years before cashing them in.

Of every $100 in the national debt, $9.71 is owed to the owners of U.S. savings bonds.

Let Henry do it. Three out of 4 American taxpayers hire someone to prepare their income tax, and 1 of those 3 hires H&R Block, Inc. In 1978, the average customer paid Block $22.14 to prepare his or her federal, state, and local income-tax forms.

Junk phone calls. According to a study by the U. S. Institute of Marketing, firms trying to sell products by phone dial 12 million numbers on an average day in America. Seven million people answer, and 4.2 million of them hang up before the end of the spiel. The other 2.8 million listen, but only 460,000 of them buy the product.

Tax mistakes. In filling out federal income-tax forms, mistakes in arithmetic are made on

1 of every 10 forms filled out by the taxpayer
1 of every 20 forms filled out by professional tax preparers
1 of every 29 forms filled out by helpers from the IRS.

Faulty arithmetic is the least of it. People make a lot more errors in trying to interpret the tax law.

In 1978, the IRS looked over the shoulders of a sampling of taxpayers and found that three fourths of them erred in figuring their medical deductions, and nearly half made mistakes in figuring their interest deductions.

At the same time, the General Accounting Office looked over the shoulder of those friendly IRS folks who answer your tax questions over the telephone. It found that the IRS gave you the wrong information 13 per cent of the time.

That leaves the professional tax preparers. In 1976, the California Department of Consumer Affairs took a typical batch of income figures to several hundred preparers. Less than 1 in 100 figured the tax correctly.

The least you can do is buy their goods. In 1977, the top 100 advertisers spent an average of $42.6 million each on television commercials alone.

Buying 30 seconds of your attention. A half-minute network television commercial during prime-time evening hours sold for an average of $60,000 in 1978. A full-page color ad in *Time* sold for $69,000.

It's flattering, in a way. In 1978, each American had $195 worth of advertising beamed at her or him through television, newspapers, billboards, and so on.

The spread of prosperity. Converting everything to 1977 dollars so inflation is accounted for, here's a breakdown of how the number of families with pretty good incomes has grown in recent decades:

	1955	1965	1975	1977
$25,000 and over	4.3%	11.8%	19.4%	22.4%
$15,000 to $25,000	17.8%	29.6%	32.2%	31.7%
$10,000 to $15,000	27.8%	24.8%	19.8%	18.5%
$5,000 to $10,000	30%	20.6%	18.7%	18.1%
Under $5,000	20.1%	13.2%	9.9%	9.3%

The energy shortage and your paycheck. Here's how the average manufacturing worker's paycheck fared in comparison with energy prices in the good old days and in the bad new days:

	From 1958 to 1969	From 1969 to 1976	From 1976 to 1980
Average hourly earnings	up 51%	up 63%	up 27%
Wholesale price of			
Coal	up 17%	up 228%	up 23%
Coke	up 24%	up 218%	up 31%
Gas fuels	up 23%	up 207%	up 161%
Electricity	up 2%	up 104%	up 42%
Petroleum products	up 5%	up 178%	up 100%

(Reprinted with permission from *Nation's Business*.)

Wages and profits. Of every $1.00 of the gross national product, $.61 is paid in wages and $.16 is made in profit. The rest goes for production costs.

The cost of living everywhere. Here's how much it costs diplomatic personnel to live in various cities around the world, according to the United Nations statistical office, with New York the standard at 100 units of currency. Where an asterisk appears, governments defray part of the cost by providing housing (rent, utilities, and domestic help) at nominal cost.

City	Cost	City	Cost
Banqui, Central African Republic	149*	Port-au-Prince, Haiti	92
Brazzaville, Congo	137*	London	91
Tripoli, Libya	131*	Lima	90
Geneva	126	Rio de Janeiro	90
Paris	124	Panama City	88
The Hague	120	Kuala Lumpur, Malaysia	88
Ouagadougou, Upper Volta	118	Belgrade	87
Bonn	116	Teheran, Iran	87
Copenhagen	116	Caracas	87
Algiers, Algeria	114*	Montreal	86
Tokyo	110*	Addis Ababa, Ethiopia	86
Ulan Bator, Mongolia	109*	Baghdad, Iraq	86
Vienna	108	Rangoon, Burma	85
Jakarta, Indonesia	107	Havana	84
Seoul	103	Bangkok, Thailand	83
Apia, Western Samoa	99*	La Paz, Bolivia	82
Sana, Yemen	99	Manila, Philippines	79
Budapest	97	Nicosia, Cyprus	79
Sydney	97	Suva, Fiji	79
Kuwait, Kuwait	96	Warsaw	78
Rabat, Morocco	96	Cairo	77
Singapore	95	Prague	77
San José, Costa Rica	95	Islamabad, Pakistan	76
Damascus, Syria	95	Santiago, Chile	75
Rome	94	Ankara, Turkey	75
Athens	93	Montevideo, Uruguay	72
Amman, Jordan	92	New Delhi	71
Washington, D.C.	92	Colombo, Sri Lanka	69
Mexico City	92	Bogota, Colombia	67
		Valetta, Malta	62
		Buenos Aires	46

It takes a heap of money. The average new house cost $36,600 in the fall of 1973 and $78,200 in September of 1979, an increase of 114 per cent.

But, considering family income, house prices used to be proportionately higher, according to *Changing Times* magazine. In 1900, the average new house cost only $4,881, but that was almost 10 times the average annual family income of $490. In 1940, the average new house sold for $6,558, 5 times the typical family's annual income. In 1977, the average new house sold for $54,200, 3 times the annual income of the average American family.

Who's poor. Of the poor in America, 1 in 3 is black, 1 in 10 is Hispanic, 1 in 8 is over 65, 4 in 10 are children, and 1 in 3 is in a family headed by a woman.

Who's on welfare. According to federal welfare officials, here is the average family on AFDC. That stands for Aid for Families with Dependent Children, our biggest welfare program.

"The average AFDC family has 3 persons—a mother and 2 children. The average AFDC monthly payment in 1977 was $237.97 per family. The average number of families on AFDC was 3,569,428. About four fifths of AFDC families are headed by women. Forty-nine out of every 1,000 people in the United States receive AFDC payments. The average AFDC monthly payment in 1977 per person was $77.09."

Think the rich are paying more and more in taxes? You're right, according to economist Rudolph G. Penner of the American Enterprise Institute for Public Policy Research.

The income-tax law has been changed several times since 1967. At the same time, inflation has pushed people into higher tax brackets. Penner took three hypothetical families and figured what percentage of their income they paid in federal income tax, year by year. In each case, the income is expressed every year in 1977 dollars. In other words, the families' income kept pace exactly with inflation.

The family with an adjusted gross income of $9,362 paid 5.4

per cent of it in federal income tax in 1967, and 4.6 per cent in 1979.

The family with an adjusted gross income of $18,723 paid 10.2 per cent of it in federal income tax in 1967, and 10.5 per cent in 1979.

The family with an adjusted gross income of $37,446 paid 14.5 per cent of it in federal income tax in 1967, and 16.7 per cent in 1979.

The American giver. The average American gave $135.20 to church and charity in 1977, according to the American Association of Fund-raising Counsel and the National Council of Churches.

Here's where the average charitable dollar goes:

Religion, $.47; health and hospitals, $.14; education, $.13; social welfare, $.10; arts and humanities, $.06; civic and public causes, $.03; others, $.07.

Dow Jones for president. According to *Stock Trader's Almanac,* the stock market has not failed since World War II to go up during the third year of a President's term. The Dow Jones Industrial Average has risen an average of 16 per cent during those years. In 1979, the third year of Jimmy Carter's term, it rose 4 per cent.

That farm's worth a mansion. Just the land of the average farm in America was worth $196,200 in 1978. That's for 400 acres.

The eroding dollar. Because of inflation and changing tax rates,

if you earned this much in 1960	*you had to earn this much in 1978 to buy as much*
$3,000	$6,473
$5,000	$11,007
$10,000	$22,671
$15,000	$34,065
$25,000	$58,522
$50,000	$118,482
$100,000	$216,553

For better or worse, richer or poorer. Marriage pays. Census Bureau figures show that the average married man outearns the average single, widowed, divorced, or separated man. But that's not the case for women. Divorced women outearn their married sisters. Here are the figures for 1977 (The figures look low because they average together people who work and people who don't.):

Status	Men	Women
Married	$13,046	$4,126
Divorced	$ 9,888	$6,962
Single	$ 4,989	$4,014
Widowed	$ 5,094	$3,811
Separated	$ 7,804	$4,574

The College Payoff (if Any)

What schooling is worth. The average family head with 4 years of college makes $25,224 a year—$5,507 more than the average high-school graduate, and $8,993 more than the average family head with only 8 years of schooling. Those are 1977 figures from the Census Bureau.

Assuming the college graduate works 43 years to age 65, the high-school graduate works 47 years to age 65, and the elementary-school graduate works 51 years to 65, by retirement the college graduate will outearn the high-school graduate by $157,933, and the elementary-school graduate by $256,851. The high-school graduate will outearn the elementary-school graduate by $98,918.

Going to the bank instead of college. But the way Caroline Bird calculates it in her book *The Case Against College,* college may not pay as well as compounded interest.

She says that if a 1976 Princeton graduate had banked the cost of his or her education plus the income lost during school, and had earned 7.5 per cent interest on it, he or she would have had well over $1 million by age 64. That's more than the average college graduate earns in a lifetime.

Help! More than half of college freshmen receive a scholarship or some sort of financial assistance. Even among those from the wealthiest backgrounds, 37 per cent get help.

Russian roots. The average grandson or granddaughter of Russian immigrants to the United States makes more money than the grandchildren of immigrants from any other country.

Here's one of those depressing big-government statistics. In a report urging the government to do a better job of figuring how many employees it needs, the General Accounting Office pointed out that you can't figure the workload without knowing how many days a month people work, on average, and how many days they're away from their desks for one reason or another.

It doesn't sound too important, but the government employs a lot of people, and a little error can add up to a lot of bucks. As the GAO put it:

"An error of one day a month in the estimated availability for work of the average civilian employee would create an annual estimating error of about 114,500 staff-years and could cost about $1.7 billion."

Does the government make errors of that dimension? Oh yes, the GAO said.

Top blue-collar dollar. The average factory worker makes more in Detroit than in any other city—$18,829. Other cities where typical earnings for blue-collar workers run high are Buffalo, Rochester, Pittsburgh, Cleveland, Houston, Indianapolis, Milwaukee, and San Francisco-Oakland.

The silver lining. Two thirds of the American people have life insurance. In 1977, the average family had $32,400 in coverage —perhaps enough to live on for two years. Counting just those families who *had* insurance, the average was $36,900.

The average insured man paid $256 a year in premiums for $28,980 in insurance. The average insured woman paid $78 a year for $7,640 in insurance.

The average family in Delaware had twice as much life-insurance coverage ($49,200 in 1977) as the average family in Mississippi ($24,600).

In 1977, the average new policy was for $18,010. More women are insuring themselves, but, still, for every woman who bought a life-insurance policy, 2 men bought a policy, and a bigger one at that.

About half those with insurance pay their premiums monthly. One in 4 pays only once a year.

The average beneficiary who collected in 1977 drew $3,552.51. That figure is so low because old people, who are the ones most likely to die, have the least insurance.

The average life-insurance policy is in effect more than 20 years before it pays a claim, and nearly half are in effect 30 years or more.

Two in 100 American adults have insured their lives for $100,000 or more.

Fuss budgets. One family in 2 keeps a budget, but only 1 in 8 draws it up in any sort of formal way.

Make more, spend more. In 1978, the average working wife made $7,200. At that rate, according to *Money* magazine, "her net after-tax contribution to the household is marginal at best and, if all extra costs are heartlessly rooted out and totted up, perhaps even a fiscal extravagance."

Two-earner households are twice as likely to eat out regularly as are families in which the wife stays home. Two-earner households also spend twice as much on education, a third again as much on transportation, have less in assets, and give less to charity.

According to studies cited by *Money,* the average working wife "is the least economy-minded of her sex, the biggest impulse buyer, and the least apt to shop for bargains."

Pump that gas, soldier. The Army says that it saves $15,000 a year by telling its drivers to use self-service pumps when they fill up military vehicles at commercial gas stations.

Democracy is expensive. The average winner in the 1978 U. S. Senate race spent $1,058,671 on his or her campaign, up from $552,423 in 1974, the last previous nonpresidential Senate election year. "Taken another way," commented the Washington *Post*, "the price tag on a U.S. senator rose almost three times as fast as the price tag on a quart of milk in that period."

The New York bargain bazaar. Prices are higher in New York than in most any other major city except Tokyo. But the average New Yorker also makes more money. The Union Bank of Switzerland calculated average wages and prices in 1976 for 12 big cities, and found that for every dollar of purchasing power of the average New Yorker, the average person has the purchasing power of $.93 in Montreal, $.87 in Sydney, $.66 in Johannesburg, $.58 in London, $.59 in Paris, $.54 in Tokyo, $.48 in Rio de Janeiro, $.45 in Mexico City, $.45 in Hong Kong, $.28 in Istanbul, and $.16 in Buenos Aires.

We're better off than we think. Here's the income of the average American over the years, adjusted for taxes and inflation. It's what the Commerce Department calls disposable personal income, per capita, and it's expressed in 1972 dollars.

Year	Income	Year	Income
1929	$1,886	1964	$3,152
1933	$1,350	1968	$3,464
1934	$1,420	1972	$3,837
1937	$1,767	1973	$4,062
1941	$2,084	1974	$3,973
1944	$2,485	1975	$4,025
1948	$2,288	1976	$4,136
1952	$2,434	1977	$4,271
1956	$2,650	1978	$4,420
1960	$2,697		

The cost of dying. The average funeral in America costs $2,000, including the grave.

Inflation. On average, consumer prices in America were about the same in 1944 as they were in 1800.

On average, consumer prices in 1978 were double what they were in 1967.

Profile of the carriage trade. *The New Yorker* is synonymous with upper-class America. In 1976, the magazine commissioned a detailed survey of its subscribers.

The average household income—in 1975, mind you—was $35,300.

One of every 6 subscribers was on the board of directors of some business. One in 5 had a Ph.D. One in 4 had written an article or a book within the past year, and 1 in 3 belonged to a tennis, golf, or yacht club. One of every 2 had flown overseas or to Alaska or Hawaii within the past 3 years, and 3 of every 4 drank scotch, at least occasionally.

During the previous year, 1 of every 4 had been asked for advice about fashions, and 1 of every 3 had been consulted about buying a car.

One of every 7 owned tax-exempt bonds (average value, $54,400). One of every 5 owned U.S. bonds (average value, $14,500), and almost 1 of every 5 owned corporate bonds (average value, $39,700). Three of every 10 owned mutual-fund shares (average value, $16,900). Seven of every 10 owned the homes they lived in (average value, $77,000), and 1 of every 3 owned other real estate (average value, $98,200).

Six of every 10 owned stock (average value $70,500, and that didn't count a subscriber who said he owned $25 million worth).

Is Howard worth all that? The average half-minute commercial on a network TV sports program cost $23,600 in 1977. Thirty seconds of commercial time cost $62,000 on "Monday Night Football." Average costs were $45,600 on other professional football telecasts, $38,000 for college football, $36,600 for horse racing, $25,000 for baseball, $20,100 for golf, $17,600 for college basketball, $17,500 for pro basketball, $17,000 for multiple sports shows, $11,400 for bowling, and $10,600 for tennis.

Turn down the heat and pull up the blankets. According to Honeywell, a thermostat manufacturer, here's how much you can reduce your heating bill by lowering thermostat settings for 8 hours a day.

In	By 5° F.	By 10° F.
Atlanta	11%	15%
Boston	7%	11%
Buffalo	6%	10%
Chicago	7%	11%
Cincinnati	8%	12%
Cleveland	7%	10%
Dallas	11%	15%
Denver	7%	11%
Des Moines	7%	11%
Detroit	7%	11%
Kansas City	8%	12%
Los Angeles	12%	16%
Louisville	9%	13%
Milwaukee	6%	10%
Minneapolis	5%	9%
New York	8%	12%
Omaha	7%	11%
Philadelphia	8%	12%
Portland	9%	13%
Salt Lake City	7%	11%
San Francisco	10%	14%
Seattle	8%	12%
St. Louis	8%	12%
Washington, D.C.	9%	13%

What are your chances of a tax audit? On average, the Internal Revenue Service audits 1 tax return of every 42. But the risk rises with income.

Taking things another step, the Criminal Investigation Division of the IRS investigates 1 of every 10,000 tax returns. Of those investigated, fewer than 1 in 6 is successfully prosecuted. Of those successfully prosecuted, fewer than half go to jail.

The Gambling American

How much we gamble. In 1975, the University of Michigan Survey Research Center surveyed the gambling habits of Americans for the Commission on the Review of the National Policy Toward Gambling. Most of the gambling facts that follow come from that study.

In a typical year, 3 out of 5 Americans gamble, and 1 in 10 does some illegal gambling.

The younger, richer, and better educated you are, the more likely that you gamble.

Here's a rundown on the percentage of adults who gamble, and who gamble illegally, by religion:

	Any gambling	*Illegal gambling*
Catholics	80%	16%
All Protestants	54%	9%
Presbyterians, Lutherans, Congregationalists, Episcopalians	74%	10%
Bible-oriented sects	33%	8%
Methodists	63%	11%
Baptists	45%	10%
Jews	77%	19%
No religious preference	40%	5%

On average, a Northeasterner is twice as likely as a Southerner to gamble. A white is more likely to gamble than a black, but a black is more likely to gamble illegally. A man is more likely to gamble than a woman, and is much more likely to place illegal bets.

Win some/lose more. The typical gambler loses $.22 of every dollar he or she wagers.

On average, you lose 55 per cent of what you bet on state lotteries, 54 per cent on the numbers game, 33 per cent at bingo, 21 per cent at New York's legal off-track horse-race parlors, 16 per cent at the track or on horse books, 15 per cent at a casino, and 4.5 per cent on sports books.

People with incomes of $5,000 to $10,000 lose $.27 of their wagering dollar, while people with incomes of $30,000 or more lose only $.17. That's largely because poor folks tend to bet on games like the numbers and state lotteries, where the take is higher.

In 1975, the average horse player wagered $512.70 at the track. Here are some other average wagers for the year:

Sports book player	$623.03
Casino gambler	$448.26
Horse book player	$416.53
Numbers player	$273.19
Bingo player	$ 74.11
Sports card player	$ 43.70

The gaming life. The average gambler spends *less* time than the average nongambler loafing, working around the house, going to church, knitting, and sewing. The gambler spends *more* time reading newspapers and magazines, fishing, hunting, camping, doing arts and crafts, and playing and watching sports. He or she spends *lots* more time than the nongambler at movies, bars, and nightclubs, and he or she dances a lot more.

Gambling itself takes time. The average numbers player plays the numbers 71 days a year. Among gamblers who deal with bookies, the average for horse bets is 29 days a year; for other sports bets, 28. The average guy or gal who plays cards with friends for money sits down at the table 25 times a year.

The odds against you at the casino. In roulette, the house has an advantage on European wheels of 1.35 per cent on even-money bets and 2.7 per cent on all other bets. On wheels used in Las Vegas, Atlantic City, and the Caribbean, the house advantage is over 5 per cent on all bets except one: the 5-number bet of 1, 2, 3, 0, and 00. The house edge on that one is almost 8 per cent.

In craps, your best bet is the "pass" or "don't pass" lines, sometimes marked "win" and "lose" or "do" and "don't." If you bet the pass line, the casinos advantage is 1.414 per cent. If you bet don't pass, the casino's edge is only 1.402 per cent.

In blackjack, casino rules require the dealer to take cards if he has 16 or less, and to stick with 17 or more. If you follow exactly the same rule, the house advantage is 5.9 per cent, according to authority John Scarne.

On chuck-a-luck (a dice game in which players bet that a certain number will come up), the house advantage is almost 7.5 per cent. On the Big Six wheel of fortune, it's more than 20 per cent. As for slot machines, some pay back as much as 95 per cent of what's put in; others pay back as little as 50 per cent.

The thrill of the bet. When asked to rate the excitement of various forms of gambling on a scale from 1 (not exciting) to 8 (very exciting), gamblers came out with these excitement averages:

Horses at the track	4.83
Cards with friends	4.53
Casinos	4.24
Slot machines	4.08
Sports with friends	3.75
Bingo	3.58
Lotteries	3.26
Dogs at the track	3.21
Dice	2.94
Horses off the track	2.32
Sports cards	2.19
Sports with a bookie	1.9
Numbers	1.74

Those figures are for all gamblers lumped together. The average guy who bets illegally rated every game more exciting than did the typical legal bettor.

__i__g__. __i__go. Bi__go. Bingo!__ The average bingo player wagers $5.93 per session. In the course of a year, she or he wagers $74 on the game.

Sixty-three per cent of the people who play have "bingoed" (that's the word they use) at least once, winning an average of $24.

Of those who play bingo, 3 per cent say they do so in the hope of winning a lot and getting rich.

Turning in the bookie. While 95 per cent of Americans say they would report a robbery to police if they saw it occurring and 64 per cent say they would report someone selling marijuana, only 30 per cent say they would turn in someone taking an illegal bet.

The odds are with the state. The average Maryland resident bets $1.40 a week in the Maryland lottery. In Michigan, the typical resident bets $.71 a week in the state lottery. In the New Jersey and Connecticut state lotteries, the average is $.67 a week for each resident.

In general, state lotteries pay back only about half of what they collect in wagers.

Let's apply at General Motors. On average, the bigger the company you work for, the more you get paid.

In 1975, people working for firms employing 9 or fewer people averaged $150.02 a week. At firms employing 10 to 99 people, the average paycheck was $169.84. For companies with 100 to 999 employees, the figure was $186.50; and at firms employing 1,000 or more, it was $229.59.

(Reprinted with permission from *Nation's Business*.)

Fighting cancer. Year after year, the American Cancer Society is America's favorite health charity. We give cancer the equivalent of $.50 a year for every American, nearly twice what we give the American Heart Association, the second most popular health cause.

I give at the office. The average donor to the United Way gave $40.39 in 1978. Of all the money the United Way received, only 2.7 per cent came from people who were solicited at home. The average person who gave at home donated $20 less than the average person who gave at the office.

Homemade vs. storebought. Food that is made at home from scratch is not necessarily cheaper than convenience foods.

That's what the Agriculture Department concluded when it computed what it would cost to concoct various foods at home.

This experiment assumed that the homemaker was paid $4.73 an hour to cook. But even when the home cook received only the minimum wage, convenience foods were often cheaper.

In 41 comparisons, the convenience food was at least $.01 per serving cheaper than the same food made at home. When the cook's wage was calculated at the higher figure, convenience foods were a bargain 3 times out of 5.

From-scratch people, take heart: Twenty-two convenience foods were evaluated by "a trained test panel" against their home-prepared counterparts for appearance, flavor, texture, and overall quality. Both rated high in quality, but homemade usually beat storebought in texture, appearance, and flavor.

Two paychecks are better than one. In 1978, 1 American family in 5 had income totaling more than $25,000, and in two thirds of those families, at least 2 members worked.

According to a study in Muncie, Indiana, working wives were 20 per cent more likely than nonworking wives to rate their marriages as "very happy." Their husbands, on the other hand, were 24 per cent *less* likely to say that they were "very satisfied" with their marital relationships than were the husbands of nonworking wives.

Three fourths of the working wives say that their husbands are "very supportive." Only 31 per cent of their husbands agree.

Big gifts. Among Americans who die and leave estates exceeding $300,000, charitable bequests average about 8 per cent of what they leave behind.

Giving to Mother Eli. One of every 3 Yale alumni gave money to his or her alma mater during the 1977–78 school year. The average gift was $204.

Home, sweet mortgage. The average family that bought a home in 1977 paid $400 a month for housing—$273 on the mortgage, $54 in real-estate taxes, $60 for utilities, and $13 for insurance.

In a 28-city survey, the highest average monthly payment was for a house in San Francisco—$614; the lowest was $333, in St. Louis.

Hovering within $10 of the nationwide average were these cities—Baltimore; Denver; Hartford, Connecticut; Rochester, New York; and Yakima, Washington.

A quart of bread, a pound of beans, and a Chevrolet. Sixteen cents of every dollar Americans spend at retail establishments go to new-car dealers.

The machine that vends. The average American spends $40 a year in vending machines. There's a vending machine in the United States for every 53 people.

Digging for gold. According to the American Dental Association, the average dentist working alone earned $89,999 in 1977.

Here is what the average dentist charged for these services:

Examination	$ 8.58
Cleaning	$ 15.35
Complete mouth Xray	$ 23.84
Single extraction	$ 15.39
A permanent filling	$ 12.75
Gold-inlay restoration (one surface)	$ 83.27
Root-canal therapy (molar, one canal excluding filling)	$166.69
Porcelain crown	$171.00
Complete upper or lower denture with six month's postdelivery care	$278.98

The hoard within. For every ounce of gold bought by an investor, 3 ounces are used to fill teeth. So reports the U. S. Bureau of Mines.

Ring it up. The average telephone—home or business—costs $23.33 a month.

Does price equal quality? From a comparison of price and independent test results for 10,000 brands of products, Professor Peter Riesz of the University of Iowa concludes that there is no necessary correlation between high price and high quality. In 35 per cent of the nondurable products he checked, higher price actually meant *lower* quality, on the average.

The price-quality correlation was weakest in frozen pizzas, fish sticks, beefsteaks, fruit pies, boil-in-bag vegetables, detergents, denture cleaners, baby shampoos, hair colorings, skin cleansing creams and lotions, boys' jeans and shoes, and men's wash-and-wear shirts.

Is it worth it? Economists Murray L. Weidenbaum and Robert DeFina claim that federal regulations cost the average American $307 in 1976.

If you bought a car that year, you paid more than your share. Seat belts, emission controls, and other items required by federal regulations added nearly $650 to the price of a new car, they said.

Consumerists argue that the regulations prevent accidents and provide other benefits that outweigh the cost.

We're sending your kids to college. Public colleges get about 13 per cent of their money from tuition and fees; private schools get 36 per cent from these sources.

The federal government pays 19 per cent of private-college costs and 15 per cent of public-college costs. States foot 45 per cent of the bill for public schools but only 2.3 per cent for private schools.

Gifts, grants, endowments, contracts, sales, and services make up the rest.

How much we owe. The average American owed $5,045.91 in 1979. He or she owed $3,748.74 on the mortgage, $517.46 on the car, $229.20 on credit-card and store accounts, and $550.51 on personal loans and other kinds of credit.

Those figures count children as well as adults. The average American *household* owed $14,836.99: $11,022.77 on the mortgage, $1,521.54 on the car, $673.95 on credit-card and store accounts, and $1,618.73 on personal loans and other kinds of credit.

On money borrowed from a bank or savings and loan association in August 1979, the average American paid 10.5 per cent interest for a mortgage, 11.88 per cent for an auto loan, 17.09 per cent on bank credit cards, and 13.76 per cent on personal loans and other kinds of credit.

How much we own. At the end of 1978, the average American had $5.10 in assets—cash, securities, house equity, and so forth —for every dollar of debts.

How much we save. The typical American was saving 3.2 per cent of his or her after-tax income in late 1979, down from 7.6 per cent in 1973 through 1975. In 1944, when, because of World War II, there wasn't much for sale, the average American saved a quarter of his or her income.

Businesswomen. A survey of more than 3,400 women who own their own businesses shows that most of them are in service industries—typically, public relations, catering, or travel agencies. A third are in retailing. About 85 per cent employ fewer than 9 people full-time. About half report gross receipts over $50,000, but 17 per cent report receipts of under $10,000. More than 58 per cent are married.

Working for less in the country. The Agriculture Department's Economics, Statistics, and Co-operatives Service says that rural working women earn on average about 25 per cent less than women in metropolitan areas.

It isn't fair. According to *U.S. News & World Report,* the average male high-school dropout makes $1,604 a year more than the average woman college graduate.

Good pay and who gets it. One of every 5 white men was making $400 a week or more in May 1978. But only 1 of every 38 white women was paid that much. The rates were 1 in 16 for black men, and 1 in 36 for black women.

If the mortgage won't get you, the taxes will. Property taxes averaged $126 for every American in 1966, and $266 in 1976. The average Alabaman paid only $57 in property taxes in 1976, while the average Alaskan paid $1,048. Those figures include property taxes paid by business, and the startling figure for Alaska resulted largely from levies on Alaskan oil reserves and the Alaskan pipeline.

Us capitalists. Only 1 American family in 4 lives entirely on wages and salaries. For the rest of us, a little extra income comes from stocks, bonds, annuities, interest on savings accounts, Social Security, pensions, or welfare.

The Pensioned American

Try living on it. The average private pension for 1977 was $1,740.74, and the average Social Security pension was $2,916.

Something to look forward to. Half the people in America working for private business are enrolled in pension or retirement plans. Three quarters of all government employees are, too. Those figures don't include Social Security.

The get/need gap. A Brandeis University study of nearly 1,000 private pension plans found that the average worker who made $15,000 in 1975 retired on $3,150 a year, after 30 years' work. Even with Social Security, the worker and his or her spouse couldn't maintain their old standard of living.

Studies have established that a couple needs 70 per cent of their working income to maintain the same lifestyle in retirement. But the average American retiree falls far short of that.

The average woman retiree with 30 years' experience receives 28 per cent of what she earned just before retirement. The average man in those circumstances gets 22 per cent.

Social Security's payoff. Nearly 1 American in 7 receives Social Security benefits.

The 33 million recipients include

21 million retired workers and their dependents
7.5 million survivors of workers
4.7 million disabled workers and their dependents

How much they get. According to the Social Security Administration, in September 1978 the average retired worker received a monthly check for $261.51. His or her spouse is supposed to get half that much, but for some reason spouses' checks averaged $132.01, a fraction more than half. Dependent children of retired workers got an average of $102.83 each.

Disabled workers, who are also protected by Social Security, drew an average check of $286.82. Spouses got $85.47, and children got $82.38.

Survivors also draw benefits. The average widowed spouse drew $240.59, and the average surviving youngster drew $180.59.

Women and pensions. According to the Pension Rights Center, only 2 per cent of widows receive anything from their husbands' pension plans, and only 10 per cent of the women who retired from private enterprise in 1970 received a pension. Retired women who do get a pension average only $81 a month, according to *Changing Times* magazine.

Will there be any left when it's my turn? In a 1978 Lou Harris poll, more than 2 in 5 working Americans said they had "hardly any confidence at all" that they would get the Social Security benefits they've earned. Another two fifths said they had "less than full confidence."

Less toil for the better life. The Association of Home Appliance Manufacturers wants you to know that wages in the United States have gone up much faster than appliance prices. Here's the proof.

The average American had to work this many hours

to buy a(n)	in 1959	in 1975
automatic washer	127.9	67.6
refrigerator	153.4	64.7
gas dryer	111.4	55.1
dishwasher	116.4	53.6
electric stove	126.9	51.1
electric dryer	98.2	50.9
air conditioner	122.8	49.9
dehumidifier	47	19.8
disposer	36.5	18.7

Rich Americans. According to statistics published by the United Nations and the World Bank, the average American has more income, and uses at least twice as much energy, as the typical resident of any other country in the world except Canada. We edge the Canadians on both counts, too, but not by much.

It helps the ins stay in. In the 1978 elections, incumbent members of the House of Representatives averaged $30,000 in campaign contributions from business and labor, while challengers averaged $12,500.

You make more, you pay more. In 1953, the average American family earned $5,000 and paid $590 of it, or 11.8 per cent, in federal, state, and local taxes. In 1977, the average American family earned $16,000, and paid taxes totaling $3,600, or 22.6 per cent of income.

Making farm ends meet. The average family farmer has to have a job somewhere else to make ends meet. In 1977, the Agriculture Department says, the average farm family made $7,440 on the farm—and $11,600 in town.

Plug it in. At $.04 per kilowatt-hour, here's what it costs the average family to operate these small electric appliances for a whole year:

Electric blanket	$6.00
Slow cooker	$5.56
Coffeemaker	$5.52
Frying pan	$4.00
Toaster	$1.56
Iron	$2.40
Toothbrush	$ .40
Corn popper	$ .36
Mixer	$ .06
Blender	$ .04
Shaver	$ .02
Can opener	$ .01

The materialistic American. In a 1975 Roper survey, a few more people named children as an ingredient of the good life than named a car. When the same question was asked in 1979, slightly more people named a car.

Other things mentioned more in 1975 and less in 1979 were a happy marriage, an interesting job, and a job that contributes to the welfare of society. Things mentioned less in 1975 and more in 1979 included a color TV, a lot of money, really nice clothes, and a second color TV.

Where income comes from. For every dollar of income, the average American gets $.74 from his or her work, $.13 from the government, $.09 from interest on savings, $.03 from stock dividends, and $.01 from rent.

Those are the proportions for all personal income in the United States in 1977, as tabulated by the Commerce Department. Of course, we're averaging together retired people on Social Security, who get almost all their money from the government, with working people who don't get any. That's the way averages work.

Of that $.13 from the government, $.07 is in Social Security pensions, and $.02 is in pensions to retired government employees. A bit less than $.01 each is paid in unemployment compensation, veterans' benefits, and welfare for mothers and their children. Another $.02 is from various other welfare programs.

Help from Washington. Of every 100 families in America, 44 get a regular monthly check from Uncle Sam—chiefly Social Security, welfare, veterans' payments, unemployment or workmen's compensation, government pensions, or railroad retirement.

The government checks are the sole source of income for 3 million of the 25 million families that get them.

Where they grow millions. Idaho has more millionaires per capita than any other state. That's because farmland has become so valuable and Idaho has so much of it. A third of all American millionaires live in the Midwest, close to the earth.

Families in the red. More than 5 families in 100 that use credit are in financial hot water; they owe more than they can pay.

Some seek professional help. The average family that consults members of the National Foundation for Consumer Credit has an income of $15,000 and debts of $7,000 to $8,000.

Harvesting Washington. Between 1970 and 1977, the average farmer got $1.00 from Uncle Sam for every $36.22 he made selling his crops and animals in the marketplace.

I have to think of my family and my old age. When asked to cite problems connected with their jobs, 1 working American in 5 said the pay wasn't enough, and half said the fringe benefits were insufficient.

The size of the government. One of every 5 American workers is employed by government, and $1.00 of every $5.00 spent in this country is spent by government. About $2.00 of every $5.00 of

Americans' income go for taxes and other government receipts, and $1.00 of every $3.80 in personal income comes from government.

Where deficits come from. The federal government takes in $.58 of every tax dollar collected in the United States. State governments get $.23, and local governments get $.19.

If you lump all our governmental units together and count both business and personal taxes, government collected an average of $2,422 from each of us in 1975 and spent $2,604 on each of us.

Beneficiaries. For every husband who collects on his wife's insurance policy, 6 wives collect on their husbands'.

Not counting proxies. A survey by *Meetings & Conventions* magazine found that 278 stockholders attend the average stockholders' meeting.

These people look forward to April 15. Three out of 4 taxpayers get a refund on their federal income tax. The average refund is $508.

The thin dime and other skinny coins. There isn't a bit of silver in today's coins. Half dollars, quarters, dimes, and nickels are 75 per cent copper and 25 per cent nickel on the face, pure copper in the core.

Rubbing, handling, flipping, and jiggling wear down our precious coin supply. In an average year, the coins in circulation lose a combined total of 132,000 pounds.

7 Everything We Do in the Bathroom and How Long It Takes

Our bathroom selves. When indoor facilities came along, bathrooms were designed to meet the needs of the plumber rather than the user. The only big design change since then has been to shrink the size of the room.

Some years ago, researchers at Cornell University set out to find what the ideal bathroom would be like. They accordingly delved into our bathroom behavior, and for that they surveyed 1,000 women in the Los Angeles area. The result was a 6-year study written by Marilyn Langford, an associate home economics professor. Here are some of the results.

Give us this day our daily bath. One third of the water used by the average American household is for bathing. Ninety-eight per cent of adult America bathes at least 2 or 3 times a week, and three quarters of us take a daily bath or shower.

A chart recording children's bath practices would be U-shaped. Nine out of 10 preschoolers get a supervised bath daily. In the grade-school years, only 3 in 4 take a daily bath. By age 12, when kids are even more free of parents' supervision, daily bathing declines still farther. By the teen-age years, when the opposite sex has been discovered, 9 out of 10 girls and 3 out of 4 boys are taking a bath a day again.

Teen-age girls, in fact, average more baths than their mothers.

The bathing hour. Adults take half their baths or showers in the evening, after dinner, or before going to bed. Men take a quarter of their baths or showers before breakfast. So do a third of working women, but only 1 housewife in 10 bathes that early.

People who insist on absolute privacy while they bathe tend to take them in the middle of the day.

Showers vs. baths. Given the choice, 4 men in 5 usually take showers rather than baths. Among women, half bathe, half shower.

But two thirds of all couples use the same method, and usually it's the wife who adopts the husband's routine. Sixty per cent of wives take showers if that's what their mates do, and 85 per cent of wives take baths if that's what their husbands prefer.

Younger people prefer showers. Under age 35, 3 couples in 5 shower.

The wealthier and more educated you are, the more likely you are to shower. This is especially true of women.

One reason people prefer showers is because of the privacy afforded by the shower curtain. One in 5 mentioned that as a reason, and the proportion rose among women with lots of children.

People who prefer showers to baths call the former "more refreshing." Bath lovers call the tub "more relaxing."

Even at age 2, boys are more likely to be showerers than tub bathers. By the time they're teen-agers, 59 per cent of all girls and 78 per cent of boys are shower takers.

It never fails. Seventy-three per cent of women who take baths say they don't leave the tub if the phone rings, and 84 per cent won't budge to answer the doorbell. Among shower users, who may have trouble hearing those interruptions, the percentages are 82 per cent and 89 per cent, respectively.

It's soooo relaxing. The average woman stays in the bathtub for a minimum of a half hour.

At least that's true when she's using a bath oil or other such additive, which is how the question was posed by the Givaudan Corporation.

Only 1 woman of 100 gets out of the tub in less than a half hour. Of the other 99, 37 stay about a half hour, 21 soak it up for 45 minutes, 31 stay an hour or more, and 10 don't know how long they soak.

The younger you are, on average, the longer you stay in the tub.

Soaping up. For every American woman who washes with Ivory soap, two wash with Dial.

Henry, I need the bathroom! Most people who take showers say they're out of the shower within 10 minutes, and almost all report being out within 20 minutes.

But not so among tub users. Only 1 in 5 is done in 10 minutes, and nearly 1 in 3 says his or her bath lasts more than 20 minutes. Of course, sometimes it's hard to keep an eye on the clock.

Asked if they "just washed" or "soaked a while," two thirds of the tub users say they soak.

Fifteen per cent of women read in the tub and 8 per cent smoke in the tub.

Please Close the Door

Modesty through sound. One American woman in 7 runs the water in the bathroom to cloak the sound of elimination, even when other members of the family are the only other people in the house. Fifty-three per cent run the water when guests are present.

Home nudity. Most mothers don't mind being seen in the nude by their babies, but their modesty increases as the kids get older.

In a survey of 1,000 women, 7 per cent objected to being seen in their underwear by their infant daughters, and 22 per cent didn't want to be seen in the nude. If the baby was a boy, the percentages rose to 10 per cent and 22 per cent, respectively.

By the time their daughters reached 16, 34 per cent of the mothers didn't want to be seen in their underwear by them, and 68 per cent didn't want to be seen in the nude.

Fifty-five per cent didn't want their 16-year-old sons to see them in their underwear, and 94 per cent didn't want to be seen naked.

Unalone in the bathroom. In families with children, 51 per cent of mothers say they want complete privacy while bathing, and 62 per cent while using the toilet. The older the kids, the more Mom wants privacy. Older and poorer mothers are more insistent on privacy than younger, wealthier moms.

Boy, girl, rubber duck. At ages 4 and 5, 4 kids out of 5 take baths or showers with their brothers or sisters. At age 9, 2 in 5 children bathe with brothers or sisters. At age 12, 2 girls in 5 still bathe with sisters, but only 1 boy in 5 shares his bath or shower.

After age 5, youngsters generally take baths only with siblings of the same sex.

Pass the soap, Junior. Two mothers in 10 bathe with their children. Even in families in which all the kids are over 6, 1 mother in 10 says she doubles up in the bath with a kid. This is equally true whether they take baths or showers.

The shared-towel syndrome. In 2 families out of 5, the bathroom hand towel is used by everyone. The bath towel is used by everyone in 1 family out of 5.

The bathroom as laundry. Fifty-two per cent of the stockings that are hand laundered in America are washed in the bathroom. Forty-nine per cent are left there to dry, too.

As for other dainties, here are the facts:

	Washed in bathroom	Dried in bathroom
Panties	38%	24%
Bras	32%	20%
Slips	28%	13%
Nighties	21%	10%
Men's shirts	8%	12%
Socks	57%	39%

We almost left this stuff out of our nice, family book. The average newborn baby pees an ounce or 2 ounces a day. By the time he or she is a year old, baby is peeing a pint or more.

A child 8 to 14 years old tinkles 1¾ to 3 pints a day. The range for the average adult is a little wider—as little as 1¼ pints, as much as 3½ pints.

As you get old, you pee a little less. The average senior citizen pees 1⅘ pints a day.

The average child defecates anywhere from 2 to 5 ounces a day. An adult on a mixed diet gets rid of 2 to 9 ounces. The typical vegetarian defecates 13 ounces a day, lots more than the adult on an all-meat diet, who defecates only a couple of ounces. Even an adult on a prolonged fast defecates a little, averaging a third of an ounce to an ounce daily.

Time to change baby. Here's how many stools the typical breast-fed baby has on an average day at

5 days old	5
10 days old	4
12 days old	3
4 weeks old	2
10 weeks old	1

It runs through you. Say you drink a quart of water at one sitting. If you're average, you'll pee away 14 per cent of it in an hour, half of it in the second hour, 27 per cent of it in the third hour, and the last 9 per cent of it in the fourth hour.

The American Toilet

What goes on there. Four people in 10 read while on the toilet. One in 5 smokes. Fourteen per cent listen to the radio. Eight per cent use the phone there—mostly people who have telephones with long cords, not bathroom phones.

Flushing. Every flush disposes of 6 to 8 gallons of water. The average family uses half its water that way—29 gallons per person a day.

Flushing II. According to Alexander Kira's study *The Bathroom: Criteria for Design,* 34 per cent of us flush the toilet while still sitting on it, while 66 per cent flush after standing up.

Missing the urinal. When 1,000 women were asked if having a urinal in the family bathroom would be desirable from a practical standpoint, 1 in 5 said yes.

Twenty-nine per cent thought it would be a good idea to have a drinking fountain in the bathroom.

Forty per cent would like a wall or divider between each fixture in the bathroom, and 38 per cent would like the toilet walled off.

Sure it's unnatural, but men like it. Of every 100 American women 15 or older, 84 shave their armpits and 68 shave their legs. But some of them quit as they get older. Of every 100 women between 15 and 44, 98 shave; of every 100 women 45 or older, only 70 shave.

For every woman who uses Nair or some other depilatory, 5 use an electric shaver, and 20 use a safety razor. Most women who use a razor shave in the tub, but 1 of every 4 does it dry.

The average American woman shaves twice a week, but picks up the pace during the summer.

What people do with their hair. The average American man washes his hair more often than the typical American woman does.

The woman washes her hair 1 to 3 times a week. The man, 4 or more times.

On average, the younger you are, the more often you wash your hair. (Of course, you have more to wash.)

One man in 10 washes his hair with soap. Virtually no women do.

More men buy Head & Shoulders than any other brand. Women prefer Prell, Breck, and Herbal Essence. But among both men and women, Prell is the brand that has been abandoned by the most people.

Two women out of 3 use a creme rinse or conditioner, and Agree is the leading brand, particularly among the young and the oily-haired.

Most women wash their hair at home when they're young, but as they get old they tend to have it done at the salon.

When people brush. Forty-one per cent of wives and 45 per cent of husbands in America brush their teeth as soon as they get up.

Bedtime is an even more popular toothbrushing time—70 per cent of wives, 60 per cent of husbands brush then, too.

Among wives, 51 per cent brush after breakfast, 19 per cent after lunch, 22 per cent after dinner, and 4 per cent after snacks.

Only 1 out of 300 people has no particular fixed times for brushing his or her teeth.

Children pretty much follow the pattern of their parents, the highest percentage brushing at bedtime. Not a child in this survey said he or she did not have a fixed time for brushing.

Now a look at toothbrushes. The American Dental Association sent new toothbrushes to 751 families, and collected and examined the families' 2,113 brushes then in use. Conclusion: Forty-five per cent were in unsatisfactory condition—caked with toothpaste, splayed, stained, or broken.

The average family that owned an electric toothbrush did not use it. Thus saving electricity.

Electrifying the hair. One out of 6 American college women bought a hair dryer in 1977. Conair was the favored brand, followed by Super Max. One in 14 bought electric curlers, and 1 of every 25 bought a curling iron, with Clairol the favorite brand for both appliances.

Twenty weeks before the mirror. The average man has 15,000 whiskers on his face, according to *Today's Health* magazine; 30,000, according to the Chicago *Sun-Times*. In either case, he spends about 10 minutes a day shaving. That's 60 hours a year or, for the man who shaves for 55 years, a lifetime total of 3,300 hours—138 days. The average man shaves off 1 pound of whiskers every 10 years.

Whiskers grow at an average rate of fifteen to seventeen thousandths of an inch every day, or roughly a half inch a month. By that formula, an average-lived fellow who never shaved would die with a 30-foot beard.

In general, old men have tougher beards than young men, and fat men get closer shaves than thin men.

Two minutes of washing with warm water expands each whisker by 34 per cent, making it much easier to shave.

The blade and the beard. Gillette research chemist Oscar Levine says that the typical shaver changes blades after 9 or 10 shaves, but needn't. He says the average man just changes blades when he thinks he ought to. But blades should last three months before becoming dull.

About 1 man in 4 owns an electric razor, but most owners use them only some of the time.

Facewashing. Seven women in 10 say they wash their faces from a stream of water rather than from the sinkbowl. Nine in 10 use a washcloth at least occasionally.

Enough to make you blush. The average American spends $41.28 a year on toothpaste, mouthwash, shampoo, perfume, cologne, lotion, moisturizer, and other cosmetics.

8 Family Life

I hate Monday. The average American family washes 8 loads of clothes a week. According to the Association of Home Appliance Manufacturers, that's 2 loads each on 4 different days. Monday is still the most popular washday: A quarter of America's laundry is done on that day.

Of every 100 loads of laundry washed in America, 83 are washed in a home machine, 4 are done at a laundromat, and 13 are done by hand.

Just over half of American families use laundry bleach. Just under half use rinses or fabric softeners. Only 1 family in 14 uses a water softener.

You can just leave them to drain. Of every 100 loads of dishes washed in America, 58 are done by hand and 42 are done in dishwashers.

Try this casserole, dear. Say a wife gives her husband a meal that she considers nutritious and delicious. He doesn't like it. What does he do?

According to two professors at Iowa State University who asked a bunch of husbands and wives just that question:

47 per cent of the husbands would eat it, and then politely ask that it not be served again.

26 per cent would be forceful, perhaps embarrassing the wife with a comment like, "Let me know when you are going to have it again, and I'll eat a big lunch."

22 per cent would fall in between. They would eat some, but be rather authoritarian in their request that it be scrubbed from future menus. "Let's not have that again," they might say.

When asked how they would respond to all this, two thirds of the wives said they would go along with their mates. The polite approach was the most effective.

Diapers. The average baby will need about 100 diapers a week during his or her first year of life, and 60 to 70 a week as she or he gets older.

Love pays off. A survey of 75,000 young, middle-class readers of *Redbook* indicates that the wives most dissatisfied with their marriages were those who married for reasons other than love.

The dissatisfied married for financial security, because they felt it was expected of them, or because they were pregnant.

The Supermarket Britannica. You know those sets of encyclopedias and china that they sell in the supermarket? You buy 1 a week until you've completed the set?

About 1 shopper in 3, at one time or another, has started a set. Only about 1 in 3 of them ever completes it.

Roomy houses. The typical American home has 2 rooms for every person. That gives us the most spacious accommodations in the world. The average Israeli home, for instance, is 3 times as crowded, with 1½ people for every room.

What worries us most. The average American thinks that the American family is in trouble.

In a 1977 *Better Homes & Gardens* survey about family life, 76 per cent of the participants said that they worried about the state of the American family. The average participant felt that inattentive parents and the lack of religion in the home were the greatest threats to family life.

Who's more average than Jim Smith? Who, indeed, asks James H. Smith, Jr., the "founder-president-newsletter editor-chief bankroller of the Jim Smith Society." Asked to describe the average Jim Smith, Jim Smith replied:

"If there's such a thing as an average Jim Smith, he must be about 5-9 or 5-10, weigh about 175 pounds, have brown hair and blue eyes. His favorite food is steak (an overwhelming choice), and the rose is his favorite flower. The dog is his favorite pet.

"Jim is unique in one way: He has a birthday every day, including January 1 and February 29. It seems like he's a graduate of every coed college and university, has served in all branches of the military, and has a double chestful of decorations, from the Purple Heart to the Silver Star. In fact, one Jim has 29 Air Medals. He has served in the Royal Navy, British Army, RAF, RCAF, and the Royal Canadian Army.

"The list of club memberships is almost endless—from service, motorcycle, and investment clubs to the Fellowship of Christian Athletes. Jim is a joiner, no question about that.

"I have tried to find out how many Jim Smiths live in the United States, but the Census Bureau says this is restricted or classified info. The VA, however, has some 16,000 Jim Smiths on its rolls.

"The Jim Smith Society, established in 1969, has 808 members in most states, Canada, Australia, New Zealand, England, Scotland, Germany, Japan, etc. But not all members are men. Three are women: Jimmie Mae Smith of Kingsville, Texas; her daughter, Jimmie Lou Smith Homburg of Cotulla, Texas; and Jim Ann Smith Oliver of Purchell, Oklahoma. Jimmie Lou and Jim Ann were full-scale Jim Smiths for 20 or more years before they married. Jim Smith is not only the father of twins, but also the mother of twins. Jim Ann has twins.

"You name the job, and it's almost a sure bet that Jim Smith is working in that line. In the world of politics, Jim Smith has held just about every elective office except President and Vice President. U.S. senator: New Jersey; congressman: Pennsylvania, North Carolina, and Oklahoma; governor: Rhode Island and Georgia; mayor: a number of cities. There is a Jim Smith Peak in New Mexico, a park and lake in British Columbia, and even a James Smith Hospital in Florida.

"My research also shows that families with several Jim Smiths seem to have an identification problem. As a result, the young Jims often wind up being called Bob or John or Randy. With Pop being called Jim, the rest of the family and other relatives seem to call James Robert Smith 'Bob,' for example."

Every year, the Jim Smiths gather for a Jim Smith Fun Festival. The founding Jim Smith, news-bureau supervisor for Bell Telephone of Pennsylvania, operates the society out of his home at 2016 Milltown Road, Camp Hill, Pennsylvania 17011.

He adds: "My membership application includes a line in which I ask applicants to list their most significant achievement. One Jim responded by writing: 'Lived up to the name by being completely undistinguished.' "

Anything but bills in the mail today? The average American family mails 4 letters or checks a week and gets 13 letters and bills, 2 magazines, and 4 ads. Only 1 of every 8 pieces of our mail is a real letter. Thursday's mail is the heaviest of the week, on average.

One of every 6 items is addressed by hand, and for 1 of every 7, the address is typewritten. Most of the rest is addressed by machines.

The average piece of mail has traveled 296 miles, and was mailed 1½ days ago. We use ZIP Codes on 28 of every 29 things that we mail.

One of every 8 Americans picks up his mail at the post office. That includes businesses.

Help! The average family gets 97 pieces of mail from charitable or other non-profit organizations a year. Most want money.

Family size. The average American family consists of a husband, a wife, and 1 kid under 18. It's been that way for years.

That leaves out all the decimals. Put them in, and you see a change.

In 1965, the size of the average family peaked at 3.7 members —2.26 of them 18 or older, and 1.44 of them under 18.

By 1975, the average was down to 3.4 members—2.23 of them 18 or older, and 1.17 of them under 18.

In 1990, the average American family is expected to round off at 3 members—2.06 of them 18 or older, and .94 under 18.

That seems like quite a change, but for the average family it'll still be 2 parents and 1 kid under 18.

In the first census, in 1790, the average household was twice as large, with 5.8 persons.

Of every 98 households in America

21 are composed of a single person
31 are two-person
17 are three-person
16 are four-person
9 are five-person
4 are six-person
3 are seven-person or more.

The Average American Day

The Robinson study. John P. Robinson, a professor at the Communications Research Center of Cleveland State University, devotes his time to finding out how we spend ours. He must be the country's leading expert on "how Americans use time," which happens to be the title of a book he published in 1977 with Praeger Publishers, Inc.

In 1965–66, when Robinson was at the Survey Research Center of the University of Michigan, he and Dr. Thomas Juster studied how 1,244 people used the 168 hours of the week. The respondents kept minute-by-minute diaries and were interviewed. A second study, in 1975, involved over

1,500 people. Using a computer, Robinson has been analyzing
the data ever since.

Where the times goes. Here is a composite day of the average
employed person in America:

	Employed men	Employed women
At the main job	6 hrs., 7 min.	4 hrs., 45 min.
On a second job	9 min.	4 min.
Hanging around the workplace	19 min.	14 min.
Commuting	42 min.	30 min.
Cooking	8 min.	48 min.
Doing the laundry	2 min.	27 min.
Grocery shopping	11 min.	14 min.
Gardening and pet care	2 min.	3 min.
Errands and nonfood shopping	15 min.	19 min.
Other household chores	29 min.	1 hr., 26 min.
Taking care of the kids	12 min.	21 min.
Personal care	59 min.	1 hr., 17 min.
Eating	1 hr., 29 min.	1 hr., 12 min.
Sleeping	7 hrs., 43 min.	7 hrs., 47 min.
Travel aside from commuting to work	44 min.	42 min.
Study	9 min.	5 min.
Religion	7 min.	9 min.
Organization work	5 min.	3 min.
Listening to the radio	5 min.	4 min.
Watching TV	1 hr., 40 min.	1 hr., 3 min.
Reading the paper	25 min.	16 min.
Reading magazines	6 min.	4 min.
Reading books	5 min.	4 min.
Other reading	3 min.	2 min.
Going to the movies	4 min.	3 min.
Visiting	32 min.	39 min.
Lunch and dinner parties	12 min.	14 min.
Going to cafes and bars	6 min.	1 min.

	Employed men	Employed women
Playing parlor games	5 min.	4 min.
Other social activities	5 min.	4 min.
Conversation	12 min.	17 min.
Fishing and hiking	3 min.	0
Active sports	8 min.	4 min.
Taking a walk	1 min.	1 min.
Going to sports events	2 min.	0
Going to nightclubs, circuses, etc.	4 min.	8 min.
Going to theaters, concerts, etc.	1 min.	0
Resting	2 min.	6 min.
Relaxing, thinking, etc.	2 min.	4 min.
Hobbies and collections	3 min.	8 min.
Making music	1 min.	0
Playing records	1 min.	1 min.
Writing letters	3 min.	6 min.
Other pastimes	2 min.	1 min.

In 1976, University of Michigan researchers Frank Stafford and Greg Duncan published more research on how employed people use their time. They found, in general, that:

Married and unmarried men devoted more time to housework in 1976 than they did in 1965–66, and married and unmarried women devoted less.

The same was true about child care: Men boosted their time with the kids, women cut back.

Married men spent about as much time as ever watching TV, but women and unmarried men cut back on tube time.

Time alone. The average working man or woman spends six hours alone on the typical work day. The average housewife spends 6 hours, 40 minutes alone. That doesn't count sleep.

Working men spend less then 3 hours with their families, on average, and only half an hour alone with the kids. They spend over four hours with coworkers.

Working women spend an hour with the children, and housewives spend almost 3½ hours alone with the kids.

More time abed. Professor Robinson conducted the same kind of study in 1965. Compared with his or her counterpart of 10 years before, the average American in 1975 was getting a little more sleep, working shorter hours, and spending more time at leisure—a bit less social life, a bit more "media" time, which may just mean more television watching.

Here's the breakdown by age, again for 1975. These figures are in hours per week rather than in hours per day:

	18–25	26–35	36–45	46–55	56–65
Sleep	55.4	53.9	54.7	55.4	56
Work for pay	27	33.4	34.4	31	20.4
Family care	15.3	21.6	20.4	23.2	23.2
Personal care	23	20.8	21.1	23.1	26.6
Leisure (total)	50	38.4	37.3	35.2	41.8
Organizations	8.4	4.2	3.3	3.1	3.2
Media	18.5	17.2	18.3	18.8	22.6
Social life	10.7	8.7	7.8	5.4	6.2
Recreation	2.6	1.3	1	1.3	1.3
Other	9.8	7	6.9	6.6	8.5

People who have been through college work longer hours than people who haven't. But people who failed to finish high school work more hours, on average, then either high-school graduates or people who had a little college.

High-school graduates with no college spent the most time on family care, college graduates the least. Those with 2 or 3 years of college averaged the most leisure time.

Time on their hands. The busiest people seem to get the most kick out of life.

Employed men who claim to be "completely satisfied" with their lives average 4½ hours of free time a day, while those "not very" satisfied with life have 5½ hours of leisure.

That's true for housewives, too. Those unsatisfied with life in general have nearly 40 minutes a day more leisure.

But women with outside jobs reverse the pattern. The "completely satisfied" employed women had nearly 40 minutes more leisure time per day than those who were not as happy.

Escaping the house. Wives with outside jobs are out of the home an average of 60 hours a week. But housewives get out only 20 hours a week.

Whom we talk to. When asked to recall the interesting conversations they had had the day before, married people mentioned only a third as many with their spouses as with other people—chiefly friends, neighbors, and other relatives.

Women mentioned interesting conversations with their children just as often as those with their husbands.

People who work talk mostly to colleagues. Housewives talk mostly to friends, neighbors, and relatives. Women with above-average educations talk chiefly to friends; less-educated women talk mostly to relatives.

What we talk about. Women talk more about other people than anything else. Health and accidents are big topics for housewives.

Working men talk about work more than anything else; it takes up 25 per cent of their conversation. Among working women, work is a big topic only for those who went to college.

The news? Rarely talked about—a remembered topic of interesting conversation less than 10 per cent of the time.

Between 40 per cent and 60 per cent of the respondents couldn't recall a single interesting conversation with anyone on the day before.

An hour saved is 36 minutes of fun. Robinson finds that every time we trim an hour off our worktime, 60 per cent of it goes into "free-time activities" and 40 per cent into family and personal obligations.

Gotta do it, but don't gotta like it. Of the obligatory, stuff-of-life chores we all have to do, what does the average person like least?

Shopping for groceries, that's what.

Grocery shopping averaged 4.0 on a scale of 1 ("terrible") to 7 ("delighted") when Robinson asked people to rank 14 obligatory activities. A rating of 4 is neutral—people neither hate it nor love it.

Here is how other chores rank:

Keeping track of household records and expenses	4.1
House maintenance, repairs	4.2
Shopping for clothes, furniture, appliances	4.4
House chores, cleaning, laundry	4.6
Cooking	4.8
Commuting to work	4.8
Working in the house or garden	5.2
Feeding and clothing the children	5.4
Sleeping	5.7
Eating	5.7
Washing and dressing	5.7
Your job	6.0
Playing and reading with the children, and teaching them	6.2

And here is how we rated some free-time activities:

Clubs and social organizations such as Scouts, union	4.4
Daily travel, except to work	4.7
Watching TV	4.8
Playing sports and games	5.0

Adult education, including classes, homework, reading for class	5.1
Reading the paper	5.2
Reading books and magazines	5.3
Visiting friends or neighbors	5.4
Going to a movie, restaurant, or sporting event	5.4
Resting or relaxing	5.5
Planning or thinking	5.5
Church and religious devotion	5.5
Hobbies	5.6
Entertaining at home	5.6

Who really cares for the kids? Eighty per cent of the time, Mom does. When Dad helps out with the kids, he's more likely to help them with their homework or play with them than tend to the more custodial aspects of being a parent—feeding, bathing, dressing, changing diapers.

Robinson says a first child will consume 5 per cent of a mother's "primary time" for the next 18 years; "primary time" is time chiefly devoted to 1 task.

Mom may also be keeping an eye on the stove, but primarily she's taking care of her child. She will spend 22 per cent of her time in the kid's company until the child is 18. "These figures can practically double if the number of children reaches 4 or more," Robinson says.

Dad is with the kid only half as much. But only 29 per cent of mothers say that they wish they had more help from him.

Parents spend no more time caring for 3 children than for 2. Each just gets a little less individual attention.

Americans versus Europeans. A 1972 study compared how the average American family and the average European family spent their time. Some of the results:

The American workweek is shorter.

Despite our appliances, Americans spend about as much time doing housework as do Europeans.

We devote more time to preschool children.

But less to older children.

We spend more time than Europeans chauffeuring our kids around.

But Europeans spend more time helping the kids with their homework.

We spend about the same amount of time in travel.

Our commute is shorter than the Europeans', even though we live much farther from work.

Americans spend more time in church, visiting, playing sports, and helping friends and relatives.

Europeans walk more and spend more time mending clothes.

How our lives have changed. The average American eats faster than his parents or grandparents. He or she spends less time doing housework. He or she travels more, shops more, spends more time with the kids. He or she spends less time reading the paper and magazines and books, and less time just visiting.

These are the big changes Robinson observed in the average family compared to its counterpart 20, 50, even 100 years ago.

Television, by far, was the biggest instrument of change in family patterns. Says Robinson: "Other notable time-related innovations of the twentieth century—the automobile, household technology, and even the 'shorter' workweek—showed surprisingly little ability to affect time usage to any consistent or significant extent."

Boy and girl, groom and bride. The average first-time bride these days is 21½ years old. The average groom is 24.

The average age at marriage has risen for both partners every year since 1958.

But in 1890, he was 26 and she was 22 when the average couple wed.

Today, 45 per cent of women aged 20 to 24 have never been married. In 1960, it was only 28 per cent.

Now, the next couple of sentences are complicated, but well worth it. Since grooms are generally older than brides, girls born during the baby boom (which started in 1947) tended to look for husbands among men born in 1944 and 1945 (who were in short supply because the birth rates were low during the war). There was a 5 to 10 per cent shortfall of eligible bachelors in the 1960s.

On the other hand, girls born since 1963 (when the birth rate was again declining) will be in scarce supply when men (born earlier, when births were still booming) begin looking for mates. Simple justice.

The bride wore white. The average American wedding costs $750, according to the American Association of Professional Bridal Consultants, but that includes $50 courthouse quickies. "You will find," says the Association, "that the middle-class working family, including many ethnic families, for a first marriage for both bride and groom, will spend $2,800 and invite 125 friends and relatives to the reception."

The average fee given to the person performing the ceremony —minister, rabbi, justice of the peace, or whatever—is $50.

The average, or most common, wedding present is a small, electrical appliance such as a toaster or warming oven. It's bought at a discount store that won't take exchanges.

Monogamous, and proud of it. Ninety-five per cent of all Americans marry, and most marry only once. Eighty-five per cent of husbands and 88 per cent of wives have never been married to anyone else. In 79 per cent of all marriages, it is the first time for both.

As for those who marry more than once:

In 6 per cent of U.S. marriages, he's been married only once, but she's been divorced (5 per cent) or widowed (1 per cent).

In 9 per cent of marriages, she's been married only once but he's been divorced (7 per cent) or widowed (2 per cent).

In 7 per cent of marriages, both have gone through it before with someone else (6 per cent shed their mates in divorces).

The marital facts. Among adults over 18:

	Men	Women
Single	21.9%	15.6%
Married	70.9%	65.3%
Widowed	2.7%	12.9%
Divorced	4.5%	6.2%

Where the power goes. In the average household, 42 per cent of the energy used is burned by the family auto, 40 per cent goes into heating and air conditioning, 6 per cent into hot water, 4 per cent into cooking, 4 per cent into the refrigerator, 1 per cent into lighting, and 3 per cent into everything else—the TV, radio, washer and dryer, and the like.

All that grass. People think of suburbia as a place filled with families with children, but it ain't so. The Census Bureau says 43 per cent of suburban families have no children living at home, only slightly fewer than the 46 per cent of city families with no children at home.

Moreover, say the Census people, there is barely any difference between city and suburban families in the average size of the family or the average number of children per family.

Refrigerators. In the course of its 15-year lifespan, the average refrigerator requires $75 worth of repairs.

Dishpan hands. One of every 7 American families does 4 or more sinksful of dishes a day. One in 10 waxes the floor at least once a week, and 1 of every 5 polishes the furniture twice a week or more.

I'll get it. Throughout the world there are fewer than 10 telephones for every 100 people. But in the United States, there are 70 per 100.

In the Soviet Union, there are 7 phones for every 100 people. There are 22 in Spain, 3 in Cuba, 2 in Iran, 23 in Israel, 38 in Britain, and 57 in Canada. There are only 3 phones for every 1,000 people in Vietnam, the Sudan, Ethiopia, and Pakistan.

Your average oldster. Eleven per cent of us are over age 65. Here are some facts about the average senior American.

Income: One old person in 7 is poor, and most of them were not poor when they were younger. By "poor," the government means a 1977 income of $2,895 for a single person or $3,637 for an elderly couple.

Work: One old man in 4 and 1 old woman in 10 are still working.

Marriage: Half the women over 65 are widows. After age 75, 7 in 10 are widows. If a husband is 5 years younger than his wife, the chances are 50-50 that she will become a widow. If the two are the same age, the chances are 2 in 3 that she'll outlive him. If he's 5 years older than she, the chances of widowhood are 3 out of 4. Widows outnumber widowers 5 to 1.

Where they live: Eight out of 10 oldsters live in the same house they did before retiring. Most who move take a smaller place in the same area. Only 4 per cent retire to Florida or Arizona. Forty per cent of older women and 17 per cent of older men live alone or with nonrelatives.

Nursing homes: Most people who enter a nursing home do not stay. Fewer than 1 oldster in 20 is institutionalized. Even after age 85, four fifths are not in institutions.

Health: Older people see doctors half again as often as younger people do. Oldsters spend 4 times as much on medicine. But 4 in 5 get along just fine, thank you.

The radio. The average household in America has 6 radios, including those in the family cars.

How long things last. If you're about to celebrate your tenth wedding anniversary, watch out. If you're average, this is the year that you're going to have to replace the dishwasher, dehumidifier, hi-fi, the mechanism for the vibrating chair, the blender, coffee maker, electric blanket, electric can opener, hair dryer, hot plate, toaster, bedspreads, oil burner, air conditioner, and on and on and on.

Here is how long things last, on average. The sources, not always entirely in agreement, are the Insurance Information Institute (III), which calculates the "reasonable average useful life" of things in order to settle insurance casualty claims; the International Fabricare Institute (IFI), whose members must know how much to compensate dry cleaners' customers when clothes are damaged in cleaning; and the U. S. Census Bureau, which conducted a survey of 12,000 households "using an actuarial or life-table method similar to the method used in estimating the life expectancy of persons."

These last 1 year: Fabric gloves, neckties, socks, uniforms, aprons, dresses, felt hats, housecoats and robes, work shoes, foundation garments, panties, and boys' shoes. Also children's bonnets, playclothes, underwear, and shoes (all according to the IFI).

These last 2 years: Bathing suits, leather gloves, straw hats, sleepwear, men's dress shirts and wool sport shirts, synthetic or cotton slacks, shorts, sport coats, and suits. Also adults' underwear, work clothes, blouses, street dresses, negligees, scarves, women's shoes, shirts, slacks, shorts, and slips, children's coats, snowsuits, dresses, and suits, sheets and pillowcases, everyday tablecloths, and bathroom towels (all according to the IFI). Ironing board covers, men's shoes, fabric pocketbooks, and toys (according to the III).

These last 3 years: Raincoats, wool or silk robes, men's fancy sport shirts and summerweight suits, sweaters, cotton blouses, afternoon and evening dresses, dress slacks, women's high-fashion suits, bedspreads, sheer curtains, drapes, and slipcovers (IFI). Sunlamp bulbs, men's pajamas, socks, underwear, handkerchiefs, and shirts (III).

These last 4 years: Men's coats and jackets, wool pants, winter suits, fancy aprons, and unlined and glass-fiber drapes (IFI). TV picture tubes (III).

These last 5 years: Tuxedos, fur hats, leather jackets and coats, women's "basic" dresses and evening shoes, lightweight and electric blankets, lined drapes, and fancy tablecloths (IFI). A house's interior paint job, electric shavers, portable record players, mattress covers and pads, pillowcases and sheets, inexpensive carpets and rugs, leather pocketbooks, children's furniture, cufflinks, earrings, necklaces, broaches, studs, rings, watches, costume jewelry and the like, kitchen utensils, lampshades, typewriters, wallets, eyeglasses, games, scooters, and tricycles (III). And washing machines, clothes dryers, and black-and-white televisions bought used (Census).

These last 6 years: An exterior paint job and dictation machines (III). Used electric stoves (Census).

These last 7 years: Clothes irons, including steam irons, men's overcoats, topcoats, raincoats, and leather jackets (III).

Lasting 8 years: Automatic washers (III, though Census says people keep them 11 years, on average).

Lasting 9 years: Used home freezers (Census).

The 10-year deluge: Fur coats, heavy blankets (IFI); oil burners, air-conditioning systems under 5 tons, galvanized gutters, room air conditioners, dehumidifiers, dishwashers (though Census finds people keep them 11 years), hi-fi or stereo sets, tape recorders, TV sets (Census gives b&w's another year, colors two more years), vacuum cleaners, vibrator chair mechanisms, blenders, coffee makers, electric blankets, can openers, fans, frying pans, heaters, knife sharpeners, roasters, hair dryers, hand massage vibrators, hot plates, table radios, toasters, vaporizers, bathroom scales, mattresses, spreads, and midpriced carpets and rugs. Also cheap clocks, drapes, window shades, card tables and chairs, slipcovers, baseball gloves, bicycles, wooden boats, camping equipment, fishing tackle, golf clubs, outboard motors, music boxes, calculators, office water coolers, duplicating machines, cigarette lighters, tobacco pipes, pens and mechanical pencils, and electric trains (III).

Reprieve! These hold out for 15 years: Air-conditioning systems over 5 tons, gas furnaces, faucet valves, asphalt roofs, attic fans, chest or upright freezers (though Census finds they hang in there for 20 years), refrigerators, space heaters, kitchen stoves (Census says gas ranges generally give out after 13 years and electric ranges after 12). And heating pads, ironing boards, sunlamps and infrareds, waffle irons, top-quality carpets and rugs, venetian blinds, furniture made of wood, table and floor lamps, office cabinets (III).

These hold out for 20 years: Boilers in hot-water heating systems, a house's wiring, shingle asphalt and five-ply tar and gravel roofs, sewing machines, bed quilts, jewel, cigarette, and collar boxes, expensive clocks, high-quality cameras; stainless steel, copper, heavy-aluminum, or cast-iron kitchen equipment; quality cutlery, ladders, Irish linen tablecloths, suitcases, mirrors, office furniture, bookcases, desks, pocket knives, picture frames, hand tools, and power tools (III).

There's a quarter century of service in these: Radiators, asbestos roofs, aluminum gutters, barometers, professional or reference books, oriental rugs, firearms, pianos, and slide rules (III).

Portraits. In an average year, every other American poses for his portrait. For every portrait shot of fathers posing alone, there are 34 portraits made of their daughters posing alone.

Where farmers live. Seven farmers in 10 live on their farm.

At the start of this century, 1 American in 3 lived on a farm. Now 1 in 28 does.

The outhouse. In 1940, 45 of every 100 American homes lacked plumbing facilities. By 1974, only 3 of 100 were without plumbing. Most were in the country.

Color on the outside, cold on the inside. These days, only 1 new refrigerator in 2 is white.

Work and marriage. The average working American spouse is happily married. But working husbands tend to be a little less happy if their wives work too, while working wives are noticeably less happy if their husbands *don't* work.

Some people call it quality of time. Three out of 4 wives say that working mothers can have just as good a relationship with their children as nonworking mothers do. Three out of 5 husbands of working wives agree.

Two out of 3 husbands of nonworking wives disagree.

Mom 'n' pop in one. One family in 8 is headed by an unmarried woman.

One family in 50 is headed by an unmarried man.

One child in 7 lives in a family without a father.

Mom alone. Of every 100 women who head families, 33 are married to an absentee husband, 23 are widows, 23 never married, and 21 are divorced.

The Liberated Woman

What became of Mom's apple pie? You know what we used to think of as the typical American family—Dad off to work, Mom taking care of the house, and two kids at home?

According to the National Commission on Working Women, that describes 7 per cent of us.

How much is a wife worth? Here's how one expert figured the value of a wife's services around the house. This was in 1977 or 1978, and he figured that she earned $15,765 a year:

	Hours per week	*Rate per hour*	*Weekly value*
Nursemaid	44.5	$2.75	$122.38
Dietician	2	$5.00	$ 10.00
Purchasing agent	3.3	$4.50	$ 14.85
Cook	13.1	$4.10	$ 53.71
Dishwasher	6.2	$2.00	$ 12.40
Housekeeper	17.5	$2.50	$ 43.75
Laundress	5.9	$2.25	$ 13.28
Seamstress	1.3	$3.50	$ 4.55
Practical nurse	.6	$4.00	$ 2.40
Maintenance woman	1.7	$3.00	$ 5.10
Gardener	2.3	$2.50	$ 5.75
Chauffeur	2	$3.50	$ 7.00
Social secretary	2	$4.00	$ 8.00
Total	102.4		$303.17

Blue-blooded singles. On average, the higher a woman's social class, the later in life she marries, and the more likely she is to remain single.

A woman's life cycle. The average American woman

marries at 21
has her first child 16 to 25 months later
has 2 or 3 children
quits having children before she is 30
is 52 when her last child marries
lives alone with her husband for another 11 years before he dies
lives within an hour's drive of her nearest child's home.

For whom the belle toils. The average woman with a job outside the home spends 50 per cent less time on housework and child care than full-time housewives do. Nevertheless, she averages 10 hours a week less free time.

Husbands of working women spend 10 per cent more time doing housework than husbands whose wives don't hold outside jobs. But the husbands don't spend any more time helping with the kids.

The time that a woman devotes to housework—whether she has other employment or not—increases by 5 to 10 per cent with each additional child.

The opposite is true about fathers. Dads of 1 or 2 children often do more housework than fathers with more kids. And husbands with large families spend less time caring for the kids than do those with small families.

Women with husbands at home spend, on average, as much time caring for the children as do women who must raise a family without a husband.

None of this generates much self-pity in women.

Asked to rate their satisfaction with housework, women—both full-time and part-time housewives—say they're generally not *unsatisfied*. Only 21 per cent say they are dissatisfied.

When women were asked in 1973 if they wished their husbands would help out more, only 23 per cent said "yes." This was a small increase over the 19 per cent who said "yes" in 1965.

About 1 wife in 3 got no help from her husband. One in 5 got 1 to 4 hours of help a week. One in 8 got 5 hours of help. One in 20 got more than that.

Of those who got no help, 35 per cent said they wanted some.

Of those who got 10 hours or more of help, less than 5 per cent said they wished for more.

The wives most likely to wish that their husbands would lift a finger around the house were younger, college-educated, working, and black.

Paymistress. In 2 out of 3 homes in the United States, the wife pays the bills.

Imprisoned women. Far from being a libber, the average female criminal thinks that women should stay home, be submissive and faithful to their husbands, and refrain from drinking, smoking, and swearing. She wishes she were that way, but admits that she isn't.

One of us has to get Sally to the doctor. When both husband and wife work, and one of them has to take time off to care for a child, it's the wife 7 times out of 8.

The crossroad years. In her book *Passages,* Gail Sheehy calls the mid-30s "crossroad years" for the average woman. Here's why:

34 is the age at which the average divorced woman remarries.

35 is the most common age for wives to leave their husbands.

35 is when the average mother sends her last child off to school.

35 is the age when most wives go back to work.

Between 35 and 39 are the ages at which most adoptions by unmarried women occur.

Who says the younger generation lacks ideals? The American Council of Life Insurance asked Americans 14 to 25 years old which of 4 life goals was most important to them. The results:

The opportunity to develop as an individual	51%
A happy family life	32%
A fulfilling career	10%
Making a lot of money	7%

My spouse, my pal. Upper-class couples tend to be closer companions than middle-class couples, who in turn tend to be more companionable than lower-class couples.

People who marry within their class have more stable marriages, on average, than those who marry above or beneath themselves. Sociologists Julian B. Roth and R. F. Peck, writing in the *American Sociological Review,* say that marital adjustment is good in 53 per cent of marriages where the partners come from the same social class and fair in 26 per cent. When the spouses are one class apart, their relationship is good only 35 per cent of the time, and fair 31 per cent of the time. And when they are more than one class apart, the relationship is good only 14 per cent of the time and fair 38 per cent of the time.

A nation of castleowners. Seven out of 10 families in the United States own their home.

Where the water goes. According to the American Water Works Association, the average American uses 60 gallons of water a day. Here's where it goes:

Taking a shower	5 to 10 gallons a minute; 25 to 50 gallons for the typical shower
Taking a bath	36 gallons if you fill the tub
Brushing your teeth	2 gallons if you leave the tap running
Washing your hands	2 gallons if you leave the tap running
Shaving	3 to 5 gallons if you leave the tap running

Washing dishes by hand	20 gallons if you leave the tap running
Washing dishes in a dishwasher	15 gallons if you go through all the cycles
Washing clothes	30 to 60 gallons for a full cycle
Watering the lawn	5 to 10 gallons a minute

Extracurricular curricula. Two kids in 3 take some kind of lessons outside of school, chiefly music, art, or sports.

Immobile homes. One American family in 20 lives in a mobile home, according to the Manufactured Housing Institute, and the homes are generally less mobile than their inhabitants. The families move, on average, once every 7 years, while fewer than 2 per cent of mobile homes ever take a trip beyond the first one, from factory to site.

The average mobile home is 14 feet wide and 69 feet long. It has 966 square feet of living space.

Are they cheaper? *Money* magazine in 1975 projected the costs of owning a $22,911 mobile home in Lake Park of LaHabra, California, against the cost of owning a $38,700 condominium apartment in Corsican Villas, next door. Both had two bedrooms and two baths, but the mobile home had more space. *Money* estimated that after 10 years the condominium owners would have been ahead by about $11,000, having spent $43,500 for taxes, upkeep, etc., against the mobile home owner's $54,500. The condominium owner got bigger tax deductions and didn't have to pay a $125-a-month site rental. But after 10 years the mobile-home owner would have paid off his home. The condominium owner would still owe $30,500.

According to the Texas Real Estate Research Center, a five-year-old mobile home is worth 60 per cent of what it cost new. But in these inflationary times, mobile homes sometimes appreciate in value just like houses with foundations, according to the MHI.

Half of all mobile homes are on individual sites and half are in community parks where, according to the MHI, "The people who live in manufactured homes are convivial without being overbearing and helpful without being nosey."

Jennifer, meet Michael. Englishman Leslie Alan Dunking, who has published an exhaustive study of first names in a book *First Names First,* says that in an average year the parents of 1 girl in 25 and 1 boy in 15 give their baby the year's most popular name.

Half of the girls' first names and 61 per cent of the boys' come from the top 50 names.

White children born in 1975 in the United States were more likely to be named Jennifer and Michael than anything else.

Where the kids are. Of every 100 kids in America

  66 live with both parents in their first marriage
   5 live part of the time with each of their divorced parents
   8 live with 1 parent and 1 stepparent
  18 live with 1 parent
   3 live with neither parent but usually with relatives.

Love those gadgets. According to *Merchandising* magazine, of every 1,000 American homes

  999 have television sets
  999 have refrigerators
  999 have vacuum cleaners
  997 have coffee makers
  733 have clothes washers
  599 have electric blankets
  448 have home freezers
  409 have dishwashers
   67 have microwave ovens

Families on welfare. The Children's Defense Fund says that the typical welfare family has 2.2 children, neither more nor less than the average family. Welfare families have decreased in size by 20 per cent since 1971.

When the children start. In the early 1960s, 48 per cent of the women who married for the first time became mothers before their first wedding anniversary. Three quarters of them were mothers by the time the second anniversary rolled around.

But 10 years later, only 39 per cent of first births occurred within the first year of marriage, and only 60 per cent within the first 2 years. This difference in "childspacing," as the Census Bureau calls it, has helped slow down the nation's population growth.

So did a delay in marrying. The bureau found that women who marry after age 21 have, on average, 1 child fewer than women who marry before age 19.

Don't call me; I'll call you. One Bell System subscriber in 5 has an unlisted phone number.

Child abuse. Dr. Vincent DeFrancis, director of the Children's Division of the American Humane Association, estimates that 30,000 to 40,000 children are "truly battered" by their parents in an average year. He says that another 100,000, at least, are sexually abused.

According to other researchers, for every child abused by parents, 6 others are neglected.

In a survey by the Texas Council of Child Welfare Boards, 1 adult in 7 reported that she or he had experienced abuse or neglect as a child. Only 1 in 4 had complained to authorities. Nearly two thirds said they do not consider spanking with a paddle to be physically abusive, so the incidents they had in mind were something more than that.

Moving day. The average American will move 14 times in his or her lifetime.

The Average American's Garbage

Garbage in, garbage out. Denis Hayes, energy expert for a Washington think tank called Worldwatch Institute, calculates that the average American, in the course of his or her lifetime, produces a pile of garbage equal to 600 to 700 times his or her own weight. A 150-pounder would create about 97,500 pounds of garbage if Hayes is right.

The garbage never lies. Archaeology pioneer Emil Haury used to say, "If you want to know what is really going on in a community, look at its garbage." Well, some ethnoarchaeologists at the University of Arizona have taken him at his word. Since 1971, under the whimsical title, *"Le projet du garbage,"* they have been analyzing what the people of Tucson discard. More than 300 anthropology students of William L. Rathje, wearing surgical masks, gloves, and white jackets, have been sorting, coding, and recording what people in representative households in Tucson (360,000 people, 110,000 households) have thrown out. These facts come from Tucson's garbage cans.

Food we don't eat. The average household buys a ton of food a year, and throws out 9 per cent of it. Plate scrapings account for somewhere over a third of food that's discarded; the rest is thrown away before it is served. And that doesn't count nonedible things like corn husks, egg shells, or banana peels. Nor does it include milk or soda poured down the sink, or food that is ground up in the garbage disposal (21 per cent of Tucson households have them), fed to the dog, put in the compost pile, or gotten rid of some other way.

Food accounts for 8 per cent of the average Tucson household's garbage, by weight. About 8 per cent of the discarded food is vegetables; 6 per cent is fruit; 5 per cent is packaged foods like TV dinners, take-out meals, canned soups, and sauces; 3 per cent is baby food; 3 per cent is sugar and sweets, including pastries; 6 per cent is breadstuffs; 1 per cent is solid dairy products; 1 per cent is fat and oils; much of the rest is meat, eggs, fish, and nuts.

Bread. Offbeat bread—rolls, bagels, muffins, hamburger buns, hot dog rolls, and the like—is almost twice as likely to be thrown out as bread that comes in ordinary loaves.

Bottles. The average Tucson household discards 500 bottles a year. About 50 of them are returnables and could be reused up to 40 times.

Wrappings. About 60 per cent of Tucson's garbage, by weight, consists of packaging. Each year, the average household tosses out 1,800 plastic items, chiefly wraps and containers; 850 tin cans; 500 aluminum cans; and more than 13,000 items of paper and cardboard.

Beer. Something about beer affects people's memory of how much they've had. In front-door interviews, 85 per cent of the households said they didn't drink beer. None owned up to going through more than 8 cans a week. But data gathered through the "back door"—from the garbage cans—identified fewer than 25 per cent with no beer cans or bottles, and 54 per cent with more than 8 beer cans or bottles per week. All told, 27 per cent of households grossly underestimated their beer consumption, as revealed by their garbage.

Detergents. Large families buy large boxes of laundry detergents; poor families buy low-priced detergents—right? Nope. On average, the garbage cans revealed, the smallest families bought the largest boxes, and the largest families the smallest boxes. The lower a household's income, the more it spent on detergents. A low-income family bought $18 worth in a year. A middle-income family spent $4.00 less.

What has 4 wheels and flies? The average garbage truck lasts 5 years. This information comes from a now-defunct government agency, the National Center for Productivity and Quality of Working Life.

Underrecycled. Back during World War II, 35 per cent of the wood fiber produced in this country was recycled; these days it's only 19 per cent.

Kids. In a survey of 7,514 kids aged 12 to 17, half said they get a regular allowance, 1 in 20 said he or she never watches television, 1 in 8 said he or she watches 5 hours or more per day, 1 in 45 said he or she spends 5 hours a week with serious books, and 1 in 5 said he or she never reads serious books.

Those new folks are real neighborly. On average, new residents of a community associate with their neighbors more than old residents do.

The vanishing bachelor. In 1890, 44 of every 100 men had never been married, and 34 of every 100 women were similarly situated.

By 1940, 35 men and 28 women were in that category.

In 1975, only 21 of 100 men and 15 of 100 women had never married.

These figures come from the Census Bureau, which until 1970 counted anyone 14 or older as a man or woman. The figures for 1975 count only people 18 or older.

Parents are a sour bunch. According to a study of 2,480 households in Alameda County, California, the average childless couple is healthier and happier than the average couple with children. The couple whose kids have grown up is happier than the couple still raising kids, but not as happy as the childless couple.

But do they vote alike? The Census Bureau says that in most marriages, if one spouse votes, the other one does, too. If one doesn't, the other probably doesn't, either.

In the 1976 presidential election, both husband and wife voted in 61 per cent of the cases.

In 25 per cent of marriages, neither voted.

In only 8 marriages out of 100, he voted and she didn't.

In fewer than 7 marriages in 100, she voted and he failed to exercise, as they say, his franchise.

Why some houses smell like lemon groves. Two thirds of American families use air fresheners. They tend to prefer aerosols, and to spray the bathroom the most, followed in order by the kitchen, the living room, bedrooms, and the dining room.

Not counting Lysol, which some folks consider a disinfectant rather than an air freshener, Glade is the favorite brand. Lemon is the favorite fragrance, followed by pine.

Among Americans who spray their garbage pails, 72 per cent do it with Lysol.

The older you are, the more likely you are to spray your garbage pail. The younger you are, the more likely that you burn fragranced candles.

Teens at the altar. By the time she's 20, 1 American woman in 5 is married. Only 6 men in 100 marry by age 20.

Age and marriage. The average husband in America is just a shade over 45 years old, and the average wife is just shy of 42.

The married years. The average American is more likely to be in a marriage between the ages of 35 and 44 than during any other decade of life.

The older wife. Fourteen wives in 100 are older than their husband.

What price clean socks. Taking into account the cost of the machinery, electricity, detergent, bleach, and water, the Agriculture Department figures it costs $.92 per load of wash if you do 3 a week, and $.80 a load if you do 4 a week. That includes electric drying.

Sending the kids to college is a full-time job. Nine out of 10 American college students work during the summer, and 3 out of 5 work during the school year. Two thirds of American college women help pay their own tuition. Only 28 per cent get an allowance; it averages $108 a month. Among college men, only 1 of every 11 gets an allowance of as much as $50 a week.

Not that parents aren't helping. Although 51 per cent of all American women work, 55 per cent of the mothers of college students work.

The average American college student spends the lion's share of his or her money on expenses related to school. For college men, automotive expenses rank second, followed in order by entertainment, clothes, sports events and equipment, booze and drugs, records and stereo equipment, and travel. For college women, clothes rank second, followed in order by entertainment and vacations, cosmetics and toiletries, automotive expenses, and then hobbies, books, records, and sports. Last come booze, drugs, and cigarettes.

Like parent/like child. Children of large families tend to have large families themselves.

Black weds white. Interracial marriages in America doubled between 1960 and 1970 and rose another 36 per cent by 1977. Even so, only 1 marriage in 100 is interracial. Three fourths of the black/white couples involve a black husband and a white wife.

Ring, ring. These days, the average woman upon getting engaged receives a diamond weighing half a carat.

Good night, dear. Good morning, dear. The average American husband and wife converse with one another 20 minutes a week, according to an article in the Washington *Post*.

What generation gap? American parents, on average, get along just fine with their teen-age children.

A Gallup poll found that 55 per cent of parents said that they got along with their teen-agers very well, and another 40 per cent fairly well. Only 4 per cent chose "not at all well."

Mothers said they got along better with the teen-agers than Dad did. He agreed.

When asked what they argued about most with their teen-age offspring, 1 out of 5 said they didn't argue about much of anything. Chores and keeping the house neat were named by 18 per cent, the general category of freedom, rights, responsibilities, and values by 15 per cent, curfew by 12 per cent, and studying by 9 per cent. Much as we read about alcohol and drug abuse by teen-agers, it was named as a source of contention by only 3 per cent of the parents.

No one asked the teen-agers what they thought of their parents.

Art and marriage. When the National Endowment for the Arts analyzed the living arrangements of a cross section of the three quarters of a million people who earn their living as artists, it found:

Actors live in husband-wife households only 58 per cent of the time. One third live alone.

Architects are more likely than other artists to be married and least likely to be divorced, separated, or single. They are more likely to be male, too; 95 per cent are men.

Dancers are the least likely to be married. More than half are unwed. Eighty-seven per cent of the nation's professional dancers are female.

Designers tend to stay married. Only 5 per cent are separated or divorced, while 75 per cent are married.

Musicians and composers also shun marriage. Thirty-six per cent are unwed, probably because they're younger than other artists. Half of the musicians and composers are under 30.

Painters and sculptors are marrying types. Two out of 3 are wed, and 46 per cent share households with children.

Photographers are family oriented, with 85 per cent living in families (as opposed to living alone or with nonrelatives). Seventy-two per cent are wed, and fewer than 6 per cent are separated or divorced.

Radio and TV announcers are singleish. Nearly 4 in 10 are unwed, again probably because more than half are under 30.

Fighting Spouses

The Friday night fights. Half of married couples have had at least 1 hitting or shoving match. In 1 of every 10 marriages, 1 mate has hit the other with an object, and in 1 of 20, 1 mate has beaten up the other, according to the National Institute of Mental Health.

They call them battered wives. One of every 26 American wives is beaten by her husband, at least occasionally. So says the U. S. Commission on Civil Rights.

Money, money, money. Fifty-four per cent of American families argue about money. As you'd expect, those who argue the most about it are those who have the least of it. The families most likely to argue about money are those with wives who work because they have to, families who rent their homes, and young families in general.

The polling firm of Yankelovich, Skelly, and White, Inc., in a survey for General Mills, asked them what they argue about. They said

Money in general	59%
Need to economize	47%
Wasting money	42%
Unpaid bills	38%
Keeping track of where the money goes	33%
Saving for the future	25%
Borrowing	17%
Bad investments	10%
Lending	8%

Sixty per cent of the husbands characterized their wives as "savers" rather than "spenders." Twenty-three per cent of the families said they talk too much about money.

More than half the families manage to put some money in the bank. One family in 5 has stocks, and 29 per cent own U.S. savings bonds.

Six families in 10 say they made at least 1 financial mistake in the past year. Mistakes mentioned most often were having to draw on savings or investments to meet current bills; overdrawing the checking account (24 per cent admit to this); waiting too long to have the car repaired; and running up a big bill on credit cards or charge accounts.

One family in 4 had to cope with a serious illness, a major car repair, or the need to replace a major appliance. Six per cent said a wedding had created a financial emergency within the past 12 months.

Those interviewed were given a list of expenditures and asked if they thought they were luxuries. Here are the results:

The temptation	Yes, it's a luxury
Having a new car every year	72%
Hiring a maid	59%
Taking an annual vacation	55%
Going out to eat in a nice restaurant	45%
Getting a second car	33%
Taking weekend trips with the family	31%
Going to a hairdresser regularly	29%
Having a color TV	24%
Drinking liquor	23%
Playing golf or tennis	21%
Smoking cigarettes	20%
Going to the movies	20%
Giving money to charity	18%
Buying a winter coat	15%
Having meat with meals	14%
Subscribing to magazines	11%
Having company for dinner	11%
Hiring a baby-sitter	10%
Taking a Sunday drive	8%
Having a phone	7%

It's so nice to make up. Two thirds of married couples say an occasional big argument is useful to "clear the air."

Dear, dear, dear, dear, Ann, Ann, Ann, Ann. In the average week, 7,000 newspaper readers write Ann Landers for advice.

"Separation" is forever. A survey by the Psychology Department of the University of Colorado suggests that few trial separations result in reconciliation. Eighty-seven per cent end in divorce.

"The poor man's divorce." Many people who can't afford a divorce just stay separated. That's why separation is sometimes called "the poor man's divorce." Black people are 6 times more likely to be separated than whites, but only a little more likely to be divorced.

The grousy spouse. In a study of 2,000 adults by the University of Michigan Survey Research Center, 62 per cent admitted they sometimes had trouble getting along with their spouses. Twenty years ago, only 48 per cent admitted it.

But the percentage of adults who said raising kids could be a problem remained just about constant—73 per cent.

Daytime grousing. On average, according to sociologists, night-shift workers scrap with their spouses more than day-shift workers do.

Turtledoves. The average American couple spends at least half of their free time together, but 1 married American in 50 dodges his or her spouse nearly all of the time.

Hi, dear. Eighty-five per cent of married couples say their marriage has worked out OK.

It's time for our divorce, dear. The average marriage that ends in divorce lasts 6½ years. That's a nationwide median. In Wyoming, couples who get divorced do so after 4 years, 4 months of marriage, on average. In Rhode Island, they wait 8 years, 1 month.

The average couple getting a divorce has 1 child.

Married at 18, divorced at 22. Marriages among teen-agers are twice as likely to end in divorce as marriages in which the partners are over 20. But women who wait until after age 30 to become brides are half again as likely to divorce as women who marry in their 20s.

One reason: Women with postgraduate degrees who marry later and who are well able to support themselves are more likely to end an unhappy marriage than are their less-educated sisters.

Men who become grooms between ages 25 and 29 are the most likely to have a stable marriage.

100 women, 51 divorces. The Population Reference Bureau estimates that if current trends hold, of every 100 women now in their 20s who marry

38 will get divorced
29 of the divorcees will remarry
13 of those will get redivorced.

The 100 women will have produced 51 divorces and 129 marriages. That means 40 per cent of all marriages for that group will end in divorce.

Anniversaries. Here are your chances of observing wedding anniversaries as the years roll by. It was calculated by population experts Paul C. Glick and Arthur J. Norton, who note that divorce is the big interrupter of young marriages, and death the big interrupter of old ones.

Anniversary	Proportion of first marriages that reach it	Proportion of remarriages that reach it
5th	5 in 6	4 in 5
10th	4 in 5	3 in 4
20th	3 in 4	1 in 2
30th	2 in 3	1 in 3
40th	2 in 5	1 in 8
50th	1 in 5	1 in 15
55th	1 in 10	1 in 50
60th	1 in 20	1 in 100
65th	1 in 50	very rare
70th	1 in 100	very rare

Divorce in Oklahoma. Here are the results of a survey of 28 men and 23 women who were divorced in Oklahoma after fewer than 3 years of marriage.

When asked what was the best part of the relationship, 35 per cent of the men and 26 per cent of the women said, "Sex!"

Men more often than women said social pressure kept them together too long.

Asked the reason for the divorce, 60 per cent of the women cited his drinking, his drug-taking, his job instability, his temper, his abuse of her, his money policies, his emotional problems, or his indecisiveness.

Sixty-one per cent of the women and 29 per cent of the men said they saw problems coming even before they married.

Eighty-six per cent of the couples slept together before they married. A quarter of them had lived together. A fifth had sex on their first date, and another 39 per cent within the first months.

In 35 per cent of the marriages, 1 or both partners engaged in extramarital relationships—the wife more often than the husband.

Who needs him? According to a study conducted in the early 1970s by the Urban Institute, a wife's chances of divorce increase by 1 per cent for every $1,000 she earns per year.

Mismarriage. Two thirds of divorce suits are filed by women, more than half of whom are 28 or younger. Two in five of these women have been married 5 years or less. One in 3 didn't finish high school.

The average divorced woman is 31.4 years old, and earns three fifths of what her former husband earns. If she remarries, she is most likely to do it within 3 years.

The price of divorce. Here are the guidelines used in 1978 by San Francisco judges to determine support payments in divorce cases. Judges adjust these figures for the wife's earnings, the length of the marriage, and the assets and liabilities of both partners.

Monthly payment if the divorce involves

Husband's monthly take-home pay	Wife only	Wife and one child	Wife and 2 children	Wife and 3 children	Child support only (per child)
$800	$325	$400	$425	$450	$100–$125
$1,000	$400	$500	$550	$600	$100–$150
$1,400	$550	$700	$800	$850	$125–$175
$1,800	$750	$900	$1,000	$1,050	$150–$250
$2,000	$800	$1,000	$1,100	$1,150	$150–$250
Above $2,000	40%	Left to the discretion of the court			

Custody. In divorces, Mom gets the kids 9 times out of 10.

But no money. Only 1 divorced woman in 7 is awarded alimony.

Fewer than half of them receive their payment with any regularity.

Not even for the kids. Among divorced, separated, and single women who are supposed to get money from the fathers of their children, 4 in 10 never get a dime.

Fathers who do come through pay out annually only 12 per cent of what they were making at the time of the divorce or separation.

A fate worse than divorce. Divorce can be stressful for parents. In one study, 60 per cent of the divorced fathers and 73 per cent of the divorced mothers said the first year apart was so miserable that they felt the divorce was a mistake.

But after 2 years, only a quarter of the mothers and a fifth of the fathers still thought so.

Mothers, cuddle your babes. The obstetrical ward of a typical hospital brings mother and baby together for feeding, and not much more. To determine whether more maternal contact might benefit babies, half the newborns in one hospital were left with their mothers for an hour shortly after birth, and for 5 extra hours a day for the next 3 days.

When the babies were a year old, the researchers compared them with babies who had been on the standard hospital schedule. At first, they found a difference only in the *mothers*. While the babies were being examined by a pediatrician, the average mother who had spent more time with her baby in the hospital spent more time soothing her baby during the exam.

At age 5, a difference was found in the babies. The average baby who had spent more time with Mommy as a newborn had a higher IQ than the average baby who had started life on a typical hospital schedule.

Samaritans. About 1 of every 5 Americans does some volunteer work for church or some other charity.

No kidding. On average, a parent is 6 times as likely as a teenager to favor a strict, old-fashioned upbringing.

The old values. From a poll conducted in late 1978 and early 1979, here are the percentages of American parents who strongly believe that

Strict, old-fashioned upbringing and discipline are still the best ways to raise children	47%
A wife should put her husband and children ahead of her own career	47%
It's up to the man to be the main provider in the family	46%
Parents should sacrifice to give their children the best	26%
Children have an obligation to take care of their parents when the parents are old	21%

Take off those running shoes and sit down. One in 4 married Americans likes to exercise in his or her leisure time. But only about a third of these energetic people have spouses who are similarly inclined. More often, the spouse prefers to sit around and relax.

Peas in a pod. The average identical twin is more likely to weigh what her or his twin weighs than to have the same IQ.

Who cries when. A little boy is more apt than a little girl to cry when frustrated. But a little girl is more likely to cry when hurt.

Like a diver. Of every 100 babies, 96 are born headfirst.

Ah progeny. Families in which mother and father are of average weight, or Dad is fat and Mom is average, have more kids but fewer sons, on average, than when both parents are fat, or Mom is fat but Dad is average.

Company's coming! In a survey, 1,000 women were handed a list of chores and asked which they would do first if they learned that guests were arriving within 30 minutes.
  Here are the priorities:

Wash the dirty dishes.
Straighten out the living room and the dining room.
Tidy the bathroom.
Make the beds.
Clean the bathroom fixtures.
Vacuum.

Making waves in California. In California, 1 home in 5 has a microwave oven.

I like it here. Of every 100 Americans, 77 consider the state they live in either a "good" or an "excellent" place to live.
  Here's how many like their home states, by region:

Mountain	97%
West south-central	90%
Pacific	89%
South Atlantic	82%
West north-central	82%
East north-central	79%
East south-central	73%
New England	66%
Middle Atlantic	57%

Who said we have a classless society? On average, lower-class parents raise their children with more authority but less supervision than do middle-class parents. As a means of discipline, lower-class parents use more physical punishment and less reasoning. The lower-class parents tend to teach sex roles at an earlier age, and to put less emphasis on achievement.

Blacks have larger families. On average, a white family and a black family are equally likely to have 5 members. But a black family is more than twice as likely to have 6 or more members.

It's so nice to have one around. The average woman lives longer if her husband is still alive.

Sibling rivalry. Of every 100 brothers and sisters, 78 have at least pushed a sibling, 47 have hit him or her with an object, and 20 have beaten up a brother or sister.

Of every 100 parents, 98 have at least mildly spanked their children. Twenty have hit the kid with some object, and 4 have beaten him or her up.

Those figures come from the National Institute of Mental Health.

2 BR w/bath. Of every 100 homes in America, 36 have 3 bedrooms, 34 have 2, 15 have 1, 13 have 4 or more, and 2 don't have any.

The house's age. Of every 98 houses in America owned by their occupants

16 were built in the 1970s
23 were built in the 1960s
21 were built in the 1950s
10 were built in the 1940s
28 were built before 1940.

Oh Mother, you're so old-fashioned! Whether they know it or not, most parents tend to raise their children the way they were raised.

Moving Americans. Americans move around a lot. Half the people who lived in the United States in 1970 lived at a different address in the United States in 1975.

Of every 100 who moved in those 5 years

Half stayed in the same county
More than 16 moved to another state.

The movingest people are Westerners: Only 4 in 10 lived in 1975 where they lived in 1970. The reverse was true of Northeasterners: Six in 10 stayed still.

In just the years 1975 to 1977

More than a quarter of us moved, but
Roughly half the movers stayed in the same metropolitan area.
One in 7 moved from a rural to a metropolitan area.
One in 14 moved from a metropolitan area to the sticks.
One in 4 of the movers went from one rural area to another.
One in 7 moved from one metropolitan area to another.

Digging for roots. About 5 of every 100 Americans have done some genealogical research into their ancestry.

Little neighbors. One family in 4 has a youngster under 6.

We should introduce them. Of every 100 Americans, 7 live alone.

No will, no way. Seven husbands in 10 die without a will.

Shared quarters. One married couple in 100 live in someone else's household.

Blacks in suburbia. The number of black people living in the suburbs increased by a third between 1970 and 1977.

But of every 100 suburbanites, 94 are still white.

You eat the tomatoes, you pull the weeds. Of every 100 households in America, 42 grow vegetables, 22 grow fruits, and 38 grow flowers. About half of the vegetable growers have a garden of 750 square feet or more, and the average garden yielded $386 worth of produce in 1979, saving the family $367. Tomatoes are the most popular crop. About 3 of every 4 gardeners freeze or can some of their produce.

About a third of American gardeners have been at it for less than 10 years, and about a third of the non-gardening households have at least 1 person who would like to garden.

Bugs bother Western gardeners the most, followed in order by gardeners in the South, the East, and the Midwest. Weeds and drought are the chief curse of the Midwestern gardener. Birds and pests infest Eastern gardens the most.

All this comes from the 1979 National Gardening Survey, conducted by the Gallup organization for an outfit called Gardens For All, which, after toting all this up, concluded that gardening is "by far the most productive spare-time pursuit of the American public."

9 Work Life

The raw numbers. Of an average bunch of 100 Americans, 25 males and 16 females work. Of the 59 who don't work, 27 are 15 or younger, 9 are 65 or older, and 23 are between 16 and 64.

Full-time work, half-time pay. Full-time women workers earn, on average, 57 per cent of what full-time men workers earn.

Women account for 41 per cent of the U.S. work force, but for 63 per cent of those making under $5,000 and only 5 per cent of those making over $15,000.

The average woman worker works 23 years.

Faith and water. Dowsers search for water (or sometimes minerals) with a dowsing rod, a forked stick that dips when the dowser gets close to what he's looking for. According to the American Society of Dowsers, Inc., "in any group of 25 adults, between 2 and 5 will obtain the dowsing reaction immediately when properly instructed." The ASD says everyone is born with the capacity to dowse.

Here are the figures behind the unemployment rate. This comes from the Bureau of Labor Statistics, and covers the third quarter of 1978, when the unemployment rate was 6 per cent.

Of every 1,000 Americans 16 and older

586 had civilian jobs
    292 of them were white-collar workers
    198 were blue-collar workers
    78 were service workers
    18 worked on a farm
13 were in the armed forces
341 didn't work and weren't looking for work
    190 of them were keeping house
    61 were retired
    39 were going to school
    28 were sick or disabled
    23 had various other reasons
60 were unemployed and looking for work; they had been looking, on average, for 11½ weeks
25 of them had been fired or laid off
18 had decided to work again after a period of not working
9 were looking for their first jobs
8 had quit their previous jobs.

Thirty-five of the 60 were living with a spouse, parent, or some other relative who had a full-time job. Specifically, of the 60 unemployed people

14 were wives, 12 of them with working husbands
10 were husbands, 4 of them with working wives, 4 with housewives, and 2 with wives who also were looking for work
17 were children or other relatives living with a married couple; 15 of the 17 were 24 or younger
4 were women heading families, and another 7 were children or other relatives in families headed by women
8 lived alone, or at least not with relatives.

Those who work and those who don't. With more older people in the population, you might think that the ratio of nonworkers to workers is increasing, but it's not; it's declining. In 1965 there were 152 nonworkers for every 100 workers. In 1990, there will be only 111. That's because the number of children is declining faster than the number of senior citizens is increasing.

Making money making things. Here's what the average manufacturing worker was paid in 1978:

Industry	Weekly earnings	Weekly hours
Steel, copper and aluminum	$430.62	42
Petroleum	$377.10	45
Automobile	$369.27	43.7
Transportation equipment	$320.67	41.7
Chemicals	$292.18	41.8
Paper	$279.48	42.8
Machinery other than electrical equipment	$277.64	41.5
Printing	$244.02	37.6
Hardware, cutlery and hand tools	$238.19	40.1
Leatherworking	$231.42	37.5
Food processing	$231.42	39.9
Electrical equipment	$228.71	39.5
Lumber	$225.83	39.9
Furniture manufacturing	$180.96	39
Textiles	$172.43	40.1
Clothes manufacturing	$140.76	36

Driving a cab with a Ph.D. About a fifth of the men and a sixth of the women who receive college degrees take jobs in fields not at all related to what they studied, a government survey shows.

Forty-three per cent of the men and 61 per cent of the women said the job they took was the only one they could find.

Who's been working on the railroad. For every 4 Americans who were working on the railroad 10 years ago, only 3 are working on it now. For every 4 Americans who were working on the airlines 10 years ago, 6 are working on them now. But the railroads had a head start, and there are still 4 Americans working on the railroad for every 3 working on the airlines.

Working at an early age. By the time she or he is 13, the average kid has worked for someone for pay. Most often, she or he has worked at cleaning, baby-sitting, waiting on tables, cutting lawns, washing cars, washing windows, or collecting trash.

No harm in looking. Three of every 10 management employees and 1 of every 3 technical employees are circulating their résumés, in search of a better job.

For every management employee who changes jobs because his or her position is insecure, 4 change from secure positions.

He or she's down in the basement, tinkering now. What of the independent inventor, working alone, relying solely on his or her own resources?

Professor Gerald Albaum of the University of Oregon's Experimental Center for the Advancement of Invention and Innovation surveyed 103 independent inventors and came up with these conclusions:

The average inventor surveyed had finished his or her first invention at 27, had received a patent for the first time at 40, and was 47 when his or her most important invention so far was finished.

Two thirds of them did nothing with their inventions. Ten per cent marketed them. The rest licensed or sold the rights.

Inventors invent chiefly because they enjoy it. But about half do it to make money or because they see an unfilled need. Only 1 in 8 said prestige was a motive.

Half said the idea for the invention just hit suddenly.

Eight in 10 work alone, without a partner or assistant. Four in 10 work on several inventions at once.

For hobbies, inventors prefer creative, indoor activities: printmaking, painting, sketching, sculpting, or playing a musical instrument. Half of them read science fiction.

Here are some cities that pay good and bad wages. On average, an unskilled factory worker is paid twice as much in San Francisco as in San Antonio. In Detroit, the average office clerk makes 38 per cent more than the average clerk in Chattanooga or Norfolk. In electronic data processing, there is the same gap —38 per cent—between the average wages paid in San Jose, California and Jackson, Mississippi. A skilled maintenance worker in Portland, Oregon, is paid more than half again as much, on average, as a gal or guy with the same job in Portland, Maine.

For every $100 earned by the average worker in those 4 jobs nationwide, here's how much the average worker gets, more or less, in the following cities. The figures are from a 1977 study by the U. S. Bureau of Labor Statistics.

	Office clerk	Electronic data processing	Skilled maintenance	Unskilled plant work
Jackson, Mississippi	−$13	−$18	−$21	−$32
San Antonio	−$17	no data	no data	−$33
Norfolk, Portsmouth, Virginia Beach	−$15	no data	−$10	−$25
Providence, Pawtucket, Warwick	−$14	−$14	−$21	−$20
Oklahoma City	−$ 8.00	−$11	−$13	−$27
St. Louis (average city)	−$ 1.00	−$ 2.00	+$ 1.00	+$ 3.00
Chicago	+$ 5.00	+$ 2.00	+$ 7.00	+$19
New York	+$ 6.00	+$10	−$ 3.00	+$21
Los Angeles	+$ 7.00	+$ 4.00	+$ 2.00	+$ 5.00
San Jose	+$ 9.00	+$13	+$13	+$14
Detroit (good union city)	+$18	+$17	+$15	+$26
Davenport, Rock Island, Moline	+$17	+$19	+$10	+$30

Where the jobs will be. In an average year between now and 1985, the Labor Department estimates, the United States will have openings for an additional:

295,000 stenographers and secretaries
160,000 janitors
 95,000 bookkeepers
 83,000 registered nurses
 79,000 cooks and chefs
 73,000 local truck drivers (and 15,400 long-
          distance truckers)
 70,000 elementary and kindergarten teachers
 67,000 carpenters
 63,000 typists
 56,500 engineers (including 1,500 aerospace,
          600 agricultural, 150 biomedical, 600 ceramic,
          2,100 chemical, 8,900 civil, 12,800 electrical,
          10,500 industrial, 9,300 mechanical, 900
          metallurgical, 600 mining, and 1,300
          petroleum)
 51,500 accountants
 40,000 construction laborers
 38,000 receptionists
 32,500 police officers
 32,000 auto mechanics
 30,000 cosmetologists
 30,000 industrial machinery repairmen
 30,000 plumbers and pipefitters
 28,000 bank officers
 27,000 painters
 25,000 social workers
 23,400 lawyers
 22,000 machine-tool operators
 21,800 physicians
 17,000 college teachers
 16,500 drafters
  9,700 computer programmers

8,500 computer operators
8,300 firefighters
8,000 librarians
7,700 office machine operators
7,600 computer systems analysts
6,400 economists
6,300 chemists
5,700 buyers
5,600 psychologists
5,200 airplane mechanics
5,100 dental hygienists
4,800 dentists
4,100 airplane pilots
3,700 photographers
3,400 business machine repairmen
3,100 architects
2,400 locomotive engineers
2,300 geologists
2,100 newspaper reporters
2,100 physical therapists
1,900 lithographers
1,800 veterinarians
1,500 statisticians
1,300 radio and television announcers
1,100 foresters
1,100 physicists
1,100 urban planners
  900 historians
  800 geophysicists
  800 sociologists
  600 geographers
  400 merchant sailors
  400 political scientists
  200 anthropologists
  200 meteorologists
  150 oceanographers
   40 astronomers

Time to change jobs. In 1978, the average American worker had been on the same job for 3.6 years, down from 4.6 years in 1963.

Old MacDonald isn't Inc. Sixty-four per cent of U.S. farmers work alone or with family members—without hired hands.

The average farm is 397 acres. But 90 per cent of the nation's food comes from one third of the farms.

Corporations with 10 or more stockholders account for only 2 per cent of farm output.

Off we go. The average Air Force recruit is 20. The average Air Force enlisted man is 27. The typical Air Force officer is 34.

It takes an Air Force enlisted man an average of 24 years to become a chief master sergeant. It takes an officer 21 years, 3 months to become a colonel.

In the Air Force, 3 in 5 enlisted men and 4 in 5 officers are married.

At retirement, the average Air Force enlisted man is a technical sergeant, and the average officer is a major.

Punching the time clock. Nearly half of American workers— 44.5 per cent, to be exact—have to punch in and out, or sign in and out, on the job.

Driving the yellow bus. The average school bus driver is a married woman, 37 years old, who has more than 1 child herself and has driven a school bus for 5 years. She works 3 or 4 hours a day, and her route is 25 miles.

The night shift. One in 10 American workers is on the evening or night shift. Among factory workers, it's 1 in 5.

Looking at it from another extreme, less than half of "protective service" workers—watchmen, guards and the like—work the day shift.

Shorter hours. The average workweek in the United States declined from 60 to 41 hours in the first half of this century, but has declined more slowly since then.

Between 1943 and 1974, the workweek declined from 48½ to 39 hours.

The hazards of work. In the average year, 1 American worker in 11 suffers an injury or illness on the job. For every 100 workers, 60 workdays are lost due to injury or illness, according to the Labor Department.

Construction work is the most hazardous, with 15 incidents of injury or illness per 100 workers. Next are manufacturing, farming and fishing, mining, transportation and public utilities, wholesale and retail trade, services, and finance, insurance, and real estate (the last 2 have a rate of 2 instances per 100 workers).

If you're looking for on-the-job safety, go into banking or the stock market. On average, 20 coal miners are hurt at work for every stockbroker injured or taken ill on the job. One of every 1,000 coal miners is killed on the job. Brokers may worry a lot, but they don't die at their desks.

What part gets hurt. If you get injured at work, the trunk of your body is most likely to be the part hurt. Next come your fingers, arms, and then legs.

Patent pending, pending, pending, pending . . . It takes 25 to 30 hours to fill out a patent application, and about 19 months will pass between when you file and when the patent is issued.

Patent lawyers say that about half the ideas that are brought to them are unpatentable or uncommercial.

Cops. There is 1 policeman in the United States for every 200 people.

She lives! The American Housewife

Who wants to be a housewife. In a survey of 17-year-old girls, only 3 per cent listed being a homemaker as their preferred life's work.

Among women 18 to 34 years old, only 9 per cent said they wanted to be full-time homemakers.

Housework. The average family in America spends 10.5 hours a day, 7 days a week, doing housework—everything from giving Fido a bath to writing a check to Visa.

Here is an unsurprising fact: Wives do the most.

In a typical day, the modern full-time housewife spends

2 hours, 18 minutes fixing meals or cleaning up after them
1 hour, 36 minutes taking care of the house
1 hour, 48 minutes taking care of clothes
1 hour, 48 minutes taking care of the members of the family
1 hour shopping and doing paperwork.

Husbands spend an average of 1.6 hours a day helping out around the house. Teen-agers chip in for an average of about 2 hours, and their younger sisters and brothers together contribute a total of 1 hour.

These figures come from investigations by the New York State College of Human Ecology at Cornell University. The results appeared in 1976 in *Time Use: A Measure of Household Production of Family Goods and Services,* published by the American Home Economics Association.

The livelong week. Breaking things down further, the average housewife works 8.5 hours on Monday and Tuesday, 8.6 on Wednesday, 8.8 on Thursday, 8.9 on Friday, 7.5 on Saturday, and only 5.5 hours on Sunday.

Her husband's pattern is the reverse. He works at home for about 1½ hours on weekdays, but for 2.8 hours on Saturday, and 2 hours on Sunday.

Teen-age kids work 3.4 hours on Saturday, but less than half that much on Sunday.

Who does what. The average husband of a housewife does 14 per cent of the housework, according to the Cornell study. If she also has an outside job, he ups his contribution to 18 per cent.

Even with help from her husband, her kids, and others living at home, the average housewife does 72 per cent of the household work. If she has a job, she still winds up doing 62 per cent.

Whether employed or not, wives do the family washing and ironing more than 90 per cent of the time.

Wives who work fix 3 out of 4 meals. Dad fixes supper 1 night in 10, and the kids do it once a week.

All told, teen-age kids do 5 per cent to 10 per cent of the household work, depending on whether Mom works. They're more likely to help with the grocery shopping and the dishes than with any other household chores.

Kids under 12 are most likely to help with the shopping, the vacuuming and dusting, and the dishes. Kids 6 to 11 do 4 per cent or 5 per cent of the work.

Husbands do 24 per cent of the grocery shopping. They also spend about twice as much time on the family car and the yard as their wives do, and even more often if their wives work.

The homemakers' laments. Housewives have job complaints, too, and the average homemaker complains most about the layout of the kitchen. In a survey in Seattle, 57 per cent said the layout caused heavy traffic, slowing them down when there was work to be done.

Other common complaints:

Half thought the windows were difficult to clean.

Half said there wasn't enough storage space at home.

Two fifths thought the kitchen or the laundry area was too small.

A third said the floors were hard to clean.

A fifth said the bathrooms were hard to clean.

Never done. For all her labor-saving devices, the average housewife today spends more time at housework than her mother did in 1926, or her older sister did in 1952.

The Cornell survey found that the average housewife put 8 hours a day into housework. Employed wives put in 5.3 hours a day.

In a study of urban housewives in Oregon in 1925–26,

homemakers were found to spend 7.3 hours a day at housework. In a 1952 study of housework in Auburn, New York, employed homemakers worked in the house for 4.1 hours a day, and those without outside employment worked at home 7.4 hours.

It turns out that technology cuts both ways: The automobile makes it possible for housewives to take on the extra role of family chauffeur.

Also, Kathryn Walker and Margaret Woods reported in the Cornell study, "There has been a decrease of 20 minutes in the homemakers' average time per day since 1927 in food preparation and after-meal cleanup, but since that time there has been an increase of more than half an hour for marketing, record keeping, and management. Possibly the time 'saved' in food preparation and after-meal cleanup went into selecting and buying convenience foods."

What the husband does. Here's what the average husband does in his daily 96 minutes of chores:

Housework	36 minutes
Kitchen work	12 minutes
Caring for the family	24 minutes
Shopping and household paperwork	24 minutes

In the kitchen. If she has only one child, the average mother spends 1.3 hours a day fixing meals or cleaning up after them. If she has 5 or 6 kids, her kitchen time rises to 4.1 hours a day.

Women holding outside jobs manage to cut 36 minutes a day from kitchen time.

But rare is the wife who sits down to a meal at home that she hasn't helped cook. Even with help from other members of the family, housewives with no outside employment do some cooking on 99 days out of 100. If they hold outside jobs, they still help prepare meals on 96 days out of every 100.

It's a good job except for the work. The average housewife says the best thing about it is that she's her own boss, and the worst thing about it is the work involved.

How wives rate the chores. Hardly anyone likes doing the dishes. That became clear when Cornell asked 1,296 housewifes to rank 16 household chores on a scale from 1 ("dislike very much") to 6 ("like very much").

Here are the rankings, from least to most popular:

After-meal cleanup: 3.1 on the scale of 6. Only 11 per cent of the wives claimed actually to enjoy such chores as clearing the table, doing the dishes (or loading the dishwasher), and finding someplace in the refrigerator for the leftovers.

Ironing: It rates a 3.5. Twenty-eight per cent said they really enjoy it. Ironing got the heaviest "no" vote, too—36 per cent compared to 35 per cent for after-meal cleanup.

Car care: It ranked down there with ironing: 3.6 on the scale, with 1 wife in 4 claiming not to mind it.

Special house care: This is the heavy, seasonal stuff, all those things that you tend to put off—washing windows, defrosting the refrigerator, cleaning the oven, waxing floors, clearing closets, repairing, redecorating. It ranks 4 on the scale, with 37 per cent claiming to enjoy it.

Special clothing care: Mending, hand washing, spot removal, taking things to the cleaners. Ranks 4.1, with a 40 per cent approval rating.

Regular house care: What we call housework—mopping, dusting, vacuuming, making the beds, watering the plants, tidying up—ranks 4.3; 41 per cent say they like it.

Record keeping: This includes paying bills and keeping track of receipts and expenditures. It ranks 4.3, with 52 per cent liking it.

Management: This is planning menus, making shopping lists, measuring space for something, figuring out if there's enough money for new venetian blinds. It ranks 4.8 on the Richter scale, with 63 per cent of wives enjoying it.

Marketing: Even though this includes standing in line at the checkout counter, it scores 4.8, with a 61 per cent approval rating.

Washing clothes: Loading and unloading the machines, sorting the dirty clothes and folding up the clean ones ranked 4.9, with 72 per cent of wives saying they enjoyed this kind of carrying on.

Yard care: This activity ranks 4.9, with two thirds of wives welcoming the chance to get out of the house, even if it is only to pull some weeds. It includes taking out the garbage.

Meal preparation: This includes breakfast, lunch, supper, snacks, baby's food, packing a lunchbag, mixing the cocktails, and serving the food, and it scores 5.0, with 71 per cent of the wives asserting that they enjoy doing it.

Physical care of the family: Bathing the baby and feeding the kids rate 5.1, with an 83 per cent approval score.

Nonphysical family care: Helping with lessons, reading to the kids, and chauffeuring them to the school play rank 5.2, with 88 per cent of wives enjoying these activities.

Special food preparation: Baking, canning, freezing, making food for guests, holidays, gifts, and parties rank highest: 5.3 on the 6-point scale, with 79 per cent approval.

Two other nonhouseworky activities were rated—volunteer and paid work. Volunteerism drew a 5.1, with 78 per cent of wives saying they enjoy it, and paid work got a 5.4 and 85 per cent approval.

The happy home life of the working mother. Four out of 5 families with working mothers eat dinner together, and the children do regular chores.

Those are among the advantages of working, according to mothers who do it. Of every 100, 97 like their jobs, 88 are proud to be working, 84 believe their job makes them more interesting, and 86 consider the setup good for their children.

Three out of 5 working mothers say that because they work, they're more tolerant of their husbands and children.

Most of them say that their husbands help out, but 84 of 100 of the mothers feel that they're still primarily responsible for household chores, and that they have more demands on their time than their husbands do.

Only 2 out of 5 working mothers do it because their families need the money. One in 5 works so the family can buy a few luxuries, and another 1 in 5 does it for personal fulfillment. The fifth didn't say why she works.

Wages vs. salary. About 1 worker in 2 is paid by the hour.

Less work, more groceries. Here's how many minutes the average factory worker has had to work to buy various grocery items over the years.

Year	10 lbs. flour	1 lb. round steak	1 qt. milk	1 lb. butter	1 lb. sugar	1 doz. eggs	1 lb. coffee
1930	50	47	16	51	7	49	43
1940	39	34	12	33	5	31	19
1950	41	39	8	31	4	25	33
1960	29	28	7	20	3	15	20
1970	21	23	6	16	2	11	16
1974	28	25	no data	13	4	11	17
1977	18	19	no data	14	2	9	37

Little guys hire a lot. Two of every 3 new jobs are in companies with fewer than 20 employees.

Money vs. time off. When a sociologist asked 750 working people in Alameda County, California, to make a hypothetical choice between a 2 per cent pay raise or a 2 per cent reduction in worktime, 85 per cent took the time.

When he raised the ante to a 10 per cent raise vs. a 10 per cent cut in worktime, 3 in 5 took the money.

The average commute. Three of every 4 working Americans get to work in less than a half hour, and only 1 in 20 commutes longer than an hour.

Three of 4 drive to work. Only 1 in 27 uses public transportation. More than twice that many walk or ride a bike.

One working American of 3 encounters a problem getting to work on any given day, and 2 times out of 3 it's a traffic jam.

Here's how American workers rate fringe benefits. They're listed in order of importance, as tabulated from the 1977 *Quality of Employment Survey,* a joint effort of the U. S. Labor Department and the University of Michigan's Survey Research Center.

Health insurance
Paid sick leave
Pensions
Paid vacation
Life insurance
Dental insurance
Profit sharing
Eyeglass insurance
Work clothing allowance
Training program to improve skills
Stock options
Free or discount meals
Legal aid

There's the job, the kids, the bowling league, the . . . One working American in 4 always feels rushed. One of every 22 has more time off than he or she knows what to do with.

Getting your mind off the job. One working American in 7 says that he or she *never* thinks of the job while off duty, and another 1 of every 5 says that he or she thinks of it only rarely.

On the road with your American business traveler. Dr. Edward J. Mayo of Notre Dame's Department of Marketing Management surveyed 1,048 business travelers in 10 U.S. cities and found

The typical businessman or businesswoman who travels spends 1 day of every 4 out of town.
He or she rarely mixes pleasure with business, except in some attractive place like New Orleans or San Francisco.

He or she likes restaurants with ethnic menus for the evening meal. French, Oriental, and Italian are particularly popular.

He or she rarely eats alone.

He or she tips 14 per cent.

Four times in 10 he or she pays for a guest's meal, too.

He or she pays in cash more often than with a credit card.

He or she spends 2.5 times more for dinner than what the average evening restaurant meal costs; it is his or her reward for working hard and being away from home.

Half the time, he or she walks to the restaurant, spending 13 to 14 minutes getting there.

Less work and more play. The average American man works 41.1 years of his life, a little less than he used to, and has 28.1 years of life without work. The average American woman works 22.9 years, a good deal more than she used to, but still has 38.7 years without a job.

Those figures are based on 1970 life expectancy tables.

Everyone gets more days off. Nowadays, the average American works only 40 per cent of all the days of his or her life. In 1925, it was 60 per cent.

I'll take that airline job. In 1977, the average airline employee made $20,049. The average railroad employee made $18,530, the average ship or barge employee made $17,342, the average trucking and warehousing employee made $14,943, and the average local transit employee made $10,494.

The jobs we have. Of every 100 American workers

15 are professional or technical	*These*
18 are clerks, or the like	*occupations*
12 are service workers not in households	*are gaining.*
6 are sales workers	*No change here.*
11 are managers, officials, or proprietors	*These*
13 are craftsmen or foremen	*occupations*
15 are what the government calls "operatives," meaning machine operators and such	*are on the decline.*

5 are nonfarm laborers
1 is a private household worker
2 are farmers or farm managers
2 are farm laborers or foremen

Part-timers. Nearly 1 member in 5 of the U.S. labor force is a part-time worker.

Lead on, maestro. Dr. Donald H. Atlas of La Jolla, California, calculated the life span of 35 prominent orchestra conductors who died between the late nineteenth century and 1978. He found that they lived an average of 73.4 years—about 5 years longer than the typical American man.

Why? Maybe, Atlas said, because conductors get a psychological lift from their work, or maybe because they get so much exercise waving their arms and jumping around. Dr. Maurice H. Cottle of Chicago, who treated Arturo Toscanini and Leopold Stokowski, subscribes to the former theory. "Conductors have very happy tissues," he said.

The Efficient American

Whew! The American worker in 1978 was twice as productive as his father in 1951, and 3½ times as productive as his grandfather was in 1924.

And he's a whiz when measured against his counterparts overseas. According to figures from the Dresdner Bank in Germany, the American worker outproduces the German worker by 24 per cent and the Japanese worker by 63 per cent.

The tempo of work. Three of every 5 working Americans say that they have to work fast on the job. Two of every 5 say that time drags.

The productive farmer. In 1870, American farmers produced enough food for 5.1 persons.

The U.S. farmer today feeds 60 people—44 at home and 16 abroad. His or her father, in 1957, fed about a third as many—23.

The Asian farmer feeds 4 people, the European 13. French farmers feed 22, Russians 10, Japanese 14.

You load 15 tons, and what do you get? Here's how our relative reliance on human, animal, renewable, and fossil energy on the job has changed over the years:

	1850	1900–10	Today
Human energy	13%	5 %	0.5%
Work animals	52%	11 %	less than 0.1%
Wind	14%	1 %	less than 0.1%
Water	9% (mill wheels)	4 %	7 % (hydro-electric)
Firewood	6%	1 %	less than 0.1%
Coal	7%	78 %	15 %
Petroleum	0	0.8%	43 %
Natural gas	0	0.1%	32 %
Nuclear	0	0	3 %

Mailman, Policeman, Army Recruit
Bricklayer, Barber, Tooter on Flute

The life of the mailman. On his route, the average American mailman drives 3.6 miles a day, walks another 7.2 miles, and delivers mail to 434 addresses. He or she carries up to 35 pounds of mail, and delivers 968 letters, bills, and such, plus 338 magazines and circulars.

In an average holiday season, he or she delivers 7,789 Christmas and Chanukah cards.

One mailman of every 9 walks his or her rounds.

Policeman of all trades. According to studies, the average policeman spends less than 20 per cent of the workday on crime-related activities. The rest is spent on rescue operations, auto accidents, family disputes, neighborhood fights, court appearances, and paperwork.

Left, right. The average Army recruit marches more than 100 miles during basic training.

Bricks and mortar. The average bricklayer lays about 300 bricks a day, according to Woodrow Orner, who has been doing it for 40 years in Washington, D.C.

Next! The average barber gives 12 to 17 haircuts a day, shearing each customer in 15 minutes, on average.

The average hairstylist fixes up 12 customers a day, in 30 to 45 minutes each.

These estimates are from Gerald R. St. Onge, national president of the Associated Master Barbers and Beauticians of America.

Dough, re, mi. The average member of the nation's major symphony orchestras was paid a base salary of $13,483.61 for the 1976–77 season, with more for overtime, soloing, recording sessions, and the like.

Working free. One American in 4 over age 13 does some volunteer work. In the course of a year their free labor is the equivalent of 3.5 million people working full-time.

More than a third of the volunteers give their time once a week, and 60 per cent volunteer at least once a month.

The typical volunteer is a married white woman, between 25

and 44, with a college degree and an upper-bracket income. But the Census Bureau found that 12 per cent of the poor donate their time and effort to worthy causes, and 17 per cent of the unemployed are volunteers.

Religious causes take half of the total. This includes teaching Sunday school, playing the organ or piano, singing in the choir, and serving as an usher or altar boy or girl.

By assigning a value of $4.76 an hour to all volunteer work, ACTION, the government volunteer agency, estimated that $34 million worth of work was done voluntarily in 1974.

Why here? The unemployment rate in the United States is consistently higher, year after year, than in Australia, France, West Germany, Italy, Japan, Sweden, or Britain.

The discouraged worker. Of every 100 Americans who are out of work and discouraged about it, 30 think no job is available, 16 have been told that they are too young or too old, 9 lack education or training, 5 have some other handicap, and 40 just plain can't find a job.

Brains in the ranks. In 1977, 94 of every 100 American officers on active duty were college graduates. Of the enlisted men, 2.7 per cent held college degrees—4.7 per cent of the recruits in the Army, 1.1 per cent in the Navy, 0.5 per cent in the Marines, and 2.2 per cent in the Air Force.

The boss's perks. Among top officials of large American corporations:

Eight in 10 get free physical exams and free parking places as fringe benefits.

Six in 10 get a company car and stock options.

Half get a luncheon-club membership, and nearly half get a country-club membership.

Four in 10 may bring their spouse along on business trips at company expense.

More than 3 in 10 get to use the company plane and get free executive vacations.

Two in 10 get deferred compensation, use of a company-owned apartment, and free financial counseling.

Hire 'em and fire 'em. The average manufacturer adds 4 employees a year and loses 3.8. That's how employment grows.

Of those 4 employees, 3 are hired for the first time and 1 is recalled from layoff. Of the 3.8 who leave, 1.8 quit and 1.1 is laid off. That adds up to 2.9; the government doesn't say where the other employee went. Must have retired, or been fired, or gone AWOL.

Teachers. According to a survey by the National Education Association, the average public-school teacher in America teaches 25 kids per class. Teachers specializing in a single subject teach 127 pupils a day.

The average schoolteacher has a required workweek of 36.3 hours and donates an additional 8.5 hours a week to school activities—coaching the basketball team or directing the band, for instance.

About 6 teachers in 10 say they would go into teaching if they had the choice to make over again.

Asked to list the chief roadblocks to "rendering better service," 17 per cent of teachers mentioned students' attitudes and discipline, and 17 per cent mentioned incompetent school administrators; 13 per cent cited their workload.

Asked why they became teachers, 7 in 10 told of a desire to work with young people. One in 5 mentioned the long summer vacation.

In 1976, the average teacher's salary was $12,005. Half of all teachers have income from other sources, averaging just under $2,000 a year. Six teachers in 10 are the main breadwinners in their households. Three teachers in 100 get food stamps.

Two thirds of all teachers are women. The average teacher is 33 years old. Nine out of 10 are white. Seven in 10 are married. One in 7 is married to another teacher.

What, me quit? One man in 5 over age 65 is still working. Among men 55 to 64, about 75 per cent are working and 25 per cent have retired.

You can't expect the kids to come down to the mill. Only 1 working American of every 4 gets any help on the job from members of the family.

The boss made me do it. One of every 4 working Americans says that he or she has to do things at work that go against his or her conscience.

This is the leisure boom? Every year, the workweek of the average American employee declines by 7 minutes.

What soldiering pays. In 1978, the average American military person drew $10,900 a year in basic pay and allowances. Officers got $22,200, enlisted people $9,200.

Between 1970 and 1977, Pfc's got a 273 per cent pay raise, while four-star generals had to settle for an increase of only 144 per cent.

But it takes 9 privates or 5½ second lieutenants to earn what a four-star general gets.

Their own boss. In 1948, 19 per cent of American workers were self-employed, including 8 per cent on farms. In 1978, only 8 per cent of American workers were self-employed, including 2 per cent on farms.

An artist's work, if you can get it. Only 1 stage actor in 20, 1 movie actor in 17, and 1 popular musician in 9 can find enough gigs to work full-time at her or his profession. Life is a little better for people in radio and television, or in serious music: There 1 performer in 5 lands full-time work.

This comes from a survey, underwritten by the AFL-CIO, of 3,211 members of 5 unions of performing artists—Actors' Equity, the American Federation of Television and Radio Artists, the Screen Actors' Guild, the American Guild of Musical Artists, and the American Federation of Musicians.

The proportion who averaged fewer than 1 day of work a week ranged from 51 per cent of the screen actors to 22 per cent of the musicians. Except for musicians, blacks had less trouble than whites in finding work. Even in Hollywood, 83 per cent of the screen actors said they had to settle for something less than full-time work.

Half the performing artists said they had to live out of a suitcase. One performing artist in 3 said he or she finds some work in New York City in a typical year.

A majority of the members of each of the unions except the musicians said they experienced some unemployment in the course of a year. Two thirds of those in Actors' Equity were out of work some of the time, and 7 out of 10 members of the 3 theatrical unions went jobless for at least 16 weeks a year.

Patter on the Hill. The average senator speaks in the Senate for 109 hours a year. Members of the House of Representatives have to settle for an average of only 2 hours of speechmaking on the floor each year.

Sorry, counselor. Only three fourths of 1978's law school graduates got jobs as lawyers. Their starting pay averaged $13,000.

I'd prefer a quiet, air-conditioned office with a nice view. One working American in 3 finds the conditions at work unpleasant.

Of those who do, 1 in 6 says it's too cold, and 1 in 7 says it's too hot. One in 6 says it's too crowded, and 1 in 7 says the furnishings aren't up to snuff.

It's too dirty for 1 in 12, and too noisy for 1 in 20. One in 17 pines for a nicer rest room, cafeteria, or lounge, and 1 in 19 needs better work equipment. One in 26 says the place lacks ventilation, one in 71 says it needs more windows, and one in 36 says the place downright stinks.

A young man's profession. The average man in the armed forces of the United States is 24 years, 5 months old.

She flies through the air with the greatest of ease. United Airlines says women business passengers were "a nontraceable percentage in United's inflight passenger surveys" as recently as 1970. Now they account for 1 passenger in 6.

The typical businesswoman passenger takes 10 round-trip flights a year, is less apt to be married than male business passengers, is 38, earns $25,600, owns a car, and is on her way to a convention.

The American Bureaucrat

We found your average civil servant. In 1977, the average civilian employee of the federal government was paid $15,873 and got fringe benefits worth $2,175. That was a nice raise from 1976, when he or she got $14,676 in salary and $1,815 in fringes.

This average toiler for Uncle Sam took 4 weeks of vacation and 8 holidays in 1977, and was home sick 9 days.

The average postal worker got $15,340 in wages and $1,574 worth of fringes in 1977. The average nurse at a VA hospital got $15,972 in wages and $1,188 in fringes. The average diplomat, or foreign-service officer, was paid $27,641 and got fringe benefits worth another $1,085. The average blue-collar worker for Uncle Sam was paid $14,237 and received $955 in fringe benefits.

You might think that White House workers would average the best pay, but they didn't. Counting fringes, the most highly paid federal employees are in the Selective Service system, draft or no draft. In 1977 they averaged $19,542 in salary and a whopping $14,361 in fringe benefits, perhaps reflecting the pension plan for military officers.

Next in line is the Office of Management and Budget, whose workers averaged $25,377 in pay and $2,028 in fringes. At the White House, the average was $20,923 in salary plus $1,553 in benefits.

The place you don't want to work is the American Battle Monuments Commission. People doing that important work averaged $7,735 in pay and $2,370 in fringes.

Guess which agency didn't report? The CIA.

Do government people work as hard? To find out, the National Center for Productivity and Quality of Working Life—a government agency that no longer exists—commissioned Sirota Associates, Inc., to compare results of surveys given to employees of 10 government agencies and 11 private companies.

Among managers, 53 per cent in companies and 45 per cent in government thought their outfits were generally effective and well managed. Among employees, 43 per cent of the business folk thought the outfit was well run; only 28 per cent of the government people did.

On whether they were expected to do too much work, there was near agreement. Among bosses, 34 per cent in government and 33 per cent in business said they were. Among workers, 35 per cent in government and 30 per cent in business said that they are overworked.

Asked to rate the performance of their boss, 67 per cent of those in private companies and 55 per cent in government thought their supervisor did a pretty good job.

Asked whether they'd stand a better chance of being promoted if they performed their job better, 49 per cent in private industry said "yes." Only 30 per cent of government workers thought that was relevant.

Pensioned by Uncle Sam. In 1977, the average retired federal worker had stepped down after 25.2 years of service; his or her pension was $7,560.

Here's a glimpse of a bureaucrat's travel expenses. In 1978, the General Accounting Office reviewed the official travel of the 5 members of the Consumer Product Safety Commission. These guys are high-level bureaucrats, just short of the very top stratum.

In a 12-month period, the average commissioner made 13 business trips and charged the government $3,741.60 for expenses—$287.82 per trip.

Not much to get excited about, eh? What's more, the GAO concluded that every single trip was on legitimate business.

They're all around us. Only 1 of every 9 federal civilian employees works in the Washington, D.C., area. One of every 8 works in California.

Of every 100 federal civilian employees, 16 are black, 4 are Hispanic, 1 is an Indian, Eskimo, or Aleut, and 1 is Oriental. The other 78 are white.

Thirty-one of every 100 federal civilian employees are women.

The pace of shuffling papers. According to a government study, the average federal employee's productivity increased by 1.3 per cent a year between 1967 and 1977. That compares with an average increase of 1.6 per cent for workers outside government.

Those darned bureaucrats. When asked in a Gallup poll what they thought of federal government employees compared with other workers in America, 2 out of 3 people said that federal employees work less and are paid more. Three out of 4 said the feds get better fringe benefits. And 2 out of 3 said that there are too many of them on the payroll, anyway.

Who works for the government? One of every 33 workers in America works for the federal government, and 1 of every 7 works for a state or local government.

The pay is good at city hall. Does the average worker make more in private industry, the federal government, or municipal government?

The Bureau of Labor Statistics tackled that question in a 1976–77 survey and found that for many jobs, city governments were far and away the most generous.

Compared with their counterparts in industry, clerks on the municipal payroll were averaging 43 per cent more in Detroit, 28 per cent more in Philadelphia, 23 per cent more in Milwaukee, 18 per cent more in Los Angeles, 16 per cent more in Seattle, 13 per cent more in Columbus, 12 per cent more in Phoenix, and 6 per cent more in New York.

Think clerks on Uncle Sam's payroll do even better? Compared with the average federal wage for clerks, municipal clerks were getting 78 per cent more in Detroit, 35 per cent more in Milwaukee, 34 per cent more in Philadelphia, 33 per cent more in Seattle and Los Angeles, 29 per cent more in San Francisco, 22 per cent more in New York, and 20 per cent more in St. Louis.

One more category: janitors. Compared with the average wage for private industry, janitors at city hall were making 56 per cent more in Phoenix, 54 per cent more in Washington, 39 per cent more in Milwaukee, 38 per cent more in Baltimore and Columbus, and 30 per cent more in Houston. Compared with what Uncle Sam pays the average janitor, the city broom pushers were averaging 11 per cent more in Detroit, 10 per cent more in Chicago, and 8 per cent more in Memphis and Milwaukee.

On the other hand, cities that pay their workers less than either private industry or Uncle Sam included Indianapolis, Jacksonville, New Orleans, and Kansas City.

Revolving doors. A quarter of the graduates recruited on campus change companies within 3 years.

Revolving doors II. According to Richard Bolles, author of *What Color Is Your Parachute?*, if you are now between 30 and 50 the chances are 1 in 50 that you'll be working for your present employer in 5 years. The chances are 1 in 100 that you'll be at the same place 10 years from now.

Revolving doors III. One of every 2 American office workers has changed employers in the past 5 years, and 1 of every 3 has been promoted and given a better office.

Revolving doors IV. In an average year, 1 worker in 6 changes jobs.

Not enough time for the third martini. Of every 10 working Americans, only 3 take off an hour or more for lunch. Four take a half hour, and 2 take less than that. One takes between a half hour and an hour.

As for regular coffee or rest breaks, 4 of 10 working Americans don't get any, 3 get less than a half hour's worth, 2 get a half hour, and 1 gets more than half an hour.

Goofing off. The average American worker goofs off for 45 minutes a day—nearly 10 per cent of his or her time at work. That doesn't include an hour off for lunch.

Men spend 52 minutes a day at the water cooler, on coffee breaks, discussing last night's game on the tube, or calling up to see if the car is going to be ready.

Women spend only 35 minutes talking with coworkers or tending to personal business on company time, according to a University of Michigan study by economists Frank Stafford and Greg Duncan.

Workers earning over $1,000 a month waste twice as much time as those earning a quarter as much.

Younger workers take longer breaks than older workers. Union members take slightly longer breaks than nonmembers.

What printers make. In July 1977, the average union member in the printing trades was making $8.46 an hour.

What professors make. The average college faculty member was paid $18,462 for 9 months' work in 1977–78. Male faculty members made $19,316, and women made $15,941.

Climbing the academic ladder, salaries went this way: instructors, $12,738; lecturers, $13,822; assistant professors, $15,356; associate professors, $18,705; professors, $24,727. In each category, men made more than women.

It was only a job, anyway. Of every 1,000 workers, 18 quit in an average month and 11 are temporarily laid off.

A piece of the action. Two University of Michigan economists have studied 98 companies that are owned partly or entirely by their employees. They averaged 350 workers each.

The conclusion: When workers own the plant, profits, productivity, and morale are higher.

The prestige ladder. From best to worst, here's how Americans rated the prestige of 15 occupations, in a poll conducted by Trendex:

Clergyman
Pharmacist
Police officer
Lawyer
Public-school teacher
Accountant
Independent supermarket owner
State legislator
Chain market manager
Appliance store operator
Factory foreman
Grocery wholesaler
Service station manager
Clothing store operator
Door-to-door salesman

Working parents. Both spouses work in 46 per cent of 2-parent households.

Woman's work hunt. Nearly 1 American woman in 2 is either working or looking for work. In 1960, fewer than 4 in 10 were.

And you expect them to work fast, smile, and say "thank you." The average supermarket employee gets $5.36 an hour. Clerks get only $3.97—and only $3.35 for part-timers.

For every man-hour, the store sells $65.71 worth of groceries.

Time and a half. One working American in 3 puts in overtime at least once a week. Of those who do, 1 in 7 averages 17 or more extra hours a week. Only 1 worker in 12 considers his or her hours excessive.

Four out of 5 Americans who put in regular overtime do it more or less voluntarily. They say they could turn it down without penalty.

Two thirds of our workers get paid for overtime, and three fourths of those employees get premium pay. One worker in 8 gets extra time off instead of overtime pay. One in 5 works overtime without pay.

If you want to get home on time, get a government job. Only 17 per cent of government workers put in overtime. If you really like to dig into your job, take up mining, where 41 per cent work overtime, or farming, where 47 per cent do.

This Job and That

Piecework. The average worker doesn't fully respond to a piecework pay system. Instead, he or she tends to do what he or she considers a decent day's work, and lets it go at that. The lower the level of work, the less likely the worker will respond to a piecework plan.

Inventors are optimists. George Udell of the University of Oregon's Innovation Center says the chances that an inventor who seeks a patent will make money from his idea are between 1 in 1,000 and 1 in 10,000.

Those Southern bugs must be easier to kill. In 1977, the average exterminator made $5.63 an hour in New York, but only $3.44 an hour in Memphis.

And all the french fries you can eat. The average teen-ager taking a minimum-wage job at a fast-food outlet quits after 4 months.

Working on weekends. Of every 100 Americans who work, 27 usually work Saturdays and 13 usually work Sundays.

Most would rather not.

A farmer's investment. The average American farmer has assets of $201,503. She or he is $37,939 in debt, owing $20,913 on the farm mortgage and $17,026 on other things.

Her or his assets include $160,988 in land, $24,308 in farm machinery, $10,611 in livestock, and $5,597 in crops and working capital—seed money in the true sense.

Fertilizer. Today's average farmer uses 5 times as much fertilizer as his father did in 1950. Gets a bigger crop, too.

Ah, water. One eighth of U.S. farmland is irrigated. But irrigated lands account for a quarter of the value of all crops raised.

No muss, no fuss, no fun. Three dairy cows out of 4 born in the United States these days are the products of artificial insemination.

Bug, drought, rain, wind, hail, flood, scorch, and general disaster insurance. More than 250,000 American farmers insure their crops with the Federal Crop Insurance Corporation, an arm of the U. S. Agriculture Department. The farmers pay an average premium of $369.46, but tomato farmers pay an average of $1,530.62, and peach growers pay $1,651.55. Oat farmers pay only $59.55.

Exporting your share of grain. Per resident, the United States and Canada together have 2.3 acres of arable land, and export 684 pounds of wheat and other cereal grains. Western Europe as a whole has a half acre, and exports 29 pounds of grain, per resident. The Soviet Union has 2.2 acres per resident, with net per-capita grain exports of 7 pounds.

Who does the work around here? In the U.S. economy, women do 41 per cent of it.

As you might expect, women are 99 per cent of the secretaries, 97 per cent of the registered nurses, 97 per cent of the receptionists, 95 per cent of the telephone operators, 87 per cent of the cashiers, and 61 per cent of the social workers.

And women constitute 83 per cent of the elementary-school teachers and 46 per cent of the high-school teachers—but only 32 per cent of college faculties (10 per cent of the professors, 18 per cent of the associate professors, 32 per cent of the assistant professors, 50 per cent of the instructors, and 43 per cent of the lecturers).

But you may be surprised to learn that women also are 45 per cent of the editors and reporters, 36 per cent of the biologists, 11 per cent of the medical doctors (but only 3 per cent of the dentists), 35 per cent of the restaurant managers, 42 per cent of the bartenders, 10 per cent of the security guards, and 17 per cent of the farmhands.

According to the Women's Action Alliance, women hold half of the graduate degrees in art history, but hold only a quarter of faculty positions in that field. Seventy per cent of English majors in college are women, but only 7 per cent of their English teachers are. Women own 5 per cent of U.S. businesses.

They're idealistic at that age. The average Peace Corps volunteer is an unmarried 27-year-old man with a bachelor's degree.

Down the pole and on the truck. The average American fire company responds to alarms within 4.1 minutes.

Fully paid fire departments arrive on the scene within 3 minutes.

Volunteer firemen, who first have to get to the station, respond within 5.1 minutes.

Why postmen get tired. In an average year, 146,000 pieces of mail are delivered for every employee of the U. S. Postal Service.

In 1978, although it took in $64.91 for every man, woman and child in America, the Postal Service lost $.39 for every 100 pieces of mail delivered. But in 1979, the Postal Service broke even, for the first time in years.

Does your salary measure up? Here are some average annual salaries that were paid around the United States in May 1978:

	Average	Men	Women
Engineers	$22,724	$22,984	$15,496
Doctors and dentists	$26,988	$27,872	$22,308
Nurses and other health workers	$12,792	$14,144	$12,480
Grade-school and high-school teachers	$13,780	$15,028	$13,156
Managers in manufacturing companies	$23,088	$24,284	$13,264
Managers in other firms	$17,316	$19,344	$11,596
Sales clerks	$ 9,048	$11,284	$ 6,604
Salesmen/saleswomen	$17,212	$18,512	$11,284
Carpenters	$13,624	$13,676	$ 8,372
Foremen	$16,328	$16,952	$ 9,932
Machinists	$14,508	$14,560	$14,300
Auto mechanics	$12,584	$12,636	$ 9,568
Miners	$17,576	$17,732	$10,348
Drivers and deliverymen	$13,780	$13,988	$ 8,736
Construction laborers	$11,076	$11,076	$10,764 (not many women)
Factory laborers	$10,972	$11,388	$ 8,840
Housemaids	$ 3,692	$ 1,300 (not many men)	$ 3,692
Dry cleaners	$ 8,684	$ 9,412	$ 7,072
Restaurant workers	$ 6,864	$ 8,476	$ 5,980
Guards	$13,312	$13,520	$ 9,672
Farmers	$10,452	$10,608	$ 6,500
Farmhands	$ 7,592	$ 7,800	$ 6,500

Firemen. In U.S. cities, there is an average of nearly 17 firemen per 10,000 people. Fire protection by paid fire departments costs an average of $32.58 per capita.

Why briefcases are carried home. According to time-management expert R. Alec Mackenzie, "the average manager is interrupted every 8 minutes all day long" and "the average manager spends 2 hours per day in meetings and most say half that time is wasted."

A busy fellow. During the summer, the national parks have 1 ranger for every 34,600 visitors.

Neither rain nor snow. An average of 1.2 pieces of mail move through the U. S. Postal Service every day for every person in America.

Stamping out the postal deficit. According to the makers of the CalcuRater postage meter, about 1 letter in 8 has too much postage on it.

A respectable age. In 1979, the average congressman was 51 years old.

It leaves me more time with the family. The average part-time job is 21 hours a week.

What the heck? In a survey of production workers at a Tennessee plant that makes automobile rear-view mirrors, 1 worker in 3 said he or she had ideas on improving his or her job or work, but didn't pass them on because the company probably wouldn't listen anyway.

Around the fringes. Four out of 5 American workers get a vacation with pay, and 4 out of 5 get health insurance. Two out of 3 come under a retirement program, and 2 out of 3 get group life insurance. Two out of 3 working women get maternity leave, and 3 out of 10 get it with pay.

Three out of 5 workers get sick leave with pay, 3 out of 10 get dental benefits, and 1 out of 5 gets eyeglass or eye-care benefits. One in 5 gets profit sharing, 1 in 6 gets stock options, 1 in 6 gets an allowance for work clothes, and 1 in 6 gets lunch free or at a discount.

Half can enroll in a training program to improve skills. Two out of 5 get a thrift or savings plan, and 1 out of 3 gets free or discounted merchandise.

One in 10 gets legal aid, and 1 in 45 can put the kids in a company day-care center during the workday.

Ever wonder what sales clerks at a department store get paid? It depends a lot on the city they live in, and the department they work in. Typically, the top salaries are earned by clerks who get part of their pay in commissions. That's usually reserved for 5 departments—furniture and bedding, major appliances, floor coverings, men's clothing, and shoes.

Here's a rundown on the average weekly salaries earned in May 1977 by clerks in various departments of the store, by city:

	New York	Atlanta	Chicago	San Francisco	Denver	Boston
Furniture and bedding	$352	$256	$283	$376	$237	$282.50
Floor coverings	$302	$215	$276.50	$291	$207.50	$257.50
Major appliances	$279.50	$293.50	$292	$350	$237.50	$284.50
Men's clothing	$232.50	$176	$243.50	$185.50	$146	$313
Shoes	$210	no data	$178	$197	$150.50	$260.50
Notions	$155	$130.50	$130.50	$143.50	$115	$130
Sporting goods	$156.50	$127	$191.50	$166	$155	$138.50
General sales	$132	no data	$120.50	no data	no data	$108

The working woman's hurry. The average working woman winds up the week with 20 minutes less sleep than does the average housewife—even though the employed woman sleeps in an hour longer on Sunday.

The employed woman eats faster, too. She spends 20 minutes less per day at the table than the housewife does. But she takes more time than the housewife to wash and dress so she'll be ready for business.

Yes, sir, ma'am. Of every 100 people on active duty in the U.S. military, 6 are women. At the peak of World War II, only 2 per cent of military personnel were women.

More than 70 per cent of the women in the military serve in two traditional areas—administration and medicine. But between 1972 and 1978, the percentage of jobs open to women rose from 35 per cent to 95 per cent of all military specialties. Still, two thirds of the women officers are health professionals.

The pilot. Somewhere in the world, according to the Air Line Pilots' Association, an American pilot is landing or taking off a commercial plane every 3.5 seconds.

The ALPA says the average commercial pilot logs 80 to 85 hours of flight time a month. He or she is 35 to 39 years old. Nine in 10 are married.

Between flights, boating is the pilot's favorite sport—20 per cent do it. Nineteen per cent play tennis and 13 per cent golf.

Son, this is oil. If you want your son or daughter to have a secure future, get the kid to study petroleum engineering. According to the College Placement Salary Survey, petroleum engineering graduates start at nearly $20,000 a year, twice what graduates in the humanities pull down.

What art pays. Among self-employed artists, the National Endowment for the Arts says, photographers earn more, on average, than writers. Writers earn more than painters and sculptors. Painters and sculptors earn more than musicians and composers.

But musicians and composers put in less time than the others; half work fewer than 40 weeks a year.

Ahhh-tennnnn-SHUN! For every 6 enlisted men in the armed forces of the United States, there is 1 officer.

For every 601 privates (or their equivalents), there is 1 general (or admiral).

For every 2 people in uniform, the military employs 1 civilian.

Let's hear it for Henry Ford. One of every 5 jobs in the United States is related to the auto industry.

Second thoughts on the job. Nine out of 10 working Americans say they're satisfied with their jobs, and 3 out of 5 say they'd recommend the job to a friend.

OK, they were asked, but what if you could go into any job you wanted?

Sixty per cent said they'd switch. Thirty-eight per cent said they'd stay. Two per cent said they'd retire.

Use plenty of ammonia and don't look down. In 1977, the average window washer was paid $4.19 an hour in Washington, $4.56 in Pittsburgh, $5.26 in Minneapolis, $6.34 in Seattle, and $7.06 in Nassau and Suffolk counties, New York.

Longer retirement. In 1940, the average man 20 years old could expect to work another 41 years, 1 month, and enjoy 5 years, 8 months of retirement.

By 1970, the average man of 20 faced 5 more months of work than his predecessor, and could look forward to 2½ more years of retirement.

Three days off a week. The average American may be down to a 4-day workweek by about 1990, at least in major industries.

So says the Delphi Forecast, which based its prediction on surveys of industrial experts.

Rating the boss. Nine of every 10 American workers say that the boss knows his or her job well, is a stickler for the rules, and leaves the workers alone unless they want help. Four in 5 say that the boss makes everyone work hard, and 3 in 4 say that the boss encourages everyone to come up with new ways of doing things.

Four out of 5 say that the boss is friendly. Two of every 5 say that the boss plays favorites.

How long would it take the average person to learn your job? A week or less, say 11 per cent of working Americans. Two weeks, say another 7 per cent.

But for 1 of every 17 jobs, it would take the average person more than 5 years to catch on, according to the jobholder.

Does your plumber really make more than you do? If you earn less than $11.64 an hour, he does. That's what the average union plumber was making in October 1978, not counting $2.97 per hour worth of fringe benefits.

Here's what other unionized building tradesmen were making:

Laborers	$ 8.42 plus $2.05	in fringes
Painters	$10.53 plus $1.74	in fringes
Plasterers	$10.68 plus $2.06	in fringes
Carpenters	$10.91 plus $2.42	in fringes
Bricklayers	$11.05 plus $2.36	in fringes

Work clothes. About 1 U.S. worker in 5 wears a uniform, according to the National Association of Uniform Manufacturers.

What industries pay the best salaries? If you're an accountant, lawyer, personnel specialist, engineer, or chemist, you should apply for work in the mining industry. On average, mining firms pay these professionals the best. Steer clear of finance, insurance, real estate, ad agencies, public-relations firms, and other such service businesses; average salaries there are quite a bit lower.

For example, while the average accountant in the mining industry makes 8 per cent above the national average for accountants, he or she would make 7 per cent below the average in finance, insurance, and so on. Personnel directors for mining firms get a premium of 17 per cent, on average, while in finance, insurance, and real estate, they're underpaid by 6 per cent. That's a total difference of 23 per cent.

There's one hitch: In the average mining firm, the 40-hour week is still standard. In those lower-paying industries, the workweek is down to about 38 hours.

Something in a V-8, ma'am? The average new-car dealership employs 26 persons and, in 1977, paid them an average of $231 a week.

Toting a briefcase. Three in 5 working Americans never bring work home from the job, but 1 in 7 totes some home more than once a week. Of those who do, nearly half say they want to, and only 1 in 15 is actually told to do it.

Science says women work harder. Through mathematical manipulations that only a social scientist would undertake, University of Michigan researchers Frank Stafford and Greg Duncan devised "an index of work intensity."

The results: Stafford and Duncan conclude that women workers, on average, expend 12 per cent more effort at work than men do.

Just treat me like him. One working woman of every 9 feels discriminated against at work. Within that group, only a third consider it a big problem.

What kind of discrimination? For 1 out of 4, it's pay or fringe benefits. For 1 of 5, it's lack of promotion. For 1 of 6, it's a lousy job assignment. For 3 of 10, it's a lack of respect, a lack of fair social treatment, or just plain mistreatment.

On average, the woman most likely to consider herself discriminated against has graduated from college, gone to graduate school, and is between 21 and 44 years old.

So you want to be an actor. Actors' Equity Association is the labor union for actors and actresses in legitimate theater, and has this to say about the profession:

"At almost any given time, 80 per cent of Equity members have no jobs in legitimate theater. In a typical year, 65 per cent of the membership earned less than $2,550. Over 73 per cent had earnings under $5,500. Over 78 per cent earned less than $8,000. Three per cent had incomes between $7,500 and $10,000. Less than 5 per cent earned over $10,000. Thirteen per cent had no earnings at all."

Working when others aren't. Eighteen of 100 working men and 13 of 100 working women work hours other than the standard Monday-through-Friday, daylight hours.

The pride of Iowa. In 1978, for the first time, U.S. corn growers averaged more than 100 bushels per acre.

Rolling in dough. On July 1, 1977, the average union rate for local bus drivers was $7.08 an hour. The average operator of a subway or elevated commuter train made $7.41. Local truck drivers under union contracts averaged $8.09 an hour, and their helpers got $7.28.

Madame officeholder. One public officeholder in 10 in America is a woman, according to the Center for the American Woman and Politics at Rutgers University, which has identified 17,000 women in local, county, state, or federal positions.

In the average state, 9 per cent of the legislators are women.

The typical woman in office is a Democrat and married. She is 48, 2 years older than the average male officeholder. She has served fewer than 4 years in her current office. She says her husband actively encourages her in politics. She is not a member of a feminist organization.

She considers herself more liberal than the average male officeholder. On issues of equal rights for women, Republican women officeholders tend to be more liberal than Democratic male officeholders.

Among women holding federal executive posts, the average says she works 64 hours a week.

Here is a table showing the proportion of women in public offices in 1975 and 1977:

	1975	1977
Congress	3.6%	3.7%
State executive and cabinet	10.3%	10.7%
State legislature	8.1%	9.3%
State judiciary	1.5%	1.8%
County commission	2.1%	3.1%
Mayor or municipal council	4.4%	7.8%
School board	13.0%	25.0%

Airports aren't so glamorous. The average married man who has to travel a lot on the job doesn't really like it. Neither does his wife.

A sociologist studied 128 big-company executives and their spouses. All the executives had to travel a lot. Only 2 liked it—a woman executive who was single, and a man who wanted to escape from his family.

Ten years before the blackboard. The average teacher in America has been teaching for 10 years. Fourteen per cent have been at it 20 years or more. These old vets are twice as likely to be teaching in an elementary school as in a secondary school, and twice as likely to be women as men.

My work is good work. You've probably heard all that stuff about people feeling like a useless automaton on the job.

Well, the average American says it isn't so.

Eighty-four per cent of American workers find their work meaningful, 81 per cent find it interesting, and 89 per cent say that their work affects a lot of people. Eighty-two per cent work at their own pace, 82 per cent say they're responsible for deciding how to get the job done, and 66 per cent take breaks whenever they choose. Seventy-eight per cent say their job makes good use of their skills and abilities, 83 per cent say that their job requires them to keep learning new things, and 88 per cent say their skills will still be valuable 5 years from now.

As for not giving a damn, 97 per cent feel personally responsible for the work they do, and 93 per cent get a feeling of accomplishment from doing a good job.

Getting fired is only half the risk. Of every 100 American workers, 40 say they're exposed to air pollution, 30 say they could be shocked or burned, 29 have to steer away from nasty chemicals, 29 fear dangerous tools or machines, and 29 have to work outside in bad weather. That's not all: Twenty-three say they could be attacked at work by people or animals, 24 risk disease, and 22 say they could be hurt in a traffic wreck on the job.

All those figures add up to a good deal more than 100 because half of all American workers say that they're exposed to three or more job hazards. A majority of them consider the hazards slight.

Here at the grind. Of every 14 working Americans, 13 report to the same place every day.

Once on the job, 1 working person in 4 moves around, whether from city to city or just from one side of a building to another. The others stay put.

Your medical team. According to a survey by the U. S. Public Health Service a few years ago:

The typical doctor was a white man in his mid-40s. He specialized in one area of medicine. He saw 129 patients a week. He worked 52 hours a week, 47 weeks a year. He netted almost $60,000 a year.

The typical dentist was a white man, too. He practiced alone. He worked 41 hours and saw 68 patients a week. He employed 1 "chairside assistant" and a secretary. He earned about $41,000 a year for his trouble.

The typical registered nurse was a white woman. She was in her late 30s. She was married and had 1 child. She made about $11,000 a year; her husband earned about $10,000.

The typical hospital had 163 beds and assets of $37,000 per bed. For every 220 of us, there was 1 hospital bed. It's good we don't all get sick at the same time.

At the Office

In and out of the cubicle. The average office worker spends only 6.4 hours a day in her or his personal work space.

During the past 5 years, 73 per cent of office workers have been moved from one location to another.

Office workers are in almost universal agreement that the work space's neatness, its organization, and the amount of privacy it offers are its most important characteristics.

What do I do next? The average American office worker wants most of all to understand clearly the scope and responsibilities of the job.

Next, in order, are whether the work is interesting, whether the right tools and equipment are available, whether he or she feels that he or she is making a real contribution and feels like an individual rather than a cog, whether the job is challenging, and whether coworkers are friendly and helpful.

After that comes the boss: Is the boss competent?

After that—way down the list—comes pay. Then fringe benefits. Even farther down come the hours.

Here are some salaries around your average American office. They were calculated in March 1978 by the Bureau of Labor Statistics.

The general stenographers were getting $9,834 a year. Secretaries were averaging $11,894, and typists were making $8,527. File clerks were making $7,914, on average, a bit more than messengers, who were at $7,595. Those key-entry operators against the far wall averaged $9,323.

Yep, this is the computer room. Our computer operators were averaging $12,506. Next door, the engineering technicians were making $14,062, and the draftsmen/draftswomen were averaging $13,709.

The average salary for engineers was $25,987, just below chemists, who made $26,013. In the personnel department, job analysts were averaging $18,354. The personnel director was paid $29,223.

Buyers averaged $17,893. Accountants averaged $18,115, auditors got $17,225, and the chief accountant was paid $30,965. Attorneys were paid an average of $30,643.

The boss? Sorry, he's not listed.

Mr. Secretary. In the United States, 1 out of every 42 secretaries is male.

Not that I'm looking for more work. In a survey, 1 in 3 office workers said that he or she probably could do more work. If conditions and circumstances at work were changed, 3 out of 4 said they could do more, and would feel better about their jobs at the end of the day.

On the other hand, the same office workers were asked what their problems were on the job, and half said they had too much work to do. Only 1 in 6 said there was too little.

Vacations. The average office worker is much more likely than the average plant worker to get 2 weeks' paid vacation after 1 year on the job. After 10 years of service, the office worker is only a bit more likely than the plant worker to get a third week. After 15 years, the office worker and the plant worker have an equal chance of getting that fourth week off.

The good old work ethic. Nine of every 10 office workers see a connection between doing their jobs well and getting what they want from life.

What does Harold know about curtains? When a company plans new offices, does the wife of the chairman or president get into the act?

Only 10 per cent of business executives say that she does. But architects and designers should know, and 27 per cent of them acknowledge the, ahem, "contribution" of the boss's wife.

Should she have a say? Only 4 per cent of the executives and 2 per cent of the architects and designers think so.

I like the air conditioning and that new photocopier. Six out of 10 office workers say that the overall quality of life in America has improved during the past 10 years, and 7 out of 10 say that life on the job has improved.

Just don't bother the papers on my desk. Based on July 1977 wages, those women who clean up your office average $2.45 an hour in Miami, $2.91 in Washington, $3.39 in Philadelphia, and $5.44 in San Francisco. They usually work fewer than 30 hours a week.

This'll do just fine. Three out of 4 American office workers are satisfied with their offices, whether private or not. That's news to the folks who design offices (and who no doubt would like to redesign yours); on average, they think that less than half are satisfied.

The appetite for energy. The average office building constructed in New York City in 1970 required twice as much en-

ergy for heat and light as a building the same size built in
1950.

During the third quarter of this century, world fuel consumption doubled, oil and gas consumption tripled, and the
use of electricity grew almost sevenfold.

Early retirement. Two out of 3 workers eligible for Social Security retire before age 65.

I'm too smart for this. One of every 3 American workers feels
overeducated for his or her job.

More important than pay. Half of American workers say the most
important thing about a job is its significance and the feeling of
accomplishment it yields. Only 1 out of 5 says income is the most
important factor. Opportunity for promotion ranks just behind
income. Job security is the most important thing to 7 per cent of
workers, and good hours to 5 per cent.

Moonlighters. On average, 5 of every 100 workers have a second
job. That rate hasn't changed much over the years.

For every 3 people who moonlight to meet expenses, 2 do it
simply because they enjoy the work.

Wages of height. According to experts who have spent years
studying the field, tall men earn more than short men, and have
less trouble finding jobs.

The bachelor works too. One of every 3 American workers is
single.

Paper mountain. Running a business means maintaining a
mountain of paper. According to the Xerox Corporation, for
every white-collar worker on the payroll, the typical business has
on file 18,000 pieces of paper. And the mountain grows at the
rate of 4,000 pieces of paper—enough nearly to fill 1 file cabinet
drawer—per employee, per year.

They don't trust us kids. On average, an old worker is less likely to suffer age discrimination on the job than is a young worker.

Among workers under 21, 1 of every 7 feels discriminated against at work. Among workers 65 or older, 1 of every 9 feels discriminated against.

Joining the union. One of every 3 blue-collar workers and 1 of every 6 white-collar workers belongs to a union. Of those who don't, 1 of every 3 blue-collar workers and 1 of every 4 white-collar workers used to.

They still don't give us blacks a fair shake. One of every 6 black workers feels discriminated against at work.

Three times out of 10, it's a bad job assignment, and 1 time out of 4 it's a lack of respect. For 1 of 5 it's lack of promotions, and for 1 of 6 the problem concerns salary or fringe benefits.

On the other side of the coin, 1 white worker in 27 complains that blacks are favored on the job.

Now, please, the groom's side. One professional photographer in 10 specializes in weddings.

Inertia at work. About half of American workers feel somewhat locked into their jobs, either because they have too much at stake to change, or because it might be hard to find another job as good.

One working American of every 4 has been with his or her employer for at least 10 years.

Say you're offered a much better job that would require you to move 100 miles or more. Three in 5 American workers say they probably wouldn't take it.

It's not just a job. About half of working Americans say that the most important things that happen to them involve their jobs. About half say that what they do at work is more important to them than the money they earn.

When you grow up. A Gallup poll of teen-agers reveals a pattern of sex stereotyping when kids are asked about their career choices.

The average girl was most likely to say she wanted to be a secretary, teacher, nurse, something else in the medical field, veterinarian, fashion designer or model, doctor, social worker, or a cosmetologist or hairdresser.

The average boy was most likely to say he wanted to be a skilled worker (such as an auto mechanic), an engineer, lawyer, teacher, professional athlete, musician, architect, farmer, doctor, or military man.

What a commuter's time is worth. Studies show that the average commuter is willing to pay up to 42 per cent of 1 hour's wage a day to shave an hour from his or her daily travel time.

More coffee, honey? In restaurants, diners, and the like, 3 out of 5 cooks are women. So is 1 bartender in 3. There are 9 waitresses for every waiter.

A third of restaurant, bar, and cafeteria managers are women.

This one separates the real workers from the rest of us. QUESTION: "If you were to get enough money to live as comfortably as you'd like for the rest of your life, would you continue to work?"

Yes	71.5%
No	28.5%

That's from a survey by the University of Michigan Survey Research Center.

Take a letter. One of every 3 working Americans supervises at least 1 other working American.

These folks don't farm. Twenty-eight per cent of American workers start the workday after 9 A.M.

Working mothers. Half the children under 18 in the United States have mothers who work, or who are looking for work. Among mothers of children under 6, 2 in 5 work.

More and more wives are working, and fewer and fewer husbands are. But wives have a long way to go if they want to catch up. Of every 100 husbands, 82 work; of every 100 wives, 48 work.

Both husband and wife work in about half the married families, and the wife is the only worker in 3 of every 100.

Among couples who both work, the median family income in 1977 was $20,722. It was $15,796 with just the husband working, and $10,449 with just the wife working.

Alibis, alibis. The average worker in America is absent from work 9 days a year—6 days because of illness, injury, or doctors' appointments, and 3 days for such personal reasons as an illness or death in the family, child care, work being done on the house, automobile repair work, or waiting at home for a delivery.

The Bureau of Labor Statistics says it would take a force of 2 million workers working 40-hour weeks to make up for the time lost by absentees. The time lost costs the average employer $100 a year for each employee.

By the way, a miner is absent 11 times more often than a bank teller.

Two weeks with cream and sugar. Each year, the average worker gets about 2 weeks of paid time off through the institution of the coffee break.

Specialized medicine. Of every 100 doctors in America

28 are surgeons
17 are internists
16 are general or family practitioners
7 are psychiatrists
6 are pediatricians
and the other 26 specialize in something else.

The others are in office buildings. One of every 4 doctors works primarily in a hospital.

Work and the immigrant. The Labor Department says the average immigrant to America catches up with the earnings of native-born workers within 13 or 14 years, and from then on out-earns the native-born American.

"These results are not surprising," says a government report, "given the fact that many immigrants have already demonstrated unusual courage, motivation, and energy simply by moving to a strange new homeland."

Light up those keys. Based on a study at the Social Security Administration, the average typist increases her or his output 28 per cent when the lighting is tripled.

Sons and daughters, take up your scalpels. One of every 7 new jobs that sprung up in the United States between 1970 and 1977 was in health care.

Burning up calories at work. An hour of typing burns up 84 calories. An hour of light assembly work at a factory uses 108. A hod carrier burns up 216 calories an hour carrying bricks, and a laborer burns up 300 an hour pushing a wheelbarrow.

Sawing wood uses 450 calories an hour. Shoveling burns up 570.

I like a little nap, myself. One working American in 3 reports coming home from work brimming with energy.

10 Food and Drink

Exactly what we eat. Here's what the average American ate in 1976, adapted from information from the U. S. Department of Agriculture.

- 95.6 pounds of beef
- 54.5 pounds of pork
- 1.7 pounds of lamb
- 13 pounds of bought fish, and 2 pounds of caught fish
- 2.8 pounds of canned tuna
- 43.3 pounds of chicken
- 9.2 pounds of turkey
- 10 pounds of liver and other organ meats and trimmings
- 92.5 quarts of whole milk
- 6 pints of cream
- 45.5 quarts of low-fat milk
- 4.4 pounds of butter
- 12.5 pounds of margarine
- 15.9 pounds of cheese
- 4 gallons of ice cream (42 per cent vanilla; 12 per cent chocolate)
- 4 cups of yogurt

129   pounds of fresh fruit, total, including
        3   cantaloupes
       50   bananas
       36   apples
        3   avocados
       0.7 pound of cherries
        3   bunches of grapes
       4.9 pounds of peaches
        7   pears
       2.1 pints of strawberries
       0.5 pounds of prunes
        1   pound of raisins
      116   tomatoes, fresh and canned
       30.8 quarts of orange juice
94.5 pounds of fresh vegetables, including
        1   pound of broccoli
       39   carrots
       12   peppers
       0.5 pound of spinach
       0.4 pound of asparagus
       1.5 pounds of string beans
        5   heads of cabbage
       13   ears of corn on the cob
        6   cucumbers
       0.6 pound of eggplant
       16   heads of lettuce
       26   onions
      140   potatoes (and another 8 in the form of chips)
24.8 pounds of frozen vegetables
56   pounds of canned vegetables
21   pounds of cooking fats and 22 pounds of other fats and
        oils
 1.9 pounds of cornstarch
 3   pounds of oatmeal and other oat cereals
 7.2 pounds of rice
 4   pounds of hominy and grits
92.7 pounds of sugar and 6.9 pounds of saccharin (mostly
        as an ingredient in prepared foods)
15   pounds of chocolate
17   pounds of candy

560 cups of coffee
160 cups of tea
124 quarts of soda pop
  6.3 pounds of peanuts, 0.5 pound of walnuts,
      0.3 pound of pecans, 0.44 pound of almonds, and
      0.66 pound of other nuts
  0.3 pound of pepper
About 7 pounds of ketchup

How our diet has changed. We eat

90 per cent more beef than we did in 1950.
Only a quarter as much butter as in 1910.
65 per cent less cabbage than in 1920.
A fifth less candy per person than in 1968, but that's because the children of the 1950s baby boom have grown up and out of the childhood habit of eating candy.
44 per cent less coffee than in 1946 (when we averaged 1,005 cups each).
Twice as much corn syrup as in 1960.
42 per cent more fresh and frozen food than in 1960.
10 times as much food coloring as in 1940.
8 times as many grapefruits as in 1910.
Nearly 7 times as much margarine as in 1910.
Nearly 5 times as many frozen potatoes as in 1960, but only a quarter as many fresh potatoes as in 1910.
1½ times as many soft drinks as in 1960.
A third more sugar and other caloric sweeteners than in 1909.
8 times more turkey than in 1910, and 27 per cent more poultry of all kinds than in 1967.
44 per cent more frozen vegetables than in 1960.
Only half as much wheat flour (including flour used in bread and spaghetti) as in 1910.
A fifth more fish than in 1969.
Only 11 eggs for every dozen we ate in 1969.
More than half again as much cheese as in 1969.

America's sweethearts. The average American is most likely to reach for a Snickers when she or he buys a candy bar, unless she or he lives in the Northeast, in which case it'll most likely be a Reese's Peanut Butter Cup.

Here, from the October 1978 issue of *Candy Marketer,* are America's favorite candy bars, in order of popularity, by region.

Northeast: Reese's Peanut Butter Cup, Milky Way, Snickers, Hershey's Milk Chocolate, Hershey's Almond, M&M's Plain Chocolate, Mounds.

Southeast: Snickers, Reese's Peanut Butter Cups, 3 Musketeers, Hershey's Almond, Hershey's Milk Chocolate, M&M's Plain, M&M's Peanut Chocolate, Milky Way, Baby Ruth, Kit Kat.

North Central: Snickers, M&M's Plain, Reese's, 3 Musketeers, Kit Kat, Milky Way, Hershey's Almond, Hershey's Milk Chocolate, M&M's Peanut Chocolate, Butterfinger.

South Central: Snickers, Hershey's Almond, Reese's, 3 Musketeers, Hershey's Milk Chocolate, M&M's Plain Chocolate, Almond Joy, M&M's Peanut Chocolate, Milky Way, Baby Ruth.

Mountain and Pacific: Snickers, M&M's Plain, Reese's, Hershey's Almond, M&M's Peanut, 3 Musketeers, Almond Joy, Hershey's Milk Chocolate, Milky Way, Baby Ruth.

Pizza. Because of the pizza phenomenon, the average American almost doubled his or her consumption of mozzarella between 1960 and 1976.

Home-grown. An Agriculture Department survey in 1976 indicated that 48 per cent of American families have home gardens.

95 per cent of home gardeners grow tomatoes.

7 in 10 grow lima or wax beans.

6 in 10 grow cucumbers, peppers, radishes, green onions (also known as spring onions or scallions), or lettuce.

Half grow onions, carrots, corn, and squash.

4 in 10 grow squash, beets, or peas.

2 in 10 grow turnips, strawberries, or apples.

1 in 10 grows melons, peaches, or pears.

7 in 10 with a home garden freeze some of the stuff they raise.

The Agriculture Department says gardens provide about 50 pounds of vegetables for every person in the country. In 1910, they provided 126 pounds per person.

Let 'em eat wrappers. Thirteen cents of the average food dollar go for packaging. Three cents go for advertising and promotion.

Wolfing 'em down for the Skins. On a warm football Sunday, the average fan at a Washington Redskins game spends $1.90 on beer, pop, hot dogs, and the like. On a chilly Sunday, he or she goes light on the cold drinks and spends only $1.30.

Averaging things out for the season, the 55,000 fans at a typical Redskins game devour 32,000 hot dogs, 8,500 kosher franks, 4,500 servings of french fries, 750 barbecue sandwiches, 350 roast beef sandwiches, 300 ham sandwiches, 300 pastrami sandwiches, 8,500 bags of peanuts, 450 soft ice-cream cones, 40,000 Cokes, 30,000 beers, 500 glasses of wine, and 1,000 packs of cigarettes.

On a cold day, the fans warm up with 10,000 to 15,000 cups of coffee.

Eating water. Cantaloupes are 94 per cent water. Apples are 84 per cent water, as are blackberries. Bananas are 74 per cent water, and avocados are 65 per cent.

That's the way it goes for most all fruits. Vegetables, too. Asparagus is 93 per cent water, and lima beans are 67 per cent. Fresh kidney beans are only 12 per cent water, but they're an exception. Green beans average 89 per cent water, and broccoli hits 90 per cent. Cauliflower is all wet, too: 92 per cent. Lettuce is 95 per cent. And cucumbers! Would you believe 96 per cent?

Whole-wheat bread is 37 per cent water, on average, and rye and white aren't much drier at 35 per cent. Cornflakes, on the other hand, are only 4 per cent water. Pancakes make a wetter breakfast, at 55 per cent. As for snacks, it's no wonder people eat them with beer. The average water content is only 4 per cent for popcorn, 5 per cent for peanuts, and 8 per cent for pretzels. And why do we eat a peanut butter sandwich with jelly? Peanut butter is only 2 per cent water, while jelly is 35 per cent moisture.

Rice averages 12 per cent water when raw, 74 per cent when cooked. Does a Hershey bar make you thirsty? Milk chocolate is only 1 per cent water. Sugar has just a trace of water, but honey is 20 per cent water, on average. Butter and mayonnaise are 16 per cent water.

Water content averages 37 per cent for cheddar and Roquefort cheese, 74 per cent for a raw egg, and 87 per cent for milk.

As for meat, water content is 13 per cent for cooked bacon, 39 per cent for smoked ham, 47 per cent for hamburger, 54 per cent for sirloin steak, and 66 per cent for broiled chicken.

In the gourmet department, caviar is 36 per cent water, and frog legs 82 per cent. Water is 65 per cent of salmon, 79 per cent of lobster, and 83 per cent of flounder.

It's hard to believe that a carrot, by percentage, has more water than a shot of booze, but it's true. Carrots are 89 per cent water, while the water content of whiskey is only 58 per cent.

The truth about white bread. Seventy per cent of all bread sold in supermarkets is good old-fashioned all-American white bread.

What goes on white bread. The average American is 3 times more likely to eat peanut butter than to eat jelly.

Yesterday's meals. One day in 1979, *Ladies' Home Journal* telephoned 500 households in 19 metropolitan areas to ask about the meals that were served the previous day and learned:

That wine was on the dinner table for only 1 family in 20, and beer for fewer than 1 family in 25.

That 58 per cent of working women had spent less than three quarters of an hour hustling together last night's dinner. But three quarters of the full-time homemakers had devoted at least 45 minutes to fixing dinner. The homemakers used frozen food or convenience foods more often than the working women. The working women served more salads.

Only one husband in 50 fixed dinner without wifely help. One husband in 25 handled breakfast solo.

Waste. The Agriculture Department estimates that 25 to 30 per cent of the food that gets to the supermarket never gets eaten. Some of it spoils in the store or at home, some is trimmed away (as with meat), some burns on the stove, and some is left on people's plates.

Yes, we can. Home canning—with its steaming pressure cookers, its hot jars, its rubber-lined lids, its promise of good things to eat in the winter ahead—is done in one third of American homes, 20 per cent of city households, and half of all rural homes.

People can at home, according to the Ball Corporation, which makes much of the stuff used in the process, mostly for reasons of economy. But, says Ball, "taste, pride, and fulfillment play important parts" as well.

Tomatoes are canned more than anything else. Three canners in 4 put up tomatoes, and 1 in 5 puts up tomato sauce.

Half the home canners put up more than 50 quarts of food, the U. S. Department of Agriculture says. Almost all use jars designed especially for home canning, but a third use peanut butter, mayonnaise, or instant-coffee jars, too.

One canning household in 4 has some trouble with spoilage.

The unsaturated American. An Agriculture Department survey of 1,400 households indicates that 1 family in 4 is cutting down on sweets and snacks, fried foods, fatty red meat, ice cream, and soft drinks, and switching to allegedly healthier foods—low-fat milk, cheese, lean meat, fish, poultry, boiled and baked foods, and fresh fruits and vegetables.

Time to put the steaks on. Three out of 4 American families barbecue. Young folks barbecue more than old folks, and high-income families more than low-income families.

The bigger your family, the more likely you barbecue.

During the summer, 1 family of every 8 barbecues more than twice a week, and 1 of every 4 barbecues once or twice a week.

In the average barbecuing family, the wife buys the briquets, usually in 10-pound bags, but the husband does the barbecuing, often with his wife's help.

Four out of 5 barbecuers use a long-handled fork, and 3 in 4 use tongs. Seven out of 10 start the fire with lighter fluid (which is usually stored in the garage), and 1 out of 6 with an electric starter. Two in 5 tenderize the meat. One out of 5 uses skewers, probably for shish kebab. Four out of 5 use seasonings, and 2 out of 3 use sauces. Only 1 in 50 uses aluminum foil.

Here, in order, are the foods barbecued most: hamburgers,

steaks, hot dogs, chicken, pork, other cuts of beef, vegetables, bread or rolls, fish, turkey, lamb, and desserts. Of every 100 barbecuing families, 96 grill hamburgers, but only 4 grill desserts.

Sweet and sour. For every 2 sweet pickles the average American eats, she or he ingests 3 dills.

Eating out the modern way. Almost 9 of every 10 Americans eat at a fast-food joint at least once a month, and the average fast-food customer eats at one 8 times a month.

In 1978, the average American spent $85.62 at fast-food restaurants.

The apple named by an adman. The average American, in the course of a year, can be counted on to eat nearly $3.00 worth of Red Delicious apples.

The Fat American

Not so fat after all. Three in 10 American adults consider themselves overweight. But only 1 in 8 is really obese, based on examinations.

An excess of plump. All told, adult Americans are 2.3 billion pounds overweight. There are 50 million overweight men and 60 million overweight women. The average one weighs 20.9 pounds more than he or she should.

Who's fat. The average American man weighs 4 pounds more than a man his age did in 1960.

The fattest Americans, on average, are black women 45 to 74 years old. The thinnest Americans are black men in the same age group.

In general, a woman is more likely to be fat than a man is, and a poor person is more likely to be fat than is someone more affluent.

The typical man gains the most between ages 25 and 34. On average, weight peaks between 35 and 44 for tall men, and between 45 and 54 for men under 5 feet, 8 inches. The average woman puts on the pounds fastest in the years from 35 to 44, but her weight does not peak until she is between 55 and 64.

The average fat person reportedly walks a good deal less than the average thin person (although it's hard to separate cause from effect here).

The fat American has a hard time. In a study in the Boston area, overweight male high-school seniors who had the same grades, IQ's, entrance-exam scores, and teachers' recommendations had only two thirds the chance of being admitted to college than did their thinner counterparts. Fat girls had only one third the chance. Nutritionist Jean Mayer says that, as a result, overweight girls tend to fall behind socially and economically, and are less likely to marry well.

It works if you stick to it. One of every 136 American women is a member of Weight Watchers.

What two (probably skinny) scientists say. If Americans all weighed what they should, the resulting energy savings would be enough to fuel 900,000 cars for a year, or to meet the annual residential electrical demands of Boston, Chicago, San Francisco, and Washington combined. That's what energy specialist Bruce Hannon and nutritionist Timothy Lohman of the University of Illinois figure.

They first calculated how much fossil fuel it would take to grow and market the extra food that was converted into the excess food calories carried around by the 110 million overweight American adults.

Then they estimated the energy savings that would be achieved if that fat were gone. (Elevators would lift more people; planes would fly faster, etc.)

The savings would be the equivalent of 1.3 billion gallons of gasoline per year.

Might be enough for all us to drive to a Howard Johnson's just outside of Joplin, Missouri, for a hot fudge sundae.

Corn-fed. The average kid in Muscatine, Iowa, is overweight. The University of Iowa studied 4,000 of them. The typical 11-year-old boy weighed 84 pounds, 5 pounds above the national average. The average 9-year-old girl weighed 70 pounds, 7 pounds above the national mean. Nineteen per cent of the 9-year-old girls were at least 20 per cent overweight. Fourteen per cent of the 11-year-old boys were at least 20 per cent over-weight.

What makes us fat. The average person has about 27 trillion fat cells. But an obese person has at least 3 times that many.

A rounded profile of the fat American. The average fat American man is 30 pounds overweight. The average fat American woman is 33 pounds overweight. (A person is "fat," according to the government, if he or she is more than 10 per cent over his or her "ideal weight." On that basis, 32 per cent of American men and 36 per cent of American women are fat.) He stands 5 feet 9 inches tall and weighs 202. She measures 5 feet 4 inches tall and weighs 176.

On average, fat people are neither taller nor shorter than average people, the government discovered. They just weigh more.

By age, here's the weight of the average fat American:

	Men	Women
20 to 24	210	174
25 to 34	212	183
34 to 44	203	182
45 to 54	202	176
55 to 64	198	172
65 to 74	190	167

What the average American weighs. From a health survey of 10,000 persons, the National Center for Health Statistics calculates that the average man who is

	this old					
	18–24	25–34	35–44	45–54	55–64	65–74
and this tall			*weighs (in pounds)*			
5'2"	130	141	143	147	143	143
5'3"	135	145	148	152	147	147
5'4"	140	150	153	156	153	151
5'5"	145	156	158	160	158	156
5'6"	150	160	163	164	163	160
5'7"	154	165	169	169	168	164
5'8"	159	170	174	173	173	169
5'9"	164	174	179	177	178	173
5'10"	168	179	184	182	183	177
5'11"	173	184	190	187	189	182
6'	178	189	194	191	193	186
6'1"	183	194	200	196	197	190
6'2"	188	199	205	200	203	194

The average woman who is

	this old					
	18–24	25–34	35–44	45–54	55–64	65–74
and this tall			*weighs (in pounds)*			
4'9"	114	118	125	129	132	130
4'10"	117	121	129	133	136	134
4'11"	120	125	133	136	140	137
5'	123	128	137	140	143	140
5'1"	126	132	141	143	147	144
5'2"	129	136	144	147	150	147
5'3"	132	139	148	150	153	151
5'4"	135	142	152	154	157	154
5'5"	138	146	156	158	160	158
5'6"	141	150	159	161	164	161
5'7"	144	153	163	165	167	165
5'8"	147	157	167	168	171	169

Once a fatty, always a fatty. A fat baby is more likely to grow into a fat adult than a skinny baby is.

Gone today, here tomorrow. Diet experts say that fewer than 10 per cent of the people who lose weight manage to keep most of it off for more than 2 years.

What makes dieting hard. Researchers have found that extremely overweight people need a third to a half fewer calories to maintain any given body weight than do people of average size. Even when the obese get down to a normal weight, they require fewer calories than other people their size.

I know I should cut down. In 1974, the average American was eating 200 calories a day more than he or she did 9 years earlier —enough to fatten up by 20 pounds per annum. Most of the increase was just that—fat.

Here is good news for thin people who don't want to be fat and a good rationalization for fat people who don't want to blame themselves. Have that second helping; obesity may be hereditary. Research published by a fellow named C. B. Davenport, who studied 1,671 progeny, established that 84 per cent of the children of parents who are both slender are slender too. But "The matings of very fleshy parents produced no slender offspring, with 33 per cent of the children classified as very fleshy, 27 per cent fleshy, and 40 per cent medium. . . . The matings of a very fleshy parent and a (merely) fleshy parent resulted in a progeny in which 28 per cent were very fleshy, 46 per cent fleshy, 22 per cent medium, and only 4 per cent slender." So reports the *Annals of the New York Academy of Sciences.*

In another study, of 1,000 fat people in Vienna, a researcher found that the parents of 73 per cent of them were also obese. In a Chicago study, it was 69 per cent; in a Philadelphia study, 80 per cent; in Edinburgh, 69 per cent. A study of fat people with life insurance found that 58 per cent had fat mothers and 43 per cent had fat fathers.

Burn, calorie, burn. To lose a pound of fat, a person must burn about 3,500 calories.

Here is how many calories the average person burns per minute in these activities

	Calories per minute
Sleeping	1 to 1.2
Watching television	1.5 to 1.6
Getting dressed	1.5 to 2
Ironing	1.7
Dusting	2.5
Cooking	2.5
Walking 2 mph	2.5
Walking 3 mph	3.5
Walking 5 mph	5.5
Cleaning floors	3.5
Making beds	3.5
Dancing slowly	3
Dancing fast	4 to 7
Bicycling 5 mph	4.5
Bicycling 9 mph	7
Bicycling 13 mph	11.1
Playing tennis	7.1
Running 7 mph (1 mile in 8.5 minutes)	10
Running 9 mph (1 mile in 6.7 minutes)	11
Skiing at a moderate speed	10 to 16
Skiing fast	15 to 19
Swimming the crawl	7
Swimming the breaststroke	11
Swimming the backstroke	14

Protein, to go. The average American eats twice as much protein as he or she needs. It is stored as fat. Nutritionists recommend that people get a third of their protein from animal sources and two thirds from vegetable sources, but the average American gets 60 to 80 per cent from animals.

Cola-Cola. If you were taking soft-drink orders from an average 100 people in 1978, 26 of them would want a Coke and 17 would ask for a Pepsi. The others would have something else.

What'll it be, honey? Here are the most popular restaurant dishes and the percentage of customers who order them:

At breakfast

Coffee	59%	Potatoes other	15%
Eggs	44%	than french fries	
Sausage or bacon	31%	Pastry	12%
Doughnuts	22%	Milk	9%
Juice	18%	Ham	5%
Pancakes	16%		

At lunch

Soft drinks	37%	Sandwich	14%
French fries	33%	Potatoes	9%
Burgers	35%	Vegetables	8%
Coffee	20%	Desserts	7%
Small salad	14%	Hot or iced tea	7%

At dinner

French fries	34%	Coffee	16%
Soft drinks	26%	Pizza	13%
Small salad	26%	Fried chicken	11%
Burgers	26%	Vegetables	10%
Other potatoes	17%	Fish or other seafood	9%

World's hungriest airport. On an average day, the snack bars at Chicago's O'Hare Airport, the world's busiest, sell 5,479 hot dogs, covered with 12 gallons of relish and 9 gallons of mustard, and washed down with 890 gallons of coffee.

Coffee that glows in the dark. The average owner of a microwave oven uses it more often to boil water for coffee than for anything else, according to the New York *Times*.

Well, pickle me in brine! The average American consumes 60 times as much salt as he or she needs.

The egg and you. If you're average, you eat fewer eggs than you used to. Americans eat 276 per annum, two thirds of what they put away in the peak year of 1945, when per-capita consumption was 403. These figures include eggs used in mayonnaise, dried egg whites in cake mixes, and the like.

The Center for Science in the Public Interest attributes the decline to the disappearing American breakfast, which it attributes to more women holding outside jobs and to the prominence of breakfast cereals. In 1950, half the eggs we ate were consumed at breakfast.

Sunny side up for gramps. One in 5 American senior citizens eats eggs every day. Fewer than 1 child in 10 eats eggs every day.

A week's chow. In the course of a typical week, the average American eats beef or lamb on 3.6 days, fresh vegetables or salad on 5.5 days, poultry on 1.8 days, candies, cookies, or cakes on 3.1 days, fish on 1.2 days, breakfast cereal on 2.7 days, and milk or cheese on 5.6 days. He or she drinks beer on 1.1 days, soft drinks on 2.4 days, water on 6.6 days, wine on 0.7 day, and hard liquor on 0.6 day.

Cackle, cackle. The average American eats 5 times a year at Kentucky Fried Chicken, and orders the three-piece dinner.

The American appetite. By his or her seventieth birthday, the average American will have eaten 150 steers, 24,000 chickens, 225 lambs, 26 sheep, 310 hogs, 26 acres of grain, and 50 acres of fruits and vegetables.

Anticarnivorism. About 1 American in 200 is a lactoovovegetarian—eats dairy products, but won't touch meat, fowl, or fish. One in 40 is pretty much a veggie—avoids meat, but maybe yields when a guest at a table of carnivores.

For every 100 who won't eat red meat, another 30 also turn down fowl, and another 19 reject fish, too, a Roper poll finds.

Skimping. To save money on food as prices have risen in recent years, 3 out of 4 families now do more with leftovers, 1 out of 4 eats out more often at fast-food spots instead of at more expensive places, and 1 out of 5 simply puts less food on the table.

Food, sex, and age. The Agriculture Department says women eat less beef, pork, grain, and dairy products than men, but more fruit. Both eat about the same amount of vegetables. Old people consume less food, in general, than middle-aged people, but the elderly eat more fruit.

It's quick and cheap. When going to a restaurant, the average American under age 35 will pick a fast-food joint 3 times out of 5.

Substandard chompers. One in 10 Americans has trouble chewing steaks and chops, and 1 in 9 has trouble biting into apples or eating corn on the cob.

What Clarence Birdseye did. Frozen foods take up nearly 8 per cent of an average supermarket's space, account for 9 per cent of its sales, and use 33 per cent of its electricity.

Why not after breakfast, too? One in 10 Americans eats dessert after lunch and dinner, every day. One in 8 almost never eats dessert.

One in 9 Americans 12 or older is on a diet.

Ground meat. The average American eats half his or her beef ground up into hamburgers, meatballs, chili, and the like. In an average week, he or she eats four fifths of a pound of ground beef at home.

Where kids eat lunch. Eleven per cent of the kids in high school skip lunch, according to the Agriculture Department. Half the kids eat lunch in the school cafeteria, a third of them carry it to school, and 3 per cent eat at a restaurant. Six high-school kids in 100 walk home for lunch.

At McDonald's

Fast food. The average McDonald's can turn out 8 hamburgers a minute.

The average McDonald's customer spends $1.90.

The average McDonald's takes in $940,000 a year. Of every $1.00, $.14 is for breakfast.

For every hamburger Americans buy at Burger King, we buy 3 at McDonald's. For every hamburger we buy at Wendy's, we buy 10 at McDonald's.

The basic hamburger. For every $1.00 the average American spends at Kentucky Fried Chicken, he or she spends $2.34 at McDonald's. He or she spends $4.30 at McDonald's for every $1.00 at Dairy Queen, $5.50 at McDonald's for every $1.00 at Howard Johnson's, and $13.90 at McDonald's for every $1.00 at Dunkin' Donuts.

In a sesame-seed bun. McDonald's sells enough hamburgers to provide everyone in America with 11 a year.

Ronald. In a survery, 96 schoolkids in 100 were able to identify Ronald McDonald. (They said in unison, "He is the clown character who is the corporate symbol of the McDonald hamburger phenomenon.")

Ohh, Henry! The average American consumed only 15 pounds of candy in 1977. Ten years earlier, he or she ate 20 pounds. Candy consumption has fallen every year since 1969.

Eating cheap. For all our grousing about food bills, Americans put out only 23 per cent of their after-tax money on food. The French spend 25 per cent, the West Germans 27 per cent, the Japanese 33 per cent, the Brazilians 42 per cent, and the Russians 52 per cent.

The spice rack. According to a survey by the American Spice Trade Association, the spices most likely to be found in the average American kitchen are:

Black pepper, dehydrated onions, dehydrated garlic, cinnamon, chili powder, mustard, parsley flakes, paprika, oregano, celery seed, celery salt, cloves, nutmeg, red pepper, sage, and bayleaf. In that order.

Calories we drink. Americans, on average, get 210 calories a day from alcoholic beverages.

I could eat a ton. Between the ages of 30 and 50, the average American eats about 10 tons of food. And gains 5 pounds.

Here's what the average U.S. service person wants and doesn't want on the mess-hall menu.

Breakfast

WANTS	DOESN'T WANT
Orange or grape juice	Cranberry or prune juice
Bacon	Grilled bologna
Eggs to order	Plain muffins
Doughnuts	Instant coffee or skim milk
Coffee or milk	

Lunch

WANTS	DOESN'T WANT
Tomato, vegetable, or noodle soup	Corn chowder
Hamburger or cheeseburger	Hot dog or cheese and bacon sandwich
French fries	Sweet potato
Coleslaw	Pickled beet and onion salad
Milkshake and chocolate-chip cookies	Butterscotch sundae and molasses cookies
Coffee, lemonade, iced tea, or cola	Instant coffee, grape lemonade, lime drink, or low-calorie cola

Dinner

WANTS	DOESN'T WANT
Grilled steak or fried chicken	Grilled lamb chops or spareribs with sauerkraut
Baked potato or hashed browns	
Green beans or plain peas	Hot potato salad or boiled navy beans
Tossed green salad with Thousand Island or French dressing	Lima beans or creamed peas
	Carrot, raisin, and celery salad
Fresh oranges or apples	
Strawberry shortcake or cherry pie	Fresh plums or honeydew melon
Beer, coffee, or milk	Spice cake or raisin pie
	Cherry drink, instant coffee, skim milk, or buttermilk

That's just a sample. Altogether, the armed forces had 378 foods and drinks rated by 3,800 soldiers, sailors, marines, and airmen.

The most popular items, were, in order, milk, steak, eggs to order, corn on the cob, orange juice, strawberry shortcake, french fries, fried chicken, ice cream, milkshake, bacon, and spaghetti with meat sauce.

What do the men and women in uniform like the least (or loathe the most)? From last place up, it was buttermilk, skim milk, fried parsnips, low-calorie soda, mashed rutabagas, french-fried carrots, prune juice, stewed prunes, french-fried cauliflower, creamed onions, kidney bean salad, and baked yellow squash.

The national sweet tooth. The average American eats about 93 pounds of sugar a year.

That 93 pounds—92.7 in 1978, to be exact—is a bit less than in preceding years. In 1972, for example, the average American treated herself or himself to 103 pounds of sugar.

But lots of food manufacturers substitute corn syrups for sugar these days, and corn syrups amount to much the same thing.

And our average American partook of 34 pounds of corn syrups in 1978, up from 21 in 1972.

He or she also poured on a pound of honey and a half pound of pancake syrup.

That's a total of 128 pounds of "caloric sweeteners," as the Agriculture Department calls them. In general, it's been edging up year by year, although the 1978 figure was down almost a pound from 1977. Maybe we've peaked on the sweet stuff.

The average American's mother or grandma did a lot of baking. In 1926, the typical American ate 103 pounds of sugar, and two thirds of it came into the house in bags. No one could dump that much in their coffee and oatmeal. Make no mistake, there was baking going on.

By 1976, less than a quarter of our average American's sugar intake was brought into the house as plain sugar. The rest was in processed foods.

These days, the average American gets a quarter of his or her calories from sugar.

In his or her first year of life, the average American baby eats 8.2 pounds of sugar in commercial baby food. How else do you get 'em to eat liver?

For the growing appetite. The average nursing mother produces about a pint of milk a day at first, increasing to a couple of quarts or more as the baby gets bigger.

People trust these brands. Three of every 4 American families who use aluminum foil pick Reynolds Wrap. Seven of every 10 salt users buy Morton's, 6 of every 10 canned-soup eaters eat Campbell's, and 6 of every 10 nut chompers chomp Planter's. Half the mustard spreaders spread French's, half the instant-tea sippers sip Lipton's, and half the corn-chip snackers snack on Fritos. Dixie Cups are the choice of 6 of every 10 throwaway-cup users, and Scott is slipped into the shopping basket by 7 of every 10 users of waxed paper. Windex is wiped on by 6 of every 10 home-window washers.

The fruit. We eat a third less fresh fruit than we did in 1936, but three times as much dried, canned, chilled, and frozen fruit.

The average American has a glass of frozen orange or grapefruit juice 1 morning out of 3.

We eat more bananas than any other fresh fruit—nearly 20 pounds a person.

Apples are second—16 pounds each. We eat 70 per cent fewer apples than our grandparents in 1910.

We eat only a third as many fresh oranges as we did in 1944: 15 pounds compared to 45.

This average is supposed to turn you off pies, cakes, and other such goodies. In 1909, the average American ate 10 pounds of fruit, vegetables, and cereal products for every pound of sugar. By 1974, the average American was eating only 5 pounds of those wholesome items for every pound of sugar.

Where beef comes from. According to the National Live Stock & Beef Board, your average 1,000-pound steer yields but 615 pounds of carcass, which, when bones and fat are cut off, yields only 432 pounds of beef and 27 pounds of "variety meats"—liver, heart, tongue, tripe, sweetbreads, and brains.

When butchered, that half-ton steer can be expected to put on your dinner table 19 pounds of porterhouse steak, 9.5 pounds of T-bone steak, 5 pounds of top loin steak, 41 pounds of sirloin steak, 21 pounds of top round, 9 pounds of brisket, and 65 pounds of ground beef and stew meat.

Little of the steer is wasted. Its by-products are used, the Board says, "in a variety of foods, cosmetics, clothing, and a host of manufactured items" and become "an important source of life-saving, life-improving medicines such as insulin and heparin."

It keeps you regular. The average American eats about one fourth of an ounce of fiber a day, much less than his forebears did a century ago.

Eating out. The average American eats more than 1 out of 3 meals away from home. In 1965, the figure was 1 in 4, and soon it is expected to be 1 in 2. If you skipped breakfast at home for coffee and Danish at your desk, you qualify as average.

In a survey, 1 person in 5 said he or she had had breakfast in a restaurant at least once in the past week. One in 2 had had lunch out, and more than 1 in 3 had had supper out.

Young people eat out more often than old people, single people more than married people, men more than women, childless couples more than families, and Westerners more than people living anywhere else.

Even poor Westerners spend a quarter of their food dollars eating out. Those earning over $25,000 spent 40 per cent of their total food expenditure in restaurants.

What people eat out. The typical patron at a fast-food restaurant is most likely, in descending order, to get: french fries, soft drinks, large burgers, regular burgers, shakes, coffee, fried chicken, sandwiches, small salads, and potatoes other than french fries.

And here, according to the National Restaurant Association, are the dishes the average person is most likely to order at other restaurants:

At a *cafeteria:* coffee, small salads, vegetables, soft drinks, desserts, potatoes other than french fries, tea, sandwiches, french fries, and milk.

At a *family-type restaurant:* coffee, small salads, french fries, soft drinks, other potatoes, vegetables, pizza, fried fish or seafood, tea, and desserts.

At *take-outs:* soft drinks, fried chicken, pizza, sandwiches, french fries, salads, coffee, other potatoes, doughnuts, and ice cream.

At *coffee shops:* coffee (of course), doughnuts, soft drinks, sandwiches, french fries, eggs, other potatoes, small salads, pastry, tea, and regular hamburgers.

At *"atmosphere" restaurants:* small salads, coffee, soft drinks, potatoes other than french fries, pizza, vegetables, french fries, cocktails, soup, tea, and steak.

How d'ya like your protein? Here's how much the Agriculture Department figures it cost in 1978 to give a 20-year-old man a third of his daily recommended allowance of protein, depending how he takes it:

Dry beans	$.13	Beef chuck roast	$.44
Peanut butter	$.17	Round steak	$.50
Eggs	$.18	Pork roast	$.53
Beef liver	$.21	Frankfurters	$.54
Fryer chicken	$.26	Bologna	$.71
Turkey	$.29	Fillet of haddock	$.72
Hamburger	$.29	Sirloin steak	$.72
Tuna	$.36	Beef rib roast	$.75
American cheese	$.36	Bacon	$.99
Whole ham	$.40		

Machines that feed us. The average American spends a nickel of each food dollar at vending machines.

What's in cereal. The average breakfast cereal is 25 per cent sugar, according to nutritionist Ira Shannon at the VA hospital in Houston.

Home-grown's better but store-bought's cheaper. Horticulturists Helen Connolly and James Utzinger of the Ohio Agricultural Research and Development Center at Wooster, Ohio, set out to determine—once and for all—if it pays to garden.

Their conclusion: maybe.

If you don't include the cost of your own labor, gardening pays. But if you charge yourself $2.40 an hour, as they did in their experiment, you'd be better off, in an economic sense—ignoring the aesthetic, spiritual, physical, and moral rewards of gardening—to buy your green beans at the Safeway.

Connolly and Utzinger gardened on a 10-by-15-foot plot 3 miles from home. They made 79 trips totaling 474 miles to the garden plus 7 trips totaling 57 miles for garden supplies and equipment. Travel expenses: $79.65.

They included in "garden expenses" $2.57 for renting the land, $11.95 for seeds and plants, $9.00 to rent a tiller, $.96 for fertilizer, $5.31 for pesticides, $4.00 for testing the soil, $13.98 for equipment, $.15 for water, and $.78 for straw, used for mulching. Garden expenses: $48.70.

They figured they put in 38.8 hours of work. At $2.40 an hour, labor costs were $93.12.

They grew tomatoes, beets, bell peppers, spring lettuce, squash, green onions, spring cabbage, Spanish onions, potatoes, carrots, green snap beans, Chinese cabbage, peas, spring spinach, fall cabbage, fall lettuce, radishes, fall spinach, and broccoli.

They harvested 197.1 pounds of first-quality vegetables and 13.42 pounds of lesser-quality produce.

They then determined what those vegetables would have cost in the supermarket: $90.45.

Conclusion I: If you subtract only the garden expenses from the grocery prices, you've saved $41.75 by growing your own.

Conclusion II: If you add in transportation and $2.40 an hour for your labor, your garden cost you $131.02 above the supermarket price.

Conclusion III: Even when you include transportation and labor, you would have saved money if you'd grown only tomatoes, beets, and peppers, all expensive items at the grocery store.

Connolly and Utzinger's further conclusion: "Maximum net returns from home gardens can be realized if the grower concentrates on productive crops with higher market value and those that require minimum maintenance in terms of pesticides and special equipment."

What's a ball game without one? The average American eats 92 hot dogs a year. Adults eat more than children, women eat more than men, and more are eaten as meal entrees than as snacks. But the average American still eats more hot dogs during the baseball season than at any other time of year.

An Olympian appetite. The average Olympic athlete consumes 5,500 calories a day. Most come from meat. During the Montreal Olympics, each athlete ate an average of 2.4 pounds of meat a day.

Breakfast champions. The real aristocrats of the breakfast table are Dr. Kellogg, Mr. Post, and Mr. Ralston. One American in 4 eats cold cereal for breakfast, and the average American eats 8.6 pounds of cold cereal a year.

One in 8 skips breakfast.

Bad eggs. The average American eats too much cholesterol. He or she can hardly help it. With two eggs for breakfast, he or she is already over the 300-milligram daily quota recommended by nutritionists. A single good-sized yolk alone contains 250 milligrams. The average American adult eats 600 milligrams of cholesterol per day, and likes them.

I'll have 1 of each. The Agriculture Department has figured out who among us is most likely to eat what kind of sweets. To wit:

Candy: boys and girls from ages 6 to 19
Soft drinks: boys 12 to 19
Cookies, cakes, pies, and doughnuts: boys 12 to 19, and men over 35
Ice cream: boys 12 to 19
Sugar, spooned on: men over 20
Syrup, honey, and molasses (often on pancakes): boys 12 to 19
Jelly and jam: boys 12 to 19

Overall sugar consumers, ranked in order:

Boys 12 to 19
Boys 9 to 11
Men 20 to 34
Girls 12 to 19
Boys and girls 6 to 8
Men over 35
Women 20 to 34
Kids 3 to 5
Women over 35

When people eat out. The average restaurant does a fifth of its weekly business on Saturday, and less than a tenth on Monday.

Well-nourished Americans. According to figures compiled by the U. S. Department of Agriculture, the average American probably eats more than he or she needs.

Not only more calories. More vitamins and other nutrients, too—lots more.

Although the figures for consumption are for raw food and the figures for recommended allowance are for food in the stomach, it sure looks as though the average American is well nourished. Here is the per-capita, per-day consumption for some important nutrients, along with their recommended dietary allowances, for a 154-pound man between 23 and 50 years old. Women and children need even less.

Nutrient	Average daily consumption	RDA
Food energy	3,380 calories	2,700 c
Protein	103 grams	56 g
Calcium	.94 grams	.8 g
Phosphorus	1.57 grams	.8 g
Iron	18.6 milligrams	10 mg
Vitamin A	8,200 International Units	3,330 I.U.
Thiamin	2.09 milligrams	1.4 mg
Riboflavin	2.5 milligrams	1.6 mg
Vitamin C	116 milligrams	45 mg

Canned peas are OK. On average, says the American Dietetic Association, canned and frozen vegetables are just as nutritious as fresh vegetables.

Eating less than Grandpa. The average American eats 4 pounds of food a day. In 1950, she or he ate 4.1 pounds. In 1910, she or he ate 4.4 pounds.

The 3,380 calories the average American eats each day exceed the 3,260 she or he ate in 1950, but are fewer than the 3,490 she or he ate in 1910.

Fat provides 42 per cent of our calories, a third more than in 1919.

Starch consumption is down 43 per cent since 1910. It now provides a fifth of our calories.

Sugar, corn syrup, and other sweeteners constitute nearly a

fifth of our calories—half again as much as for the people of 1910.

The seventh-inning stretch. In 1976, the average baseball fan at Wrigley Field, where the Chicago Cubs play, drank 1 beer and 1 soft drink (actually, 1.04 beers and .94 soft drink), and ate .75 hot dog. The tab was two bucks.

The franchise that feeds us. Because the average American now eats so often at fast-food places, per-capita consumption of ketchup, pickles, beef, chicken, fish, potatoes, and ice milk (used in fast-food shakes) have risen sharply since the early 1960s.

The additive and I. To improve the texture, culture, and shelf life of their products, America's food processors add about 1 billion pounds of additives a year—the equivalent of 4.5 pounds for each of us.

The colors we eat. The Food and Drug Administration certifies enough coal-tar-based colors (95 per cent of which end up in food) to provide a third of an ounce for each of us each year— 11 times as much as in 1940.

I'll just have a third of a cup more. Four in 5 American adults drink coffee, and they average 3⅓ cups a day each.

Coffee accounted for 55 per cent of all the beverages we consumed in 1973, but by 1977 it accounted for only 46 per cent.

Instant and freeze-dried coffee make up 35 per cent of all coffee purchases.

A flood of quench. The average American drinks about a bottle of pop a day—to be precise, 359 12-ounce containers in 1977. That's 3 times as much as the average American drank in 1954, and twice as much as he or she drank in 1965.

Three out of 5 soft drinks downed by the average American are colas. Lemon-lime sodas, such as 7-Up, account for 12 per cent of sales. Orange and root beer are tied at about 3 per cent, and grape and ginger ale at 1.5 per cent each.

Of every 8 soft drinks drunk in America, 1 is a diet pop.

Three out of 5 sodas are purchased at grocery stores, and 1 out of 5 from vending machines. Two out of 5 sodas are in cans, 1 out of 5 is in a throwaway bottle, and 2 out of 5 are in returnables.

In 1879, the average American drank 3 bottles of pop.

Sweet and wet. A quarter of all the sweeteners we eat is in the soda pop we drink.

What red tastes like. The average person tends to taste with his or her eyes as well as taste buds. When researchers added red coloring to a lemon-flavored drink, people generally said it tasted like strawberry. The test was expanded to include drinks flavored orange, strawberry, grape, and blueberry, and colored yellow, orange, red, purple, and blue.

When colors and flavors matched, 72 per cent of the tasters identified the flavor correctly. But when colors didn't match flavors, the tasters were fooled 78 per cent of the time.

In another experiment, a white wine colored to resemble rosé was called "sweeter" by tasters than the same wine uncolored.

Milk through a straw. In the school lunchroom, the average child drinks 86 per cent of her or his milk. The rest is thrown away.

Including both authors of this book. One in 5 American men drinks at least 5 cups of coffee a day.

Bottled trickle. Commercial bottled water is drunk in 1 U.S. household in 500. All told, each American drinks 1.8 gallons of it each year, on average. The Perrier invasion notwithstanding, only 3 per cent of it is imported.

Just one cup. The average American cut his or her coffee consumption by 25 per cent after prices suddenly zoomed in 1976, and still hasn't returned to the old level.

Good to the last drop. One in 3 cups of coffee brewed by Americans is made from General Foods products—Maxwell House and Sanka, mostly. So are half the cups of instant coffee we drink. Maxim is General Foods' big instant brand.

Something to think about when you can't sleep. The average cup of brewed coffee contains about 85 milligrams of caffeine—just 15 milligrams less than a No-Doz pill. Instant coffee has about 60 milligrams, and espresso averages 150.

A cup of hot tea has about 38 milligrams of caffeine. (Iced tea has more.) A cup of cocoa has 50 milligrams.

A Coke or a Tab has 24 milligrams of caffeine. A Pepsi or a Diet Pepsi has 18. Royal Crown and Diet Rite average 21. Dr. Pepper beats them all with 32.

Does this give you a headache? Excedrin, Anacin, Dristan, and Sinarest each have about 30 milligrams of caffeine.

All these figures are from the *American Journal of Clinical Nutrition*.

Breast versus bottle. According to the National Institute of Mental Health, a study of 200 children in Oakland, California, showed that the average baby is better off bottle-fed than breast-fed if his or her mother lacks a warm personality.

The Hard Stuff

The average American drinker. In the words of the National Institute on Alcohol Abuse and Alcoholism, here's what the average American *drinker* drank in 1970:

"The average drinker . . . consumed 3.93 U.S. gallons of absolute alcohol. This allows, for one drinker, about 44 fifths of whiskey; or 98 bottles of fortified wine; or 157 bottles of table wine; or 928 bottles of beer. Or, for a drinker with eclectic tastes, about 12 fifths of whiskey plus 15 bottles of sherry plus 30 bottles of table wine plus 350 bottles of beer.

"The average may also be calculated as a little over 3 ounces of whiskey a day, or the equivalent in other beverages—for example, 1 cocktail, 1 glass of wine, and a bottle of beer a day."

Youth at the Bar

Underage. One 12- or 13-year-old boy in 4 is a moderate drinker—that is, he has a drink a week, or 2 drinks 3 times a month, or 5 drinks once a month.

Two out of 3 young men age 18 to 20 drink that much. After age 17, only 1 boy in 5 drinks infrequently or not at all.

One girl in 5 age 12 or 13 drinks moderately, and nearly half the young women 18 or over do.

Alcohol goes to high school. Ninety-three per cent of male and 87 per cent of female high-school seniors have drunk alcoholic beverages, at least to try them.

Three fourths of American teen-agers drink at parties, and half of them drink in cars.

Have another, kid. On average, according to a Gallup poll, the parents least likely to restrict the drinking of their teen-age children are drinkers who went to college and live in the East or the Far West.

Where the drinkers are. College students are more likely to drink than anyone else. Four out of 5 drink, and on some campuses 92 out of 100 drink. The average college student has 400 drinks a year.

In a survey at the University of Delaware, 7 students in 10 said they had made a purchase in a liquor store within the past year.

The average college man said he drank on 107 days and spent at least $264 on the stuff. College women drank on 73 days, spending $133. Half of it went for beer.

An average night out at a bar cost the college man $5.70, and the college woman $3.25.

How much can you safely drink? In the nineteenth century, Francis Edmund Anstie, a fellow of the Royal College of Physicians and a student of alcohol's effects, devised this formula for figuring out how much the average drinker could consume without impairing his or her health. This was "Anstie's limit"—to be imbibed only with meals:

1.5 ounces of absolute alcohol per day, to be taken as:
   3 ounces of whiskey, well diluted; or
   a half bottle of table wine; or
   4 glasses of beer.

The National Institute on Alcohol Abuse and Alcoholism says, "In the absence of further evidence, the classical 'Anstie's limit' seems still to reflect the safe amount of drinking which does not substantially increase the risk of early death."

When you drink, don't walk. Not counting children under 18 and adults over 65, 3 out of 4 pedestrians hit by cars have been drinking.

Which wine. Among young adults who drink wine often, 17 per cent prefer Gallo, a marketing study shows.

The next most popular brands: Almaden, 9 per cent; Italian Swiss Colony and Paul Masson, 4 per cent each; Manischewitz, Mogen David, Boone's Farm, Christian Brothers, and Inglenook, 3 per cent each; Taylor, 2 per cent. Nineteen per cent preferred other brands, and 30 per cent couldn't name their brand.

Drinking customs. People on the East Coast are more likely to drink at parties or other special occasions. Southerners and Westerners tend to drink at home. Midwesterners drink equally at both places. City residents drink most at parties, rural residents at home, and suburbanites an equal amount at each. Relatively little booze is consumed at bars—9 per cent of all drinking is done in taverns and restaurants in the East and Midwest, even less elsewhere.

People on the West Coast and in New England drink more alcohol than other Americans.

People with less than an eighth-grade education are more likely to refuse a drink than anyone else. People with high incomes are more likely to drink than people with low incomes. As a group, farm owners have a lower proportion of drinkers than any other occupational class.

Moderate drinkers, as a class, live longer than abstainers and ex-drinkers. Heavy drinkers have the highest death rate of the three groups.

Alcoholism is a big problem. The National Institute on Alcohol Abuse and Alcoholism estimates that there are 9 million problem drinkers, that their problem affects the lives of 1 person in 6, that drinking is a factor in close to 30,000 highway deaths a year and that 20,000 of these deaths are caused by drivers with "ongoing drinking problems," that half the murders and a quarter of the suicides—11,700 deaths a year—are related to drinking, and that the whole problem represents an annual $15 billion drain on the economy—$10 billion in lost work time, $2 billion for the health and welfare of alcoholics and their families, and $3 billion in property damage, medical expenses, insurance costs, and the like.

A nice domestic, steward. California produces 85 per cent of the wine Americans drink. We drink 400 million gallons of wine a year—twice as much wine today as we did in 1967. But we still drink 16 times more soft drinks than wine.

California had 315,175 acres in wine grapes in 1977, and we Americans take almost every drop that California makes. Only 1.5 per cent is exported, and that includes wine shipped to Puerto Rico and other U.S. possessions, wine drunk on ships and aboard planes, and wine sent to commissaries and embassies overseas.

The Wine Institute says that half the wine California produced in 1967 went into appetizer and dessert wines, but now we drink like Europeans: Eighty per cent is table wine, drunk with the meal.

The Agriculture Department surveyed 7,000 households and found that 4 out of 10 of us didn't care for any wine, thank you.

About those abstainers: Nearly 40 per cent of them have a

beer now and then and 30 per cent also drink hard liquor. The rest don't take alcohol in any form.

Mr. Drunk, meet Mrs. Moderate. Here, from the National Institute on Alcohol Abuse and Alcoholism, is the "profile analysis" of the Americans most likely and those least likely to have an alcohol problem.

Our heavy drinker is a man, separated from his wife but not divorced. He's mostly a *beer* drinker, and he has no religious affiliation. Ask him about drunkenness and he's likely to say things like this: "Drunkenness is usually not a sign of social irresponsibility," and "Drunkenness is usually a sign of just having fun."

Our American least likely to have a drinking problem is a woman. She's Jewish, over 50 years old, has a graduate degree, and lives in the rural South. She drinks mostly wine, and she's either married or a widow. What she says about drunkenness is not recorded.

The 2-month hangover. Americans drink almost as much hard liquor in December as in the next 2 months combined.

If the year were rearranged with the heavy-drinking months first, the calendar would reel along in this order:

December, November, June, March, October, September, April, August, May, July, January, February.

A dry statistic. Three out of 4 adult Americans drink.

Six-pack America

Beer, to go. Half the adults in America drink beer. On the average summer day, 29 per cent of them will have a beer. On the average winter day, 21 per cent will.

The average beer drinker is not too loyal to a single brand. Market researchers say 45 per cent of beer buyers buy a particular brand more than others, but switch from brand to brand from time to time. Only 1 in 4 buys the same brand every time. The rest are more interested in price than label, or buy any brand they recognize.

Men buy most beer, except in supermarkets. Women tend to buy their husbands' brand. About 44 per cent of beer is purchased cold. Most beer drinkers buy some every week. Half of what they buy goes directly into the refrigerator, not the pantry.

The typical customer who prefers cans will switch brands before switching to bottles. The typical customer who prefers bottles will switch brands before switching to cans.

Choice malting barley. Each year, the brewers of America use more than half a bushel of choice malting barley for every man, woman, and child in the nation. That's enough for 56 billion 12-ounce bottles or cans of their golden fluid.

Where the beer goes. The typical Nevadan downs more beer than the average adult in any other state, according to the U.S. Brewers' Association. He or she drinks 605 12-ounce beers a year, more than twice as much as the typical Arkansan.

Here are the ranking states for consumption and eschewal of beer:

The most	The amount (per capita)	The least	The amount (per capita)
Nevada	605 beers	Arkansas	265 beers
New Hampshire	543 beers	West Virginia	275 beers
Wyoming	522 beers	Alabama	286 beers
Wisconsin	520 beers	Utah	294 beers
New Mexico	494 beers	North Carolina	302 beers

When'll you have it? Beer drinkers are most likely to drink beer in the early evening, after supper.

How'll you have it? The average beer drinker is most likely to take it direct from the can or bottle when outdoors, and poured into a glass when indoors. But 24 per cent of beer drinkers drink it both ways, both places.

The conglomerated brew. Americans drink more beer than ever, but it comes from fewer places. Between 1933, when Prohibition ended, and 1978, when only 44 of them were left, brewing companies disappeared at an average of nearly 16 a year.

In 1968, the 5 largest brewing companies produced half the beer drunk in this country. Ten years later they produced 7 beers in 10.

The disappearing draft. The average American drinks 9 cans or bottles of beer for every draft brew.

When you're having more than one. During the summer, 40 per cent of all beer drinkers drink 75 per cent of all the beer drunk. In the winter, the heavy drinkers—those who down 2 bottles or more a day—account for 35 per cent of the beer drinkers and 70 per cent of the beer drunk.

Seventy-seven per cent of the 2-bottles-or-more crowd are men. According to marketing researchers for the American Can Company, they tend "to be people who like the taste of beer unreservedly, on any occasion, at any time and place, in cold or hot weather."

People who drink less beer tend to have snacks with it. Heavy beer drinkers take it straight.

The booze gap. The people of only two countries—the Soviet Union and Poland—outdrink Americans. In the United States, the equivalent of 5.8 liters of 100-proof alcohol is drunk per person per year. The Russians drink 14.8 liters, and the Poles, 6.8. West Germans drink 5.5, Swedes and Yugoslavs 5.2, East Germans and Spaniards 5.

The people's choice. Based on sales popularity, this is what the average liquor buyer is most likely to have on the shelves of his or her bar at home:

BLEND: Seagram's 7 Crown, the most popular spirit in America
VODKA: Smirnoff
RUM: Bacardi
CANADIAN: Canadian Club
BOURBON: Jim Beam
GIN: Gordon's
SCOTCH: J&B

Three-martini lunches. Several years ago, 528 executives from the country's biggest companies were asked about their drinking habits. Only 1 in 14 drank less than once a month. Half were moderate drinkers. One in 6 worried that he or she was "doing too much drinking."

What these folks need is a good stiff drink. According to the National Institute on Alcohol Abuse and Alcoholism, the average American who doesn't drink has "a somewhat gloomier perspective than others on life in general."

Harvey, the winner. Here's how it goes on the vodka-drink front. For every 1 white russian, 1 vodka collins, 3 bloody marys, 3 black russians, and 6 screwdrivers that the average young American drinks, he or she drinks 13 harvey wallbangers.

Your old granddad couldn't leave it alone. The average American today drinks only half as much hard liquor as the typical American drank in 1850.

Drinking demographics. In cities and suburbs, 1 of every 8 adults drinks pretty heavily. In small towns, only 1 in 11 drinks that much. In rural areas, only 1 in 13 rates the heavy-drinking label.

The truth about bourbon. Here is what the folks down at Marketing know about the young bourbon drinker.

Fifty-five per cent of the men and 45 per cent of the women aged 25 to 34 have had a bourbon, or a drink containing bourbon, within the past year. Those who drink it more often than that tend to be white-collar high-earners, on the younger side of that age group, and southern, by golly.

Eleven per cent of those who drink it drink it frequently. Of them, 11 per cent drink it straight, 13 per cent drink it on the rocks, and 76 per cent drink it with a mixer.

Of those who use a mixer, 28 per cent say they mix their bourbon with a cola, 27 per cent with Sprite or 7-Up, 24 per cent with water, 7 per cent with ginger ale, 6 per cent in sours (mostly women), 1 per cent in old fashioneds, and 7 per cent some other way. Water is the mixer of choice in the Northeast, colas in the South.

Blue-collar straight-bourbon drinkers outnumber white-collar straight-bourbon drinkers by nearly 3 to 1. Men here outnumber women, but just marginally.

Booze and religion. On average, you are more likely to be a heavy drinker if you are a:

Catholic rather than a liberal Protestant
Liberal Protestant rather than a Jew
Jew rather than a conservative Protestant.

When to cut loose. The average American drinks less than usual with relatives, neighbors, and church acquaintances, and more than usual with close friends.

Like Gatsby, like son. On average, the higher your social class, the more you drink. So says the United States Government.

Puts hair on your chest. On average, a man in America is 3 times as likely to be a heavy drinker as a woman is.

The average American man does his heaviest drinking between the ages of 18 and 20, and again in his late 30s. The average American woman drinks the most in her 20s.

11 Wheels

Getting there by all means. The average American travels 8,080 miles a year.

Of those 8,080 miles of travel, the average American drives 3,899 miles and rides in cars 2,917 miles. He or she rides 8 miles in taxis, 513 miles in trucks, including pickups, 191 miles in buses, another 210 miles in school buses, 56 miles in subways or elevated trains, and 66 miles in other trains.

He or she flies 200 miles in airplanes, and rides a motorcycle 11 miles.

That adds up to 8,071 miles. The other 9 miles are unaccounted for. Could he or she possibly have *walked?*

Time for a drive. The average drive in America is 8.9 miles.

The average drive to work is 9.4 miles, and the average drive for business related to the job is 16.1 miles.

The average drive to the doctor or dentist is 8.4 miles. For shopping, the average is 4.4 miles, and for other kinds of family business it's 6.5 miles.

The average drive to visit friends or relatives is 12 miles, and the average pleasure ride is 20 miles.

All these figures are one-way.

Breaking down the odometer. On average, every 99 miles of car travel includes 42 miles to earn a living, 33 miles for social and recreational purposes, 19 miles for errands and other family business, and 5 miles for educational, civic, or religious travel.

Fill it up. The average car in America burns either 709 or 789 gallons of gasoline a year, depending upon whether you ask the auto industry (709) or the government (789).

City and country. Of every 100 miles the average American drives, 58 miles are in the city and 42 are in the country.

Going places. The average car is driven 12,000 miles a year.

I'll take a blue one. Based on sales of 1977 models, the average family buying a new car is more likely to pick a medium-blue model if the car is full or intermediate in size, but leans toward medium red for a compact.

Next most popular colors for full and intermediate-size cars are, in order, silver gray, white, medium red, and brown. For compacts, it's silver gray, medium blue, white, and brown.

Carpool savings. Back in 1976, when gasoline cost $.61 a gallon, it cost the average commuter $500 to drive to work alone in a subcompact car and $750 in a standard-sized car. That's for a 20-mile round trip every workday, and includes a prorated share of the car's maintenance and depreciation.

By carpooling with just 1 other person, the commuter in the subcompact would save $224. The commuter in the standard car would save $337.

So figures the U. S. Department of Transportation.

Lonesome drivers. The average American drives half the time alone, and half the time with a passenger or 2.

Instant recall. For every new car sold in the United States in 1977, 1.1 cars (of all model years) were recalled to fix safety defects. That's right—more were recalled than sold!

Taken to the cleaners at the garage. About $455 is spent each year to repair the average American car. The National Highway Traffic Safety Administration estimates that two fifths of that goes for unnecessary or fraudulent repairs.

It's OK, it's covered. In an average year, about 1 out of every 8 new cars is damaged enough to prompt a collision-insurance claim. For new 1978 models, the average claim was $790.

The cost of coverage. The average American family spends $2.33 of every $100 of income on auto-insurance premiums.

Driveaholics. In response to a Gallup poll, 36 per cent of drivers said that they sometimes drive after drinking, and 18 per cent said that they had, at least once, driven when too drunk to drive safely.

Most of those were men. In fact, 26 per cent of the males said that they had driven while drunk. Only 8 per cent of women made a similar confession.

Let me see your driver's license, Bub. The average driver's license in America costs just under $2.00 a year, and 2 of every 3 Americans have one.

In every state, the license shows your name, address, birthdate, signature, the license expiration date, and restrictions on what sort of vehicle you can drive. Most states also include your sex, weight, height, and eye color, but only 18 list the color of your hair. In 44 states, your license shows your picture, 43 of them in color. The driver's license in 21 states shows your Social Security number, and in 28 states it also says—conveniently—whether you automatically donate your organs for transplant when you die.

It's a nice day for a drive. The average American uses a car most often in the spring, drives the most miles in the summer, and drives the fewest miles in the winter.

The tune-up. Three car owners in 4 get a tune-up for the family car at least once a year. In New England, where the winters are rough, 94 in 100 do. According to a survey by the Champion Spark Plug people, 35 per cent of tune-ups are do-it-yourself-in-the-driveway jobs.

Champion tested 216 cars that needed tune-ups. It said that tune-ups improved fuel economy by 11 per cent, and reduced carbon-monoxide emissions by 45 per cent and hydrocarbon emissions by 55 per cent at idle.

The average tune-up in 1977 cost $47.13, but do-it-your-selfers spent an average of only $16, all on parts.

Long lonesome highway? There are 29 cars for every mile of highway in America. There are 57 Americans for every mile of roads, streets, and highways. For every mile of interstate highway in the United States, there are 17 miles of dirt and gravel road.

The auto business. The average new-car dealer sells 383 cars a year.

Well, it worked for Dillinger. A stolen getaway car is used in 43 per cent of bank holdups.

Let's talk cars. For everyone who buys a new car in America, 3 people buy a used car.

According to the Hertz people, a 3-year-old car that's been driven 10,000 miles a year costs about half as much to run as it did during its first 3 years. It may not have been Simonized, but it's been amortized.

One car in 8 is traded in after a year's use.

Another car in 7 is traded after 2 years.

Nearly a fifth of all cars are traded in the third year.

One car in 7 is traded in during its fourth year of operation.

Four cars in 10 are still on the road 10 years after they were made.

How long we keep our cars. The average car on American roads is 6.2 years old. The average car traded in for a new model is 4.3 to 4.6 years old.

Wha'ddya driving that heap for? In 1978, 53 per cent of the cars on the road were over 5 years old. It was only 47 per cent in 1968.

Starts the minute you drive it away. Cars depreciate an average of 25 per cent the first year, 15 per cent the second year, and 10 per cent the third year.

Buy in January; sell in November. On average, according to the National Automobile Dealers' Association, used cars are cheapest in January and most expensive in November. They are also cheap in August and February.

Loaded. Nineteen out of 20 American cars are made with automatic transmissions. Nine out of 10 have power steering and power brakes.

Four out of 5 are air conditioned, and 4 out of 5 have steel-belted radials.

Here are the percentages of 1977 American cars that included these other options:

Vinyl roof	48%
Stereo tape player	14%
Stereo AM/FM radio	30%
Mono AM/FM radio	13%
AM only radio	34%
Power door locks	25%
Power seats	21%
Power windows	27%
Sun roof	3%
Clock	46%
Adjustable steering column	41%
Cruise control	33%
Rear-window defogger	35%
Bucket seats	19%

Car Costs. On average, if you bought a new, standard model car in 1967 and drove it for 10 years, it cost you $11,024.45, which averages out to just over $.11 a mile for 100,000 miles.

That includes everything—the price of the car, gas, oil, insurance, parking, repairs, taxes, tolls, etc.

For a '72 model, the average cost would be $13,552.95, or $.13 a mile. For a '74 model, it would be $15,892.36, or just under $.16 a mile. For a '76 model, it would be $17,878.96, just under $.18 a mile.

You need a tune-up, mister. By far the most frequent car repairs are replacement of spark plugs, oil changes, oil-filter changes, and grease jobs.

Next in order of frequency are brake jobs, wheel balancing, tire repairs, new transmission fluid, tune-ups, new air filters, new belts, battery recharges, wheel cylinder jobs, new shock absorbers, new headlights, new radiator hoses, front-end alignments, new mufflers, new thermostats, air-conditioner jobs, new water pumps, new universal joints, radiator repairs, new starters, and new ball joints.

Ain't she a beaut? Here, according to the National Automobile Dealers' Association, is what the average new car sold for in these years:

1968	$3,240	1974	$4,390
1969	$3,400	1975	$4,750
1970	$3,430	1976	$5,450
1971	$3,730	1977	$6,120
1972	$3,690	1978	$6,470
1973	$3,930		

Men drive more. Although the average American driver drives 8,686 miles a year, distances vary a lot by sex and age.

The average male driver drives 11,352 miles, more than twice as much as the average woman driver's 5,411.

Male drivers drive the most—14,496 miles a year—between the ages of 30 and 34. The average woman driver reaches her peak a bit later: 6,232 miles a year between the ages of 35 and 39.

Teen-agers and senior citizens drive the least. The average is

4,633 miles a year for teen-age drivers, 4,644 miles for drivers 70 and older.

There are more male drivers than female drivers, but the women are gaining fast. Read on.

Who drives? A few more men (53.8 per cent) than women (46.2 per cent), according to the Federal Highway Administration.

Here's a breakdown by age:

Under 20	9%
20 to 34	37%
35 to 49	24%
50 to 64	20%
65 and older	10%

The car–people ratio. For every 10 cars bought in the United States in recent years, only 7 old ones have been scrapped. This leads to a diminishing car-to-people ratio, to wit:

Year	Persons per car
1910	202
1920	13
1930	6
1940	5.2
1950	4.1
1960	3.2
1965	2.8
1970	2.5
1972	2.3
1974	2.16
1976	2.09
1977	2.02
1978	1.9

Projected by the National Automobile Dealers' Association:

2000	1.4

Stop and go. Three out of 5 car trips in America are less than 5 miles. Only 2 in 25 are over 21 miles.

The auto gap. There is 1 car for every 25 people in Mexico, 1 for every 18 in Brazil, 1 for every 6 in Japan, 1 for every 37 in Hong Kong, and 1 for every 23,378 in China.

Statistically, the average Russian has to share a car with 85 others. There is a car for every 3 people in Switzerland, Sweden, West Germany, and France, and a car for every 4 in Britain, Austria, Belgium, Iceland, Denmark, Italy, Norway, and Holland.

The Communist country with the most wheels seems to be East Germany, with a car for every 8 people.

No wonder the bus is so crowded. There is a motorcycle for every 43 people in America, a bus for every 4,098, and a private plane for every 1,187.

You can't tell it by the traffic. There are 5 people for every car in New York City, but only 2 people for every car in Los Angeles. In fact, no other big city comes close to New York for scarcity of cars relative to population. Pittsburgh is second, with 2.4 people for every car.

In Dallas, there are only 1.8 people for every car.

We just can't afford it. For every American who buys a Cadillac, 5 buy a Ford and 6 buy a Chevy.

Who makes what you drive. Of every 1,000 new cars sold in America in 1978

General Motors made 476
Ford made 228
Chrysler made 101
American Motors made 16
And 179 were imports.

In 1979, 220 of every 1,000 new cars sold in America were imports.

And you think you got a good deal. According to *Money* magazine, auto dealers average a profit of $600 on each new car they sell.

The payments aren't bad. The average loan for a new car in 1977 was $5,561. For a used car, it was $2,823.

Driving frenzy. The average American family with 2 or 3 cars drives each of them more miles than the average one-car family drives its car.

The average car bought new is driven more than the average car bought used. In fact, the newer a car, the more it's driven, on average.

More MPG. A car with manual transmission will get 2 to 5 more miles per gallon than the same model with automatic transmission, on average. Air conditioning will eat up as much as 4 more mpg.

It didn't come cheap. Because of government regulations, the average new 1979-model American car gets 36 per cent better mileage than the average 1974 model; 1985 models must get 100 per cent more. Auto exhaust emissions have also been reduced four fifths.

The average 1977 Ford weighed 4,100 pounds. The average 1985 Ford will weigh 1,000 pounds less. So says Ford Motor Company.

Diesel hardly pays. According to the AAA, the average diesel car has to be driven 100,000 miles to get back in fuel savings the extra cost of buying a diesel in the first place.

Drive on, he said. Back when gasoline cost about $.65 a gallon, business executives were asked how high the price of gasoline would have to go before they would quit driving to work. The average answer was $2.08 a gallon.

One in 5 said he or she would continue driving no matter what the price of gas.

Your move is a gamble. Reports filed with the Interstate Commerce Commission by the country's 20 largest moving companies on 452,588 moves in 1978 show:

Your chances of getting an underestimate of 10 per cent or more of the cost of the move are 22 in 100.

But your chances of getting an *overestimate* of 10 per cent or more are even greater—28 in 100.

Nearly 18 moves in 100 result in a damage claim for $50 or more.

Seven shipments in 100 are delivered a few days later than promised, and another 6 are more than 5 days late.

Which government department do you believe? Forty-two per cent of American kids walk or ride their bikes to school, and 38 per cent ride a school bus. About 14 per cent get a ride, 2 per cent drive, and 3 per cent take public transportation.

That's from a study by the U. S. Department of Transportation. Just down Independence Avenue, the folks at the U. S. Department of Health and Human Services did their own study, and announced that 55 of every 100 schoolchildren ride a bus. In 1976, it cost an average of $104.22 to transport each of them, the Department said.

The school bus is safer. A child is at least 9 times safer on the school bus than in the family car.

There is 1 school bus in America for every 126 schoolchildren.

Foot power. Fifteen per cent of the average person's travel time is spent walking or riding a bicycle.

Farewell, choo-choo. Nearly 2 out of 3 U.S. communities have no rail service at all, not even freight.

Flying your own. Based on membership in the Aircraft Owners' and Pilots' Association, the average private pilot is 44, has a management or professional job, and makes $40,377 a year He or she flies 115 hours a year, mostly for pleasure.

And don't forget to take your shots. About 1 American in 15 has a passport. Six passport applicants in 10 say they are going to Europe. One in 4 plans to visit Germany.

Staying the night. Thirty per cent of the people who stay in hotels and motels account for 68 per cent of all visits. Sixty-eight per cent of these frequent visitors (those making 6 or more ho-tel/motel visits a year) are on business. Fifty per cent of them stay more than a night at a time. Seventy-seven per cent stay in a motel rather than a hotel. Sixty-eight per cent of them are men.

People who stay in a hotel or motel less than that are more likely to be women, and to be traveling on pleasure, not business.

Here's why people pick one hotel/motel over another:

Its appearance	66%
Its convenient location	50%
Its name or reputation	33%
Its reasonable rates	25% (nearly twice as important with vacationing guests as with business-trip guests)
Its quietness	9%
Its swimming pool	9%
Its type of beds	8%
Its good service	6%
Its TV/radio	5%

And when people are asked why they've come back to a place they've lodged in before, the place's cleanliness is mentioned first by 57 per cent of those responding.

What gripes guests. Mostly poor service. The next most frequent complaint is about the bathroom. Guests say there weren't enough towels, the bars of soap were too small, there were no washcloths, or no bathmats, and the plumbing made noise or didn't perform well.

Other frequent grounds for complaint: lack of cleanliness, including that stale, hotel smell; noise; uncomfortable temperature; the bad restaurant; the lack of an ice machine; the lumpy bed; the malfunctioning TV.

Seven guests in 10 have some complaint, but they don't all speak up.

Leave the driving to them. The average American rode 117 miles on intercity buses in 1977. For every 1 who rode Amtrak, 19 rode an intercity bus, like Greyhound or Trailways. For every 2 Americans who flew, 3 took the bus.

For every American city or town served by commercial airlines, 21 are served by bus. For every city or town served by passenger trains, 30 are served by bus.

The average bus passenger is older and poorer than the average Amtrak or airline passenger. Two out of 3 airline passengers are men; 3 out of 5 bus passengers are women. Ever wonder how many of your fellow passengers are on personal or family trips rather than business trips? It's 88 per cent on the bus, 84 per cent in private cars, 70 per cent on the train, and 50 per cent in the air.

People per gallon. A government study says 1 gallon of fuel (gas or diesel) can move

270 to 360 railroad passengers 1 mile
282 bus passengers 1 mile
112 passengers in subcompact cars 1 mile
72 luxury-car passengers 1 mile.

Going. The government's National Travel Survey finds that between January and April, the average American traveler takes 2.2 trips, is away from home 7.6 nights, and travels 1,494 miles. Eight times in 10 he or she travels by car or truck. Three times in 10 he or she is going to a convention.

Fun City. For every person who lives in New York City, 2 others visit in an average year.

One of every 9 visitors to New York is from overseas. One of every 5 is attending a convention. New York hosts 840 conventions a year. The average convention delegate spends between $150 and $200.

New York has 39 taxicabs for every square mile, 1 skyscraper for every 67 miles of city streets (6,400 miles of streets and 95 skyscrapers, at last count), and 1 restaurant for every 5 hotel rooms.

Consult your travel agent. One airline ticket in 2 is sold through a travel agent.

There'd better be an airport there. The average airline passenger, here and abroad, travels 829 miles in a typical flight, at 370 miles per hour, with 84 fellow passengers in the plane.

Oh, let's drive. The average American would rather go by car. When a pollster asked people what means of transportation they'd prefer for a 100-mile trip, 56 per cent chose cars, 28 per cent airplanes, 8 per cent buses, and 6 per cent trains.

The Naderized American

Underbuckled. According to a Gallup poll, 4 out of 5 Americans on the road at any given time are not wearing seat belts.

The safest way to go. Railroads, with an average of 0.1 fatality per 1 billion passenger miles, are by far the safest way to travel. In 1977, according to the National Transportation Safety Board, commercial airlines averaged 0.4 death per billion miles. The rate was 33 for automobiles and taxis.

Wrecks versus war. Anyone living in the United States from 1900 through 1976 was 3 times as likely to be killed in a car wreck as in a war.

Auto wrecks. Americans drive 1 trillion, 400 billion miles a year.
   Every 33 million miles, someone is killed.
   You are statistically almost twice as likely to be killed in a car wreck in a rural area as in an urban area. But you are twice as likely to be injured in an urban accident.

As far as fatal accidents go, you are 4 times safer on a turnpike than on the average rural road. Your safest turnpikes include the Audubon Parkway and the Purchase Parkway in Kentucky, the Dallas North Tollway in Texas, the Maine Turnpike, Florida's turnpike and toll roads, and the Hutchinson River Parkway in New York.

According to the National Safety Council, the only turnpike more dangerous than rural roads is the West Virginia Turnpike.

Slower. Two out of 3 American drivers drive slower than they used to as a result of the 55-mile-per-hour speed limit.

On the highway, a majority of drivers exceed the 55-mph limit, but the percentage varies from state to state. According to the U. S. Department of Transportation, only 35 per cent of drivers in Virginia drive over 55, while in Missouri and New Mexico 74 per cent of drivers exceed the limit. In Texas, 16 per cent of cars on the highway are going over 65.

The truth about woman drivers. According to various studies, the average woman driver takes fewer risks than the typical male driver. She drives more slowly through pedestrian crossings, and is less likely to run a red light. She yields the right-of-way to a man driver twice as often as he yields it to her, but is less likely than a man to yield to a motorcycle.

Thanks, America. On average, you're safer driving in the United States than in any other country in the world. Our highway death rate is less than half what it is in many countries, including Belgium, France, West Germany, Italy, Holland, and Japan.

Better drive a truck. Of every 100 people killed in collisions between cars and heavy trucks, 97 of them are in the cars.

You never know when. For every hundred miles you drive you face 1 chance in 303,030 of being killed in a wreck. The risk was almost 5 times as great 50 years ago, but people didn't drive so much back then.

Give that car a wide berth. The more often a driver has been convicted of a traffic offense, the more likely he or she is to have an accident. The driver with 9 or more traffic convictions in the past 3 years is 9 times as likely to have a wreck as is the driver with no convictions during those 3 years.

All this was worked out in a study by the California Department of Motor Vehicles.

Compared with the driver who had no convictions during the past 3 years, the driver with 1 conviction in that period is almost twice as likely to have an accident, and the driver with 2 convictions is almost 3 times as likely to have an accident.

Where Americans go. Of every 99 Americans who take a trip abroad:

- 53 go to Canada
- 12 go to Mexico
- 2 go to Austria
- 1 goes to Ireland
- 2 go to Italy
- 4 go to France
- 4 go to West Germany
- 10 go to the Caribbean or Central America
- 2 go to South America
- 2 go to Israel
- 7 go to Britain

Conventional American. The average delegate to the average convention spends $50 a day, although auto dealers and Kiwanians spend more than Adventists and librarians. If all the conventions held in America were spaced out evenly over the calendar, half a million of us would be off to a convention at any given time.

Bring a camera and a pair of good walking shoes. The most popular activities at national parks, in order, are sightseeing, pleasure driving, walking around to look at nature and taking pictures of it, picnicking, swimming, camping, hiking, and back-packing.

Yes, we have a room. On an average day, the average hotel or motel is three quarters full.

Shall we see the Amazon, walk on the moon, or ride the roller coaster? More than 69 million people visit America's 30 busiest theme parks in a typical year.

If you count each admission as a separate person, Disneyland and Disney World alone attract 1 of every 9 Americans every year.

Mpg/mph. Driving faster doesn't *always* increase your gas consumption. When the government tested 13 cars, it found that 7 of them got better mileage at 40 mph than at 30. Three did better at 50 than at 40.

The cars ranged in weight from 2,050 to 4,880 pounds, and were driven with the air conditioning off. Here's what happened to the average car in this experiment:

Speed	30	40	50	60	70
Mpg	21.05	21.07	19.49	17.51	14.93

Increase in gas consumption as speed increased:

30 to 40	40 to 50	50 to 60	60 to 70
0%	8.11%	11.31%	17.28%

Lots of reasons, Mac. When asked what keeps them from spending more time at federal recreational areas, Americans said they didn't have the time, didn't like the crowds, couldn't afford it, didn't know much about it, and had other fish to fry.

Those were the reasons cited most often, in order.

Fill her up for her. Women are behind the wheel of 2 out of every 5 cars pulling into gas stations. One car in 4 is registered in a woman's name.

Flights of fancy. In a poll, people were asked where would they go if they had the time and money. The United Kingdom was the first choice of 13 per cent of Americans. Italy was first for 10 per cent.

With the exception of the residents of the Benelux countries, who'd rather see Spain, Europeans' leading choice was the U.S.A. Nineteen per cent put America first.

In Latin America, 13 per cent said they most wanted to see the Yanquis up North, except for Brazilians, who put France and Italy first.

Sub-Sahara Africans chose the United Kingdom first and America second. Far Easterners also wanted to see America first, with Japan their second choice. The Japanese wanted to see the United States most, Switzerland next.

Do you get good mileage? In 1978, the average car got 14.06 miles per gallon, according to the Highway Users' Federation. Motorcycles averaged 50 miles a gallon, commercial buses 5, school buses 7.35, one-piece trucks 10.1, and combination trucks 5.4.

Whoosh. U.S. airliners fly at an average speed of 406 miles an hour on domestic flights and 484 miles an hour on international flights.

Uncle Sam on wheels. The federal government owns 1 vehicle for every 6 people it employs.

Look at those young singles go! According to *The Travel Agent* magazine, young singles take 3 times more pleasure trips, go farther, and spend 60 per cent more on vacation than other adults. Young singles are 3 times more likely to go abroad, too. The average young single vacationer, male or female, is more likely to search out beautiful beaches than any other feature.

One in 8 young singles vacations with a member of the opposite sex.

The Commuting American

They tell us to ride the bus, but we don't. Of every 10 bread-winners in America, about 7 get to work by driving their own cars. Of those who commute more than 60 miles round trip, 4 in 10 drive.

And no wonder. The person who takes public transportation to the job takes twice as long to get there as the commuter who drives, even when both work the same distance from home.

And: Whether you're driving or taking public transportation, the closer you are to work, the slower the going. People who live 20 miles from work average 34 mph in making the trip. Those 10 miles away average 21 mph. Those five miles away average only 16 mph.

If you live in a city, you are 5 times more likely to ride public transportation to work than if you live in the suburbs. One city resident in 12 and 1 suburbanite in 16 walks to work.

Only 1 person in 200 goes to work by cab.

Please have exact change. In 1977, the average American commuter paid $.38 a ride for public transit. He or she paid $.56 to ride the ferry boat, $.48 to take the subway or elevated, $.35 to ride the bus, and $.28 to ride the trolley.

What did he or she get in return? Well, the average ride was 5 miles on the ferry, 7 miles on the subway or elevated, 5 miles on the bus, and 4 miles on the trolley.

To get the folks where they were going, the average transit employee was paid $14,885.

We'll be there in 3 hours, kids. The typical vacation trip by auto in America is 160 miles, 1 way. On average, there are 3.4 people in the car.

Let's go. Nearly 2 of every 3 Americans took at least 1 trip of 100 miles or more in 1977. Of those who did, the average traveler went on 4.9 trips, spent 19 nights away from home, and traveled 3,330 miles.

About 4 of every 5 trips were by car or truck. Another 15 per cent were by airplane, and 4.5 per cent were by train or bus.

One trip in 3 was just for the weekend. One traveler out of every 25 took camping equipment along.

As for the reasons people travel:

Visits to relatives and friends	31%
Business	29%
Conventions	3%
Outdoor recreation	11%
Sightseeing	4%
Personal or family affairs	10%
Shopping or medical	3%

Our glorious national parks. There are more visits to our national parks, national battlefields, and national monuments than there are people in our country—262,603,433 visits a year, or 1.2 visits for every man, woman, and child in America.

The average visitor stays 4 hours, 24 minutes.

One visitor of every 15 spends the night. Of course, you can't spend the night at the Lincoln Memorial or the White House. But more than half the visitors spend the night at Yellowstone and Yosemite. One of every 13 spends the night at Acadia National Park in Maine, and one of every 4 sleeps over at Glacier National Park in Montana. It's 1 of every 3 at Grand Canyon and 1 of every 6 at Shenandoah National Park in Virginia.

More than half of the overnight visitors are campers. Of the campers, 57 per cent sleep in RV's (recreational vehicles) and 43 per cent in tents.

On average, the Park Service spends $1.01 on every visitor. The cost is $.30 at Acadia, $.68 at Grand Teton in Wyoming, $.94 at Shenandoah, $1.08 at the Statue of Liberty, $2.25 at Yosemite, $2.74 at Yellowstone, and $3.37 at Everglades in Florida.

On an average July day at Yellowstone, there are 7,791 campers, who generate 27 tons of trash. There is an act of vandalism every 43 hours, causing an average of $34 in damage.

Here's how many people visited some of our parks in 1977:

Great Smoky Mountains (North Carolina and Tennessee)	11,621,606
Hot Springs (Arkansas)	5,152,047
Grand Teton (Wyoming)	3,973,462
Acadia (Maine)	3,181,269
Shenandoah (Virginia)	3,055,000
Grand Canyon (Arizona)	2,848,519
Yosemite (California)	2,535,846
Yellowstone (Idaho, Montana, and Wyoming)	2,487,084
Mammoth Cave (Kentucky)	1,979,351
Hawaii Volcanoes	1,816,836

Neighbors of the grizzlies and the geysers. Half the people who visit national parks, national forests, and other government lands live so close that they're there just for the day. A quarter of the visitors are more than 8 hours from home, and the other quarter are somewhere in between.

Europe on $35.83 a day. Of the 4.1 million Americans who went to Europe in 1978, the average stayed 20 days and spent $35.83 per day.

All aboard! On Amtrak trains, the average commuter rides 40 miles and the noncommuting passenger rides 269 miles. Combine them and you'll find that the average Amtrak passenger is on board for 214 miles.

Devil-may-care on the road. When vacationing American motorists at 21 popular vacation areas were asked whether they had made unscheduled stops en route, three quarters said that yes, they had visited places and done things they hadn't planned on before leaving home. One in 8 said that he or she didn't have a trip plan at all upon leaving home. And a survey of 736 campers on the Maine coast showed that 38 per cent made the decision to go camping less than 6 hours before leaving home.

12 Having Fun

Outside pep. In a survey, adults were asked what sort of physical activity they do on a regular basis. Here's what we say we do.

Of every 100 Americans:

22	walk for exercise	2	ice skate
17	swim	2	play badminton
14	do calisthenics	2	do yoga
13	bicycle	2	sail
13	bowl	2	cross-country ski
11	jog	1	plays soccer
9	play tennis	1	participates in archery
7	play basketball	1	climbs mountains
7	hike	1	does gymnastics
6	play baseball	1	does karate
5	play golf	1	boxes
5	play volleyball	1	plays handball
4	play football	1	plays squash
4	toss a Frisbee	1	participates in track-and-field events
4	play table tennis	1	plays hockey
3	lift weights	1	wrestles
3	ski	1	does judo
3	water ski		
2	play racquetball		

What we do in the national forest. The National Forest system encompasses 187 million acres, or 37,443 square feet for each American.

Americans spend an average of 12 hours a year each in a National Forest—185 minutes camping, 29 minutes picnicking, 168 minutes in motorized recreation, 25 minutes boating, 18 minutes engaging in other water sports, 38 minutes in winter sports, 55 minutes fishing, 49 minutes hunting, 36 minutes hiking or mountain climbing, 10 minutes riding horseback, 4 minutes in nature study, and 103 minutes, the Forest Service says, "in a wide variety of other activities."

The Forest Service sold enough timber to provide every American with 50 board feet of it in fiscal 1978. One American in 414 collected free firewood from National Forests, taking an average of 5.6 board feet each. One salmon was caught in National Forest streams for every 8 Americans; 1 deer was taken for every 609 Americans; 1 elk per 2,731 Americans; 1 turkey for every 12,139 Americans; and 1 moose for each 97,111—hardly enough to go around.

One American in 1,515 started a forest fire in the National Forests, either carelessly or deliberately, in 1977.

America at the flicks. The average American goes to 5 movies a year.

But 27 per cent of Americans over age 12 go to the movies at least once a month, and these movie lovers account for 87 per cent of the total audience, according to the Motion Picture Association of America.

On the average day, 3 million people go to the movies. That's way down compared to the peak year of 1946, when 11 million went to the movies each day.

If everyone in America went to the movies at once, the average theater would be jammed with 13,017 people.

Thirty-five per cent of the adult public says it never or almost never goes to the movies.

What did we do before television? Several years ago, Gallup pollsters asked people to name their favorite leisure activity. Nearly half—46 per cent—named television.

You might think that television replaced radio as the national favorite. But when the same question was asked by Gallup in 1938, only 9 per cent named radio as their favorite activity. Reading ranked first, with 21 per cent naming it as their favorite.

Here are the results:

	Per cent of respondents naming it as their favorite leisure activity in	
	1938	*1974*
Reading	21%	14%
Movies and theater	17%	9%
Watching television	0%	46%
Dancing	12%	4%
Radio	9%	5%
Playing cards and games	9%	8%
Staying home with family	7%	10%
Visiting friends	4%	8%

Do not collect $200. People who own Monopoly sets play the game an average of 9 times a year, according to Parker Brothers.

Marijuana and friends. Half the people in America between the ages of 18 and 25 admit to having tried marijuana at least once, the government reports (although it spells it "marihuana").

One adult American in 4 has tried marijuana.

One in 10 smokes it regularly.

One kid in 4 aged 12 to 17 has tried marijuana.

In the older generation—people over 35—only 1 in 14 has smoked marijuana, but 40 per cent of those 26 to 34 have.

Virtually everyone knows someone who uses marijuana. According to the National Institute on Drug Abuse, "The experience of knowing someone who used marihuana is now pervasive in our society. Almost all young adults and 3 out of 4 youth reported knowing someone who had used marihuana, as did a majority of older adults."

Here are our drug preferences. Among Americans 12 and older, marijuana is used by 1 of every 11 persons. Leaving out people who take them on doctor's orders, stimulants such as amphetamines are used by 1 of every 95 persons 12 and older, cocaine by 1 of every 107, tranquilizers by 1 of every 122, sedatives such as barbiturates by 1 of every 155, and LSD and other hallucinogens by 1 of every 155.

One of every 2 Americans 12 and older drinks alcohol, and 1 of every 3 smokes cigarettes.

These figures are from the government, which counts as a "user" anyone who has taken the drug within the previous month.

Work versus play. Two working Americans of every 5 say they work too long, at the expense of play. One of every 12 says work leaves him or her too tired or irritated to enjoy any leisure activities, and 1 of every 59 says the pay is so lousy that he or she can't afford to have any fun.

One of every 9 has a different problem: His or her leisure activities interfere with work.

How to make 30 seconds last long. The average sports parachutist often freefalls—dropping without her or his parachute open—for 30 seconds, routinely starting from 7,200 feet up. During that time, she or he drops at a speed of 120 mph, or even 200 mph in a dive, before pulling the ripcord at 2,500 feet. The average 'chutist takes 6 to 10 jumps per outing.

Those darned commercials. One of every 3 adult Americans is willing to pay a yearly television fee in order to get rid of commercials. When asked how much, the average adult came up with $82 a year.

When asked whether they considered TV commercials annoying and in poor taste, 40 per cent said yes in 1960, 43 per cent said yes in 1970, and 54 per cent said yes in 1978.

Three of every 5 Americans consider television commercials too long, and almost that many consider them too loud. Two of every 3 think they're inaccurate.

But 2 of every 3 adult Americans said that commercials constitute a fair price to pay for television entertainment.

The Sultan of Swat. On average, Babe Ruth hit a home run 1 of every 12 times he came to bat, not counting walks. (OK, baseball experts, it was 1 homer for every 11.764705 at-bats.)

Back so soon? According to boomerang expert Ben Ruhe, boomerangs rarely stay aloft more than 10 or 11 seconds. Observers, though, impressed "by the magic of it all," typically guess that the boomerang they've just seen soared through the air for 55 to 60 seconds.

Buckle on those skis. In 1977, the sport the average American was most likely to have just taken up was cross-country skiing, and the sport she or he most wanted to take up was downhill skiing.

Here are the runners-up, in order:

Just took up	*Want to take up*
Downhill skiing	Tennis
Tennis	Water skiing
Sailing	Horseback riding
Snowmobiling	Cross-country skiing
Water skiing	Camping in primitive areas
Canoeing, kayaking, or river running	Sailing
Golf	Golf
Off-road motorcycling or driving	Snowmobiling
Horseback riding	Canoeing, kayaking, or river running

What we watch. The average family watches prime-time situation comedies more than anything else.

Sitcoms especially attract women and teen-agers. Adventure programs rank highest with children, movies with men.

No fun for me. When asked what they do for relaxation, working Americans said they read, watch television, visit with friends and relatives, putter around the house, and play games and sports—all the same old things.

They were also asked what they *don't* do. That proved a little more interesting (at least for us):

One in 5 working Americans never goes to the movies.
One in 4 never goes to parties, nightclubs, or dances.
Three in 10 never go to museums, concerts, plays, or lectures.
One in 5 never does anything athletic.
One in 5 never works around the house or yard for pleasure.
One in 5 never goes to church or temple.
One in 5 spends absolutely no time on hobbies.
One out of 25 never eats at a restaurant.
One out of 33 never reads.
One out of 53 never watches TV.
One out of 125 never visits with family, friends, or neighbors, even by telephone.

The swift and the idle. In a recent poll by the Gallup Organization, 47 per cent of the respondents said they exercised daily—twice as many as in a 1961 poll.

Eleven per cent told Gallup they jogged. That's 24 per cent of those who exercise regularly.

Of the joggers, 16 per cent of the men and 35 per cent of the women did less than a mile; 76 per cent of the men and 94 per cent of the women did less than 3 miles. Democrats were more likely to jog than Republicans, Catholics more likely than Protestants, and single people twice as likely as married people.

Why we do it. In a survey, people who exercise regularly were asked why they do it.

Eight in 10 said it made them feel better in general.
Half said it was relaxing.
Half said it made them sleep better.
More than 4 in 10 said it made them more alert, made them look better, and would help them live longer.
A third said it improved their concentration, gave them more self-discipline and a better self-image, improved their outlook on life, enhanced their ability to cope with pressure, and improved their output.
One in 4 said it made her or him more assertive or more creative.

One in 5 said it improved his or her sex life.
One in 10 said it helped him or her cut down on smoking.

Ballplayers' revenge. Does the average ballplayer who's been traded or sold come back to play better against his old team than against the league as a whole?

You bet, say researchers Richard Kopelman and James Pantaleno. At least for the following season.

Searching through the records for the 1968 and '69 major-league seasons, they found 47 players who had been traded or sold and who had stayed with their new teams for at least 2 seasons. On average, they batted .254, but against their old teams they hit .273.

That was the first season. The next year, the players batted an average of 5 points *lower* against their old team than against the league as a whole.

Fisherwomen. For every girl or woman who fished in 1972, 3 fished in 1977. For every girl or woman who scuba dived in 1972, 4 scuba dived in 1977.

What we belong to. Of every 100 Americans surveyed recently, 40 belonged to various church-affiliated groups. Nineteen belonged to sports groups, 16 to labor unions, 14 to school service groups, 12 to professional or academic societies, 11 to fraternal groups, and 10 to youth groups.

Three-penny opera. Box-office receipts provide only 45 per cent of the budgets of the nation's 68 biggest opera companies.

The Jogging American

Just one more lap. Take heart. The average American jogger is no marathoner.

A Gallup poll asked joggers a couple of years ago how far they jog. Only 14 per cent said that they jog as much as 3 miles at a time, and that is practically the last thing that anyone would underestimate.

Twenty-three per cent said that they jog less than a mile, and another 23 per cent said that they jog 2 miles. The biggest chunk, 37 per cent, said that they jog a mile. There's your average jogger.

Eating on the run. Forty-six per cent of runners say they eat more because they run. Twenty-nine per cent say they eat less.

A running average. A check with 20 champion runners shows that it took an average of 10.4 years of competition before they ran their fastest time.

What makes Speedy run? Of every 100 joggers, 21 say they do it to stay in shape, 17 because it's good for maintaining stamina or wind, 17 because it's fun, 15 because it tones up their muscles, 14 because it helps keep the heart pumping, 12 because it's relaxing or gives them time to think, and 12 because it helps them lose weight. Some had multiple reasons.

How Rodgers runs. Bill Rodgers ran an average of 131 miles a week in 1977 and 125 miles a week in 1978.

Was Achilles a jogger? A jogger's heel strikes the ground 1,500 times a mile, or 10,000 times an hour. Each. In that hour, he or she contacts the ground with 4.5 million cumulative foot-pounds of force.

The home-field advantage. The average major-league baseball team wins 54 per cent of its home games and 46 per cent of its road games. Batting averages are 5 per cent higher at home. Home teams score runs at a rate 10 per cent higher than visiting teams, but since the home team doesn't bat in the last of the ninth if it's ahead, actual run production is only 5 per cent greater.

Some parks seem to have more of an advantage than others.

From 1934 through 1977, for example, the Boston Red Sox played .594 at home and .459 away.

Fenway Park in Boston is a hitter's park, and Yankee Stadium in New York is not. For instance, Ted Williams batted .361 at Fenway and .328 away. Lou Gehrig batted .329 at Yankee Stadium and .351 away.

In other sports, home teams have an even a greater advantage. The average National Basketball Association team plays .620 at home and .380 on the road, and the average National Hockey League team plays .610 at home and .490 on the road.

Nothing but shop talk. Three working Americans in 4 socialize with friends from work.

Tuning in. The average radio listener listens for 21.3 hours a week, and has 2 or 3 favorite stations.

Here comes WHOOSH there goes your average American skier. Based on a survey commissioned by the U. S. Forest Service, the average American skier is 26 years old, has an income of $20,200, has been a skier for 4⅓ years, and skis 9 days a year.

Counting only persons over 16 years old, 1 American of every 13 skis. One in 11 used to ski and hopes to take it up again, and another 1 in 11 is thinking of becoming a skier.

Those temporarily inactive skiers have an average income of $19,200, and are 27 years old. Marriage was the prime factor taking them off the slopes.

There are 7 downhill skiers in America for every cross-country skier.

Not counting casts and splints. According to a survey published in *U.S. News & World Report* in January 1979, the average skier spends $400 for equipment.

What's a six-letter word for "fan," beginning with "a"? One grown American in 5 works crossword puzzles, making this the nation's most popular sedentary addiction. (Addict.)

Just like the concert hall. According to a 1977 reader survey conducted by *High Fidelity* magazine, the average hi-fi buff spent $812 on his or her stereo gear.

Wha'ddya read? One American family in 4 gets *TV Guide*. One in 4 gets *Reader's Digest*. One in 7 (and Lord knows how many doctors' offices) gets the *National Geographic*. One family in 14 takes the *National Enquirer*. One in 15 gets *Playboy*. One family in 47 takes *Elks Magazine*. One in 97 gets *Weight Watchers Magazine*. One in 97 gets *The New Yorker*. One in 100 takes *1,001 Decorating Ideas*. One family in 136 gets *Catholic Digest*. One in 145 gets *Ms*. And 1 in 240 takes *The United Church Observer*.

Among every 100 books sold in America in an average year are

15 hardcovers
6 quality paperbacks
34 mass-market paperbacks
6 religious books
4 children's books
6 professional books and manuals
15 books sold through book clubs
17 elementary and high-school textbooks
6 college texts
2 mail-order books

The antimovement movement. In a survey conducted by Lou Harris for Great Waters of France, Inc., the importers of Perrier, Americans were asked their attitudes about exercise.

Nearly half agreed with the statement, "Too many people, such as joggers and weight lifters, become fanatical about physical fitness, which is not healthy." Among highly active people, 30 per cent agreed; among inactive folks, 54 per cent said yes, that was so.

Thirty per cent of the public agreed with this one: "These fads about physical fitness come and go, and I'm not impressed by this current emphasis on it." Forty-one per cent of the inactives agreed; 17 per cent of the actives did.

"People who exercise work up big appetites and then eat too

much, making exercise useless." Ten per cent of the jocks agreed with that statement, compared to 38 per cent of the rocking-chair set.

You could look it up. Casey Stengel was about average as a baseball manager.

That's not really true, but it shows how long years of managing tend to even things out.

Stengel managed the New York Yankees to 10 pennants. But he also managed the New York Mets through 4 last-place seasons, and he finished in the second division 9 seasons, ending in 1943, as manager of the Brooklyn Dodgers and Boston Braves. Altogether, Casey's teams won 1,926 games and lost 1,867 for a percentage of .508—just 8 one-thousandths better than the absolutely average record.

Let's catch some action on the box. When asked to name his or her favorite television program, 1 adult American in 6 picks a sports show. The typical American man devotes more than a quarter of his TV time to sports, compared to 15 per cent for the average American woman.

Here are the 10 favorite regularly scheduled shows of the average American adult, in order. The poll was taken in October 1978, and the results were published in February 1979; you can check how many are still on the air:

1. "Little House on the Prairie"
2. "60 Minutes"
3. "The Waltons"
4. "M*A*S*H"
5. "All in the Family"
6. "Mork and Mindy," tied with
7. "Happy Days"
8. "Three's Company"
9. "Soap"
10. "Family"

The tube is everywhere. There's a television set in 98 per cent of American homes. In three quarters of U.S. households, it's a color set. Half of us have 2 or more TVs.

That's the way it is. Two thirds of us catch a network evening news program on 3 nights of the average week.

More channels. Back in 1964, 22 per cent of the homes in America could get only 1 to 3 channels on their TV sets, and only 4 per cent could get 10 or more.

Now a third of all homes get 10 or more channels, and two thirds get 7 or more. Only 4 per cent receive fewer than 4.

Tippy canoe and kayak too. Here is the canoe story from Mike Reynolds, cruising chairman and spokesman for the Wisconsin Canoe Association and the United States Canoe Association:

"The average paddler will own his canoe for about 7 years and trade or sell for a different one. They just don't wear out. One half of 1 per cent (or a very small number) are destroyed each year by one cause or another—whitewater or traffic accidents, etc. Make that figure about 100 per year.

"The average canoeist will paddle about 300 miles per year, while the serious racers will paddle 300 miles per year in competition alone, not counting practice sessions. Racers put on about 1,000 miles per year total. Most canoeists reside in the Midwest and the East. I think there is a direct ratio between canoeists and rivers in their state, but I can't figure it out; for example, we've got 3 members in Arizona and 150 in Ohio."

Reynolds says there is 1 kayaker for every 18 canoeists.

The television week. We watch less television on Friday night than any other night of the week, and most on Sunday night.

In terms of "gross evening audience," this is how the average week arranges itself: Sunday, Tuesday, Monday, Wednesday, Thursday, Saturday, Friday.

Recreation and education. On average, college-educated Americans go for sightseeing, boating, sailing, canoeing, skiing, golf, tennis, hiking, bicycling, and walking. Americans with fewer than 8 years of education prefer fishing, hunting, and picnicking.

Who sees skin flicks? One American out of every 3 polled by Gallup in 1977 said that he or she had seen at least 1 X-rated movie.

Big, tough football players. In 1978, the average National Football League player was 6 feet, 1.95 inches tall, weighed 221.84 pounds, and was 25.99 years old. Those figures, precise decimals and all, come courtesy of NFL statisticians.

The average player in 1948 was a little older (26.38 years) but otherwise didn't measure up. He had 2.82 years of NFL experience, stood 6 feet, 0.88 inch, and weighed 209.84—exactly 12 pounds less than the 1978 average.

By 1958, the average NFL player had grown to 6 feet, 1.42 inches, and 216.47 pounds. He was 25.87 years old, and had been in the league for 3.65 years.

The year of the football behemoth was 1968, when the average player was 6 feet, 2.03 inches tall, weighed 222.95 pounds, was 26.23 years old, and had been in the NFL for 4.88 seasons.

Who has the biggest team? The 1978 Cincinnati Bengals weighed in at an average of 225.09 pounds. The lightest players that year were the Atlanta Falcons, at 217.57 pounds.

How they stand. Here are the standings for an average major-league baseball season, going back through 1900 for the National League and 1901 for the American League. The percentages reflect each team's total won-lost record through 1978, and include all their incarnations.

AMERICAN LEAGUE

EAST	Won	Lost	Pct.
New York Yankees	6,698	5,009	.572
Detroit Tigers	6,209	5,810	.517
Cleveland Indians	6,192	5,813	.516
Boston Red Sox	6,084	5,909	.507
Baltimore Orioles (formerly St. Louis Browns)	5,571	6,279	.469
Milwaukee Brewers (formerly Seattle Pilots)	707	905	.439
Toronto Blue Jays	113	209	.351

WEST	Won	Lost	Pct.
Kansas City Royals	835	776	.518
Chicago White Sox	6,036	5,951	.504
Minnesota Twins (formerly the original Washington Senators)	5,742	6,244	.479
California Angels	1,378	1,527	.4744
Oakland Athletics (formerly Philadelphia and Kansas City Athletics)	5,669	6,290	.4740
Texas Rangers (formerly the second version of the Washington Senators)	1,271	1,625	.439
Seattle Mariners	120	202	.373

NATIONAL LEAGUE

EAST	Won	Lost	Pct.
Pittsburgh Pirates	6,401	5,747	.527
St. Louis Cardinals	6,257	5,983	.515
Chicago Cubs	6,249	5,915	.514
Philadelphia Phillies	5,456	6,664	.450
Montreal Expos	705	907	.437
New York Mets	1,194	1,550	.435

WEST			
San Francisco Giants (formerly New York Giants)	6,641	5,498	.547
Los Angeles Dodgers (formerly Brooklyn Dodgers)	6,360	5,780	.524
Cincinnati Reds	6,115	6,044	.503
Atlanta Braves (formerly Boston and Milwaukee Braves)	5,639	6,486	.465
Houston Astros	1,259	1,483	.459
San Diego Padres	651	959	.404

The price of luxuries. *Medical Economics,* a magazine for doctors (naturally), figured out a few years ago how much the following luxuries will set you back:

Tennis Court: An all-weather, hard-surface court will cost you $12,000, and a 10-foot-high fence and lighting for night play will cost another $12,000.

Your court will add about $300 to your real-estate taxes, and you'd better budget $300 a year for insurance, electricity, and entertaining your tennis friends.

After the first 3 years you'll need a new net, and you can expect to have to resurface the court with an acrylic layer, and repair the fence, all of which will set you back another $2,100.

Yacht: You can pick up a nice 41-foot Chris-Craft commander yacht with appropriate accessories for $95,000.

Assuming you'll use it for 550 hours during the summer, expect these annual expenses: $1,750 for gas and oil, $575 for overnight docking, $1,025 for slip space in season, $1,000 in yacht club dues, $1,025 for winterizing, storing, and servicing your boat, and $1,465 for insurance. You might also want to figure in the first year's depreciation: $19,000.

Sauna: You can put yourself in a cozy 5-by-7-foot redwood hot box for $1,695 or a larger, 6-by-8 unit for $2,175. Figure $300 for electrical wiring, and maybe $100 in annual utility bill increases.

Saddle horse: Here's one where the annual expenses exceed the original outlay. The horse can be had for about $1,000, plus $500 for the saddle and bridle and $20 in grooming tools.

But look out. Board will cost $1,800, shoeing $132, shots for the horse $40, filing its teeth $20, worming $20, and lessons and vets' care another $150. Total annual expenses: $2,162.

Swimming pool: Seven thousand dollars will buy you an in-ground, 16-by-32-foot pool with a filter and cleaning tools. But extras—a diving board, a ladder, a heater, an automatic cleaner, a chlorinator, masonry for a concrete deck and patio, and electrical work—will add another $2,827. For operating expenses, figure $200 for chemicals, $200 for winterizing and opening the pool, $250 for electricity and insurance, and $300 in extra property taxes, for an annual total of $950.

Airplane: A discounted 4-seater Piper Cherokee Archer will run you $38,000 to $40,000. Figure $10,000 as the first year's depreciation, in addition to these annual expenses: $3,700 for fuel and oil, $600 for inspections and maintenance, $1,200 in hangar rent, and $1,800 for insurance; that's a total of $7,300.

Why get all sweaty? Of every 4 Americans, 2 prefer to spend their leisure time sitting around, relaxing. One prefers going out to a movie, bar, or restaurant. The fourth chooses exercise of some kind or other.

How much TV we watch. According to the A. C. Nielsen Company, the average American watches 27 hours, 19 minutes of television a week during a prime watching month, such as November.

But the amount varies from young men, who watch the least, to older women, who watch the most:

Women over 54	35 hours, 1 minute
Men over 54	31 hours, 57 minutes
Women 25 to 54	29 hours, 44 minutes
Women 18 to 24	29 hours, 22 minutes
Children 2 to 5	27 hours, 35 minutes
Men 25 to 54	24 hours, 29 minutes
Children 6 to 11	24 hours, 26 minutes
Male teens	22 hours, 42 minutes
Female teens	21 hours, 25 minutes
Men 18 to 24	20 hours, 12 minutes

Who likes television best? In a 1974 Gallup poll, 46 per cent of the people named television as their favorite leisure pastime.

Television was named the favorite by 51 per cent of the males and 41 per cent of the females, by 58 per cent of the blacks and 44 per cent of the whites, by 62 per cent of those with only a grade-school education, 48 per cent of those who went through high school, 29 per cent of those who went to college, 52 per cent of the widowed and divorced, 48 per cent of the married, and only 25 per cent of the single people.

Among adults, the older you get, the more likely television will be your favorite activity. The richer you get, the less likely it will be your favorite.

And going up. The average movie ticket cost $2.37 in 1978 and $2.52 in 1979.

The athletic gap. Woman athletes are closing the gap between their best performances and the best performances of male athletes. *WomenSports* magazine reached that conclusion on the basis of research by Linda Bunker of the Motor Learning Laboratory at the University of Virginia, and Australian scientist K. F. Dyer.

For example:

In 1934, female world record holders in the 100-meter run were 13.6 per cent slower than the male record holders. In 1954, they were 11.8 per cent slower, and in 1976, their times were only 11.1 per cent slower.

In 1934, the female champions ran the 800-meter run 24.6 per cent slower than the male winners. But they were only 11.2 per cent slower by 1976.

In 6 swimming events, the gap between women's and men's world records narrowed from 12.28 per cent in 1945 to 9.08 per cent in 1976.

Concluded *WomenSports,* "The biological differences may be much less significant in sports than has always been assumed. . . . (Once) social limits are removed, women may reach peak performances commensurate with the ultimate world-record performances of men."

Scouts' honor. More than a third of all boys in America become Cub Scouts, 1 in 5 becomes a Boy Scout, and 3 per cent become Explorer Scouts, according to the Boy Scouts of America.

About 2 per cent of Scouts attain Eagle rank.

A study in Dallas showed the differences between boys who join Scouting and boys who don't:

Scouts like noncompetitive outdoor activities; non-Scouts prefer team sports.

"Making the team" is the most important thing to the non-Scouts, and least important to Scouts.

Of those who don't join, 30 per cent say Scouting is boring, 25 per cent say they don't have time, 20 per cent say they'd rather be involved in sports, 10 per cent never had the chance, 9 per cent weren't asked, and 7 per cent are in some other group like the Scouts.

Seven Scouts in 10 say they like their adult Scout leaders.

Culture vultures. Of every 100 Americans

36 go to museums
29 go to plays
25 go to rock or folk concerts
13 go to classical concerts
11 go to dance performances.

Here's a profile of your average tennis and golf buffs, taken from surveys of subscribers to *Tennis Magazine* and *Golf Digest,* respectively.

The average *Tennis* subscriber is 34, has an income of $33,307, owns at least 1 car, drinks or at least serves liquor, wine, and beer, and spent 24 days on vacation last year at a cost of $1,800. In an average year, he or she plays tennis on 103 days and buys 33 cans of balls. Moreover, 73 per cent of the subscribers bought a new racket last year, 93 per cent bought a new pair of tennis shoes, and 78 per cent belong to a club. Three of every 4 *Tennis* subscribers own their homes, 1 of every 10 owns a vacation home, and 1 of every 25 has a private tennis court. La de da.

The *Golf Digest* subscribers don't have their own golf courses, but otherwise they seem to be pretty much the same kind of people. Their income averages $32,000, they have an average net worth of $155,000, they drink and vacation, and 3 out of 4 own 2 or more cars.

Tennis describes its subscribers as "a young, affluent, active target market," and *Golf Digest* describes its subscribers as "an affluent, influential target market." We might deduce that the average golf buff is a bit older.

Hobbies. Of every 100 Americans:

48 garden
39 do handicrafts of one kind or another

22 paint or draw
18 play a musical instrument
11 sing in a choral group
 9 use a CB radio
 7 collect stamps
 5 play bridge
 5 play chess
 3 dance
 1 is an ardent photographer

Most likely to sweat. According to a Gallup poll, the Americans most likely to exercise vigorously most every day are single college graduates, 18 to 29 years old, who live out West and make $20,000 or more per year.

Licensed for sport. In an average year, 1 American in 9 buys a hunting license, 1 in 6 gets a fishing license, and 1 in 100 buys a federal duck stamp.

Are we watching less television? Yes, according to a nationwide poll of 1,693 Americans 18 and older, conducted in late 1978 by the Washington *Post*. Altogether, 53 per cent said they were watching less TV than they did 5 years before; 32 per cent said they were watching more.

Nevertheless, according to the poll, the typical American 18 or older watches 3 hours of TV on an average weekday, and 3 hours, 25 minutes on an average weekend day.

Two of every 3 adult Americans watch TV every day. Nineteen of every 20 watch at least twice a week. Only 1 in 50 never tunes in at all.

Two of every 5 adult Americans say that the quality of TV entertainment is better than it was 5 years before, and 2 of every 5 say it is worse.

They'd rather make waves. The average boater likes a motor, as you might imagine, and the average motor is getting bigger. Here's a trivia quiz. The most popular motor is:

a.   1 to 5 horsepower
b.   6 to 10
c.   11 to 30
d.   31 to 50
e.   51 to 100
f.   over 100

per cent.
for 10 per cent, 6 to 10 hp for 12 per cent, and 1 to 5 hp for 9
Motors of 31 to 50 hp accounted for 14 per cent, 11 to 30 hp
motors that big, and 15 per cent had motors of 51 to 100 hp.
Answer: f. In 1976, 16 per cent of U.S. pleasure boats had

Snapshooters. The average family in America takes 118 snap-shots a year. Ninety per cent of them are in color. Four out of 5 of the color pictures are prints, and 1 is a slide.

The average American spends $24 a year on photography. Nearly 9 families in 10 own a still camera, and almost half of those are self-developing of the Polaroid type. A third of all American families own movie cameras. Thirty per cent of us take our film to a drugstore for processing.

The career of the average pro athlete. The average big-league baseball player plays in the majors for 4.5 years. That's just long enough to qualify for a pension, which, in 1979, began at age 55 and consisted of $574 a month for a player with 4.5 years in the majors, regardless of his salary.

In the National Football League, the average player hangs on just a little longer—4.6 years. For that much service, he gets a pension of $500 a month, also starting at age 55.

Hockey is a fast sport, but the average player skates 8 years in the National Hockey League. He sustains 5 serious injuries in that time. For 8 years of service, he gets a pension of $667 a month, starting at age 45.

In the Ladies' Professional Golf Association, the average player stays on the tour for 8 years. She's 24 years old, and in an average tournament she grosses $562.50, having paid an entry fee of $50 plus $12 for locker-room and driving-range privileges. In an average round, she uses 2 to 3 balls. She's not entitled to a pension.

Where the chatter is good, good buddy. In Wyoming, nearly 9 people of every 100 are licensed to use citizens' band radio. Other states where CBers constitute more than 7 per cent of the population are Alaska, South Dakota, Oklahoma, North Dakota, Kansas, Nebraska, West Virginia, Texas, and Iowa.

On the other hand, barely 3 Hawaiians in *200* are CBers. Other places with relatively few are Washington, D.C., Rhode Island, New York, California, Massachusetts, New Jersey, and Connecticut.

Apparatus over art. Two or 3 people go to science museums for every person who goes to an art museum.

The young play more. As part of the 1977 National Outdoor Recreation Survey, the U. S. Interior Department asked all kinds of Americans what sports they played, and broke down the results by age.

Say what you will about hale and hearty oldsters, the results showed that most of us stop participating as we get older.

Take swimming. Between the ages of 12 and 17, 53 per cent of Americans swim at the beach and 75 per cent swim in pools. By middle age, 45 to 54, it's down to 28 per cent at the beach, 37 per cent in the pool. Among those 65 and older, only 6 per cent swim at the beach, 11 per cent in the pool.

Fishing isn't what you'd call an exhausting sport. But the percentage of Americans who do it declines from 51 per cent for teen-agers to 36 per cent for the middle-aged and to 21 per cent for those over 65.

Golf is the sport of the aging, but not of the aged. The peak golfing years are 55 to 64; 15 per cent of Americans in that group play golf. But only 5 per cent of Americans 65 or older are golfers.

Tennis playing declines steadily with age, from 46 per cent for teen-agers to 38 per cent for those 18 to 24, 34 per cent for the 25-to-34-year-olds, 25 per cent for the 35-to-44-year-olds, 13 per cent for the 45-to-54-year-olds, 4 per cent for those 55 to 64, and 1 per cent for those 65 or older.

Here are the participation figures for a few other outdoor activities:

Age	Attending sports events	Sightseeing	Hunting	Bicycling	Hiking	Sailing	Camping in a developed area
12–17	66%	30%	17%	80%	19%	9%	14%
18–24	57%	39%	19%	56%	23%	7%	18%
25–34	52%	41%	13%	47%	23%	5%	13%
35–44	42%	42%	20%	38%	21%	4%	15%
45–54	31%	42%	14%	26%	11%	3%	11%
55–64	28%	32%	13%	11%	10%	2%	11%
65 and older	13%	24%	6%	9%	6%	1%	3%

More Mozart, more Chablis! According to the distributors of Christian Brothers wines, people who listen to classical music on the radio drink, on average, 2½ times more wine than people who don't.

Exercise: the truth. Lou Harris & Associates found that 59 per cent of the public "claim to have participated in some form of sport or athletic activity in the past year." (In 1961, only 24 per cent made that claim.)

All exercise isn't alike. On the basis of a Caloric Expenditure Index, the Harris people calculated that:

15 per cent of adults are highly active, spending an average of 5 hours, 6 minutes a week participating in sports or exercise.

16 per cent are moderately active, spending 3 hours, 24 minutes weekly doing their thing.

28 per cent are low-active participants, giving it 2½ hours a week.

On average, the highly active group are men under 35, in the higher income brackets, living in the suburbs in the Midwest or West.

Having fun with the news. More than half of television watchers surveyed in Albany County, New York, said they liked television news because it often was funny. Three out of 4 said that joking by newscasters makes the news "easier to take."

These are pretty avid average music lovers. *The Schwann Record & Tape Guide* is a monthly publication listing every new record, cassette, and cartridge on the market. The November 1977 issue included a questionnaire, which was filled out and returned by 3,847 readers. Based on that, here's your average home music buff:

He or she is 35, has an income of $19,550, and owns 1,192 records, worth $5,789.64. He or she buys a new record every 3 days and spends $445.48 a year on records. In 1977 dollars, mind you.

Fifty-four per cent graduated from college. A full third have a graduate degree. Fifty per cent are married, and 50 per cent are single.

Nearly half of the records they buy are classical. Next come rock at 16 per cent, jazz at 11 per cent, opera at 9 per cent, and popular at 7 per cent.

What the athlete makes. On the Ladies' Professional Golf Association tour, the average player wins a total of $13,500 a year. She picks up another $3,000 on the outside with exhibitions, endorsements, and the like.

Those are 1978 figures. So is this one: The average National Hockey League player's salary is $95,000.

In the 1978–79 season, the Washington Bullets, defending champions of the National Basketball Association, were paid an average of $183,000 each.

The average major-league baseball player made $99,876 in 1978.

That same year, the average National Football League player made $62,585.

Here are the average National Football League salaries, by position:

	1979	1978	1977
Quarterback	$113,932	$102,606	$89,354
Running back	$ 74,194	$ 66,516	$60,414
Defensive lineman	$ 75,246	$ 66,063	$59,644
Offensive lineman	$ 66,584	$ 60,241	$52,250
Receiver	$ 64,631	$ 59,824	$53,760
Linebacker	$ 63,377	$ 58,061	$50,416
Defensive back	$ 58,874	$ 54,838	$47,403
Kicker	$ 53,030	$ 48,354	$41,506

In 1977, the average rookie quarterback made $36,612. That jumped to $53,120 for quarterbacks in their second year, to $141,583 for those in their fifth year, and to $177,750 for quarterbacks in their eighth year in the NFL.

Backing up the line is less lucrative. The average rookie linebacker was paid $31,541 in 1977. Second-year linebackers averaged $35,920, linebackers in their fifth year in the NFL were paid $53,771, and linebackers in their eighth year got $82,077.

The average baseball rookie made $28,490 in 1978. The average salary was $51,674 for players in their second year, $124,175 for those in their fifth year, and $181,557 for players in their eighth year in the major leagues. There were 41 baseball players with more than 12 years in the majors, and they were paid $180,224, on average, in 1978.

Here's the average major-league salary lineup for 1978:

First base	$143,796
Second base	$130,745
Shortstop	$121,923
Third base	$143,641
Outfield	$153,515
Catcher	$144,374
Designated hitter	$163,786
Starting pitcher	$126,936
Relief pitcher	$ 87,268

Here it is by team:

	1978	1977
New York Yankees	$188,880	$132,417
Philadelphia Phillies	$159,039	$143,160
Boston Red Sox	$147,803	$108,131
California Angels	$141,814	$ 97,210
Los Angeles Dodgers	$135,884	$ 97,885
Cincinnati Reds	$132,847	$112,525
Pittsburgh Pirates	$127,852	$ 98,567
Texas Rangers	$121,244	$ 83,487
San Diego Padres	$106,759	$ 73,727
Kansas City Royals	$106,532	$ 95,000
San Francisco Giants	$106,346	$ 87,620
Montreal Expos	$105,589	$ 65,820
Chicago Cubs	$ 96,222	$ 69,018
Milwaukee Brewers	$ 91,986	$ 54,435
St. Louis Cardinals	$ 89,333	$ 69,726
New York Mets	$ 86,235	$ 58,440
Baltimore Orioles	$ 82,860	$ 71,710
Chicago White Sox	$ 81,321	$ 63,442
Cleveland Indians	$ 77,013	$ 67,254
Houston Astros	$ 70,558	$ 55,832
Atlanta Braves	$ 69,699	$ 67,435
Toronto Blue Jays	$ 63,593	$ 34,240
Detroit Tigers	$ 61,012	$ 47,144
Seattle Mariners	$ 58,484	$ 38,161
Minnesota Twins	$ 51,317	$ 39,648
Oakland Athletics	$ 49,258	$ 45,673
Overall average	$ 99,876	$ 76,066

In 1969, the average major-league baseball player made $24,090. In 1975, he made $44,676.

Who needs sunshine? Of every 100 Americans, 21 bowl, 17 shoot pool, and 15 play Ping-Pong.

Regards to Broadway. If you go to Broadway shows, you see an average of 8.3 of them a year if you live in New York and 3.8 if you are an out-of-towner.

Here's more about Broadway tendencies from a *Playbill* audience survey. The average theatergoer earns $30,806 a year, and is 38 years old. He is most likely to be male and single. Four in 5 own cars, and 80 per cent own stocks worth an average of $55,500. Half go out for something to eat or drink after the show. The average Broadway ticket cost $11.92 in the 1977–78 season.

Only 42 shows got to Broadway in 1977–78, fewer than in other years, but 1 out of 2 of them was a hit, a big improvement in the 1-to-3.5 hit-to-flop ratio of the 11 previous seasons. The League of New York Theaters and Producers says it costs an average of $1 million to get a large musical to Broadway, and $300,000 to stage a dramatic play.

The Video Kid

The tube and the tot. The average preschooler watches up to 30 hours of TV a week—a total of 6,000 hours before he or she sets foot in a first-grade classroom.

What kids watch. On average, small children prefer situation comedies and cartoons. Sixth graders like family situation comedies and adventure programs. Tenth graders prefer adventure programs and music and variety shows.

Most children and adolescents go for programs featuring characters their own age.

He or she just sits there. According to 3 social scientists, dull, insecure children tend to watch more television than bright, well-adjusted children.

Hilde Himmelweit, A. N. Oppenheim, and Pamela Vince, writing in *Television and the Child* (Oxford University Press, 1958), say that this is because the problem child's maladjustment seems "to impel him toward excessive consumption of any available mass medium."

Good TV shows make good kids. According to a sociological study, the average preschooler who watches "Mr. Rogers' Neighborhood" is nicer and more sociable than the average preschooler who doesn't.

Buy, buy, small fry. Every year, the average American kid watches 25,000 television commercials.

Go watch TV, you little brat. On average, the adults who are most concerned about the effects of television on children don't themselves have any children under the age of 16.

Here are the results from an October 1978 poll of 1,693 adults conducted by the Washington *Post*.

	Overall percentage who say it's a serious problem	*Percentage of parents of children under 16 who say it's a serious problem*
Children see things they shouldn't see	53%	45%
TV keeps kids from doing other things they should be doing	57%	49%
TV advertising has a bad effect on children	38%	34%

I prefer the murders. By the time he or she graduates from high school, the average American has watched 15,000 hours of television and has seen 350,000 commercials and 18,000 murders.

They need it. The American who works more than 40 hours a week is more likely to participate in outdoor recreation than is the American who works fewer than 40 hours a week.

On the water. Here is what folks tell the Coast Guard they do on their boats.

Most take along something to drink. Four out of 5 bring soda pop, coffee, or something like that. One third say they bring beer, and the Coast Guard had this to say about that particular response: "The interviewers felt that many of the interviewees hedged somewhat in answering this question."

One boater out of 16 admitted to bringing along something else alcoholic, like wine or gin.

Not that they're out there just to drink. If you divide up an average hour on the water, 27 minutes are spent fishing, 19 minutes cruising or sailing around, 8 minutes water skiing, and 47 seconds racing. The rest of the hour was spent just dawdling.

The average boat outing is 5 hours, 18 minutes. It's 12 hours for houseboats; 7 hours, 12 minutes for cabin cruisers; 5 hours, 29 minutes for runabouts; 4 hours, 42 minutes for sailboats; and 4 hours, 30 minutes for canoes.

He spins, hands off to the fullback, who . . . Crashes the line for 4 yards. That's the average gain on a rushing play in the National Football League.

The average NFL quarterback completes 53.1 per cent of his passes, and the average completion gains 12.67 yards. When a pass is intercepted, it's returned for an average of 12.97 yards.

The typical punt is booted 38.6 yards, and is returned 8.4 yards. The average kickoff is run back 21.4 yards.

One of every 159 punts and 1 of every 194 kickoffs are returned for a touchdown.

Life in the bleachers. For every American who attends a professional football game:

   1 goes to a professional basketball game
   3 go to a college football game
   1 goes to a professional hockey game
   4 go to a major-league baseball game
   8 go to horse races
   2 watch greyhound racing

The life cycle of TV watching. The surgeon general's Scientific Advisory Committee on Television and Social Behavior says television watching follows a predictable pattern for most people.

The average kid is 3 when he or she begins watching frequently. By the first grade, he or she has favorite programs. Viewing remains high until age 12, then declines, reaching its low point during the teen years.

When young people marry and have families, they spend more time before the tube. Viewing remains at a stable, high level, then climbs again when the kids marry and leave home.

According to one study, the average kid, during the first 16 years of life, spends as much time with television as in school.

In a study of sixth graders, over a quarter said they watched more than 5 hours on school days. But another quarter said they hadn't watched any TV the day before they were asked.

The committee says TV viewing is not the "universal, global, nonrational, automatic manifestation of behavior" it seems. That's a relief.

Don't look for your plumber at the ballet. The average income of people who go to the ballet, dance, symphony, opera, or indoor theater is $20,318. The operagoer, at age 41 and an income of $21,024, constitutes the oldest and wealthiest segment of the arts audience. Blue-collar workers make up a third of the work force but only 2.4 per cent of the arts audience.

We were strolling through the park one day. The average American spends a day a year in a federal park.

The average neighborhood park is used by only about 18 per cent of the people living close by.

Ahoy, there! And there! And there! In 1976, when the Coast Guard last took a boat census, there were 12,750,000 pleasure craft in the United States—1 for every 17 people.

The average boat operator is 32 years, 5 months old, and is twice as likely to be a male as a female. But more women are starting to take the helm: In 1973, a full three fourths of boat operators were men. If it's a woman at the tiller, she's 3 years younger, on average, than the guy skippering the boat alongside.

The typical boater is better educated than the average American, but he or she is not of the idle rich. Only 7 per cent of boat operators are retired, and only 2 per cent are unemployed. Students account for 11 per cent. Seventy-eight per cent of boaters work, a bit more than half of them in white-collar jobs, and the rest in blue-collar, farm, or service jobs.

Almost 9 out of 10 boaters fish. Half hunt, 7 out of 10 camp out, 7 out of 10 play outdoor sports, and 7 out of 10 plunge into other forms of outdoor recreation.

Two members of the average boating household actually run the boat.

Two-wheelers. The Bicycle Manufacturers Association of America says that nearly 1 American in 2 rides a bike, at least occasionally. Three American bikes in 10 sold these days are 10-speeders. In 1970, only 5 per cent were.

A nation of pianists. Two out of every 5 American children take piano lessons at some time or other. The average plinker sticks to it for 3 years, at a cost of $35 a month. The average private piano teacher makes $12,000 a year.

Roughly half of the kids who took lessons can still play, at least a little bit, as adults.

More time than at work. The average household in America has the television on for 45½ hours a week.

That's almost equally true regardless of income. Households with income under $10,000 a year watch 44 hours, 9 minutes. Households with over $20,000 in income watch 46 hours, 24 minutes.

But in households where no one is under 18 years old, the television is on only 38 hours, 11 minutes in a typical week, compared to 55 hours, 20 minutes in households with at least 1 kid.

501 fans per player. In 1978, the average home game of a college basketball team in the NCAA's Division 1—meaning the larger schools—drew 5,015 fans.

Hiking in my Gucci's. The average American with a low income is more likely to take up tennis than any other new outdoor activity. That's true for the average middle-income American, too. Among Americans with big incomes, hiking and backpacking are the most popular new activities.

Games. According to a 1977 survey, American families own 5.8 table games each.

We can put you into a nice little runabout. That's America's favorite boat. Runabouts, or small motorboats, accounted for 28 per cent of our pleasure fleet in 1976. Rowboats totaled 14 per cent, johnboats and other open, lightweight boats 10 per cent each, sailboats and canoes 8 per cent, and cabin cruisers 4 per cent. Only 1 boat in every 250 was a houseboat, and only one 1 of every 132 was a kayak.

About 48 per cent of the boating public buy their craft new, 48 per cent buy theirs used, and 4 per cent make them themselves. More than 2 out of 5 houseboats and kayaks are homemade.

The typical pleasure boat is 8 years, 4 months old. The oldest boats, on average, are rowboats and cabin cruisers; they're both 10 years old. Inflatables are the newest, averaging 3 years old. The average runabout is 9 years old, and so is the average sailboat.

If it moves, watch it. A professor asked 791 people this question:

"Were there any times yesterday when you wanted to watch television but did not because there were no programs worth watching on at that time?"

Only 12 per cent said yes; 88 per cent said no.

Cookies and exercise. People who exercise regularly do not sleep less, eat less, or smoke less than people who don't, a survey discovers.

A third of people in both groups said that they eat too much. But people who exercise least eat more candy, cookies, cake, breakfast cereal, and fried foods, and drink more beer, wine, and liquor than people who exercise a lot.

Forty-six per cent of the active people say exercise has increased their appetites. Only 9 per cent say they eat less. About a quarter of them have gained weight in recent years. Another quarter have shed some weight.

Whoreadit? The average addict of mystery books is said to read 3 whodunits a week.

How tall is the average college basketball player? Among major colleges, the answer is 6 feet, 4.67 inches.

That was in 1978. Between 1972 and 1976, it increased by an average of .33 inch a year. Between 1976 and 1978, the average player grew by only .13 inch a year.

One of every 9 players in 1978 was 6-9 or taller. One of every 118 was a 7-footer. One of every 18 was under 6 feet.

For the average team, the leading scorer was 6-5, 6-6, or 6-7. There were 24 players who stood 7 feet or taller, but none of them led their respective teams in scoring. Nineteen players were 5-8 or shorter, and one of them—James Horton of Alcorn State—was his team's leading scorer.

Spending for fun. Of every $8.00 spent by the average American in 1978 $1.00 went for leisure and recreation, from books to bowling balls to vacations.

Other people need it. One government survey found that 86 per cent of Americans consider outdoor recreation important. Another found that 45 per cent of American adults never exercise.

Some are strikes, some are balls, some are hits. A major-league pitcher throws 14 or 15 pitches in an average inning.

Sleeping-bag demographics. A sampling of 2,003 households establishes that the average camper is most likely to be between 18 and 29, a craftsman or foreman, a big-city resident in the north-central states, white, with kids under 18, a homeowner, and high-school-educated.

This crystal ball went awry. In 1960, the U. S. Outdoor Resources Review Commission predicted how many Americans would be participating in various outdoor recreational activities in 1977.

The forecasts turned out to be just awful, greatly underestimating American pep.

Here are some of the predictions, and the actual participation rates as gleaned from a 1977 survey. In this list, it counted if you did the particular activity just *once a year*.

	Prediction	Actual participation
Pleasure driving	56%	69%
Walking or jogging	37%	68%
Sightseeing	47%	62%
Picnicking	57%	73%
Fishing	32%	55%
Bicycling	11%	47%
Attending sports events	27%	61%
Rowing or motorboating	28%	35%
Nature walks	16%	49%
Hunting	14%	20%
Camping in developed areas	11%	30%
Horseback riding	8%	15%
Water skiing	9%	17%
Hiking	8%	28%
Attending outdoor concerts, plays, etc.	12%	40%

13 Lord Knows What Else

Longevity in the animal kingdom. Owls outlive elephants, on average. Spiders outlive worker honeybees, ants outlive spiders, and giant tortoises outlive them all.

According to Mutual of Omaha (which, after all, should know about longevity): "In general, big beasts live longer than little ones. Among mammals, vegetarians and animals that eat mixed kinds of foods live longer than meat eaters. Slow-maturing animals live longer than early-maturing animals. Sluggish, cold-blooded animals live longer than hot-blooded mammals. Teeth are also a controlling factor. Teeth take a definite time to grow and a less definite, but still limited, time to wear away. When the teeth of a mammal become useless for procuring food, the animal will die."

Here are some average life spans in the animal world:

butterfly	6 months	shrew	2 years
moth	6 months	spider	2 years
worker honeybee	6 months	armadillo	3 years
housefly	2 years	starling	3 years

iguana	4 years	stork	24 years
kudu	4 years	tiger	24 years
mouse	4 years	zebra	24 years
otter	4 years	dolphin	25 years
squirrel	5 years	giraffe	25 years
worker ant	5 years	lion	25 years
wren	5 years	peacock	25 years
aardvark	6 years	camel	29 years
giant panda	6 years	gibbon	31 years
rabbit	6 years	polar bear	34 years
sable antelope	6 years	wild horse	34 years
skylark	6 years	hawk	35 years
woolly monkey	6 years	toad	36 years
queen honeybee	7 years	gorilla	39 years
lemur	9 years	pelican	39 years
black bear	10 years	rhinoceros	40 years
hyena	10 years	chimpanzee	44 years
bullfrog	12 years	ostrich	48 years
eel	12 years	hippopotamus	51 years
kangaroo	14 years	whale	52 years
queen ant	15 years	orangutan	56 years
rhesus monkey	15 years	elephant	57 years
cheetah	16 years	halibut	60 years
wolf	16 years	owl	68 years
bat	17 years	pike	70 years
goat	17 years	raven	70 years
sea lion	18 years	swan	70 years
rattlesnake	19 years	eagle	80 years
cougar	20 years	crocodile	100 years
herring	20 years	eider duck	100 years
moose	20 years	salmon	100 years
sheep	20 years	shark	100 years
panther	21 years	parrot	120 years
canary	24 years	box turtle	138 years
deer	24 years	giant tortoise	190 years

Here's the average weather, based on decades of records kept by the National Weather Service.

An average July day:

City	Highest temperature (°F)	Highest humidity (%)	Wind (mph)	Rain probability
Phoenix	105	28	7	13%
Miami	89	65	8	53%
Washington, D.C.	88	52	8	33%
New York	85	55	8	33%
Chicago	84	57	8	33%
Los Angeles	83	54	5	0%
Portland, Maine	79	60	8	29%
Duluth, Minnesota	76	58	10	35%
San Francisco	64	74	8	3%

An average January day:

City	Highest temperature (°F)	Highest humidity (%)	Wind (mph)	Rain or snow probability
Phoenix	65	43	5	10%
Miami	76	84	9	23%
Washington, D.C.	41	68	10	33%
New York	38	68	11	35%
Chicago	31	76	12	35%
Los Angeles	67	51	7	19%
Portland, Maine	31	77	9	35%
Duluth, Minnesota	18	75	12	39%
San Francisco	56	72	11	35%

Mr. President! The average American President was 27 when he married, 54 when he was inaugurated, and nearly 69 when he died. He served an average of 4.89 years and had 5.4 brothers and sisters, 2.12 sons, and 1.43 daughters. He died fewer than 3 years after leaving office. Nineteen per cent of our deceased Presidents have died in July. More than half outlived their wives.

On most of these criteria, your average President would have to be Rutherford B. Hayes or Lyndon B. Johnson.

Hayes was 30 when he married, 54 when he took the presidential oath, and 70 when he died. He served 4 years. He had 4 siblings.

Hayes would have been even more average, except he overdid it in the children and post-presidential-survival departments. Untypically, he had 7 sons and 1 daughter and lived for 12 years after leaving office.

L.B.J. had 4 siblings, married at 26, took office at 54, and died at 65, 4 years and 2 days after leaving office. He served 5 years, 59 days.

Forty-three per cent of Presidents have lacked a middle name or initial. None was an only child. Eighteen per cent had the same given names as their fathers. Thirty-seven per cent were Republicans, 32 per cent were Democrats, and the rest belonged to other parties—or occupied the office before we had political parties.

"There she is . . ." Here's the lowdown on Miss America. Here she comes! The winner! America's dream girl, Miss America!

She is 5 feet, 7 inches tall.
Her bust measures 35.7 inches.
Her waist is 23.4 inches.
Her hips are 35.5 inches.
She is 20 years old.
Fourteen times out of 18 her hair is brown.
One eye is brown, 1 green. (That's what happens when you average out eyes.)
She is most likely to hail from the Midwest or the South. She is unlikely to hail from the East.

The father of our country was a 42 long. A survey by *Men's Wear* magazine shows that the average American man wears a 42 regular suit (it used to be 40 regular) and a 15½-33 shirt.

When Hart Schaffner & Marx orders suits for their stores, it buys 65 per cent regular, 10 per cent short, and 25 per cent long.

Big suits are reportedly in strong demand in the Upper Midwest (where, H, S & M note, a substantial number of men are of Scandinavian stock) and Texas (where men are just bigger). In San Francisco, because of the large population of Orientals, the average suit sold is smaller, H, S & M says.

Men's Wear calculates that George Washington, at 6 feet, 2 inches, and 200 pounds, would have taken a 42 long. Something in a pinstripe, no doubt.

Timber! For each American, we use up 590 pounds of paper and cardboard, 216 board feet of lumber, and 102 square inches of ⅜-inch plywood per year.

Eaten by the bookworms. In the average public library, 1 book in 20 can be counted on to vanish from the shelves within 6 months of its purchase. Most are novels.

Too much crime. A Gallup poll asked a cross section of Americans whether anyone in their household had been the victim of a crime during the past 12 months. One out of every 5 said "yes."

Who robs banks. According to Sergeant Edward Dory of the Washington, D.C., police department, the typical bank robber is an unemployed, unskilled man, 18 to 25 years old, with previous criminal convictions. Of every 10 men convicted of bank robbery, 3 do it again after they get out of jail.

Why rob banks? Willie Sutton says he robbed banks because "That's where the money is." But psychiatrist Donald A. Johnston, who interviewed more than 200 bank robbers in prison, said the average stick-up man has other motives.

He said the typical robber is emotionally troubled and frequently psychotic and acts out of impulsiveness and a self-destructive rage.

Johnston cited FBI statistics showing that in a typical year 1,747 of 2,200 bank robberies were committed by men who didn't even case the joint.

The loot. The average bank robber got away with $4,858 per job in the United States in 1977.

Spring forward, fall backward. After Daylight Saving Time was extended in 1973, the government asked people whether they liked it. More than half said they did, because it gave them "more light in the evening." But three quarters of Americans didn't change their behavior one bit to take advantage of that extra daylight.

The American Pet

Going to the dogs. For every person in the United States, there are 4 or 5 pets.

But you needn't put up a fence. Most of them are fish. In fact, pet fish outnumber people in this country by at least 3 to 2. Only 1 household in 16 has fish, but those who do own them by the tankful.

One of every 19 American households owns birds—6 feathered friends each, on average. One of every 100 households owns a creature in the category that the pet industry refers to as "other," which includes turtles, snakes, gerbils, and hamsters. The average "other" owner keeps a slew of them.

One in 3 American households owns a dog, 1 of every 8 owns a cat, and 1 in 10 owns both.

The average dog-owning household has almost 1½ dogs. The average cat-owning household has a little over 1½ cats.

Not counting strays, there is a dog for every 5 people in the United States, and a cat for every 9 people.

The average pet dog is 4 years old and weighs 32 pounds. Half are pedigreed. Almost half of the females are spayed, but only one eighth of the males are neutered.

The average dog consumes $47.09 worth of dog food a year. The average cat eats $38.48 worth of cat food.

Every year, more than a quarter of the dogs and cats in the United States die from something other than old age. The Humane Society says that 13.5 million of them are put to death in animal shelters.

In an average year 1 American in 147 complains to authorities that she or he has been bitten by a dog. One in 50 of them takes painful rabies vaccine injections, at an average cost of $50.

How to combat cat loneliness. Have 2 cats or more. According to Star-Kist cat foods, 1 of 3 cat-owning families has more than 1. One in 5 cat-owning families also has 1 dog.

I wuv my doggie. In 1975, National Analysts, a subsidiary of Booz, Allen & Hamilton, surveyed pet ownership in the United States. Here's what their report had to say about those among us who have dogs and cats:

Of dog owners, 27 per cent are "championship owners" who have such fun with their dogs that they take them along on vacations. Another 17 per cent are "enthusiastic owners," who also love their dogs a lot but are a shade less committed to them. "Valued-object owners" make up 19 per cent of the group; they love their dogs the way they love their antiques.

We now come down to "worried owners," who comprise 24 per cent of dog owners. They like their dogs, but cannot control them that well, and are embarrassed by the lack of modesty in animal sexual activities. Their dogs often disappear for a day or more at a time. The average "worried owner" is likely to describe his dog as stupid and spoiled.

At the bottom of the list are "dissatisfied owners," who include 19 per cent of all masters. They consider their dogs a nuisance. They don't like the way the animal smells, and they think it's too affectionate. Lots of dissatisfied owners were given their dogs as gifts, or got them for their children.

Among cat owners, 59 per cent are "low-involvement owners," who seem to have picked a cat as a pet because it requires little attention. "Low-involvement owners," report the researchers, "seem less to own their cats than to merely have them around."

Moving up the ladder, we have "quality/status-conscious owners," 21 per cent of the group. They take great pride in their homes and great pride in their cats, both of which they consider signs of their own good taste. They believe that their cats depend on them for love, affection, and care, and they disagree with the notion that pedigrees for cats are absurd.

"High-involvement owners" account for 20 per cent of all cat owners. They love their cats a great deal and play with them a lot, but don't consider them status symbols.

Unfat cat. When a boy asked the Boston *Globe* whether his cat was likely to get fat from eating mice, the *Globe* asked nutritionist Stephen L. Blythe of New England Deaconess Hospital.

Nutritionist Blythe said *Mus musculus* averages 25 calories; *Microtus pennsylvanicus* has about 43 calories; and *Oryzomys palustris* averages 127 calories each.

The mouse, he reported, is a nutritious part of any cat's diet, especially valuable for minerals such as iron and calcium. Next question.

Feeding dogs. Americans spend $2.5 billion a year buying commercial food for their pets—the equivalent of $11.50 for each human in the country.

A pencil's work. Your average pencil would draw a line 35 miles long.

What America is used for. About a third of the real estate in America is covered by forests. A quarter is grassland, pasture, or range. A fifth is under cultivation. Recreation and wildlife areas claim 4 per cent. Cities and towns occupy 1.5 per cent of the total area. Roads and other transportation facilities take 1 per cent, and public installations and facilities take another 1 per cent. Of the 14 per cent that remains, much is mountain, desert, or swamp, never claimed by private owners and remaining in the public domain.

All told, there are 2,264 million acres in the United States, according to the Agriculture Department, which provided these figures. Of every 100 acres:

58 are owned by individuals and businesses
34 are owned by the federal government
 6 are owned by state and local governments
 2 are owned by American Indians.

Mr. ZIP thanks you. Ninety-seven letters in 100 mailed in the United States are addressed with ZIP Codes.

Fire!

If you can't stand the heat, get out of the kitchen. One in 14 American households has a fire in the average year.

Appliances are the source of two thirds of the blazes, and kitchen stoves the cause of two thirds of the appliance fires.

In appliance fires, the fire department is called only 3 per cent of the time.

Looks like a torch job. In 1975, the average fire caused $2,700 in damage. For fires started by arson, the average loss was $4,000, and $6,433 in 1979.

But it looks so warm and cozy. When it's about 20 degrees Fahrenheit outdoors, the average home fireplace generates just enough warmth to make up for the heat that's lost up the chimney. You're out the price of the firewood.

The Yellow Pages. In an average year, we use the Yellow Pages 17 billion times, according to the American Telephone & Telegraph Company.

The average user is most likely to be searching for information on auto parts or repair, restaurants, building materials, hotels and motels, or banks.

The typical American is more likely to be able to match AT&T's walking-fingers emblem with the Yellow Pages than to match any other corporate emblem with its sponsor, a survey showed. CBS's "eye" came in second.

Windy cities. In Chicago, the wind blows at an average of 10.4 miles an hour. But there are windier cities in America.

At Kennedy and LaGuardia airports in New York, for instance, the wind blows at an average 12.2 miles an hour.

At a typical moment, the wind blows at 14.1 miles an hour in Dodge City, Kansas, 13.7 miles an hour in Amarillo, Texas, 13.3 miles an hour in Cheyenne, Wyoming, 12.8 miles an hour in Oklahoma City, 12.6 miles an hour in Boston, 12.3 miles an hour in Buffalo, New York, and 11.8 miles an hour in Honolulu.

There now, Chicago.

The criminal hours. The average police department gets most of its calls from 5 to 6 P.M., when people come home from work to find their places burglarized, and from 9 P.M. to midnight, when most violent crimes occur.

Stick 'em up! This is a heat wave! The crime rate seems to rise with the thermometer and the barometer. In a study of 40,000 crimes in Philadelphia, medical climatologists found that murder, rape, and aggravated assault increased by 45 per cent when the weather turned warm and muggy, with clear skies and temperatures about 80 degrees. Violence increased by about 30 per cent on overcast, humid days when the temperature was only about 70 degrees. On nice days—dry and crisp after a period of bad weather—the crime rate dropped by 75 per cent. The climatologists concluded that humidity may be an "accessory to the crime."

Caws célèbre. For his own reasons, Dr. Nicholas S. Thompson, associate professor of psychology at Clark University in Worcester, Massachusetts, has measured the caws of crows. He says the American crow's caws last an average of .2 second each, and come typically in a burst of 3.03 caws at a time. European crows, on the other hand, manage an average of 3.2 caws per burst, with each caw lasting an average of .43 second.

Commissions by the numbers. Since 1844, the government has created an average of 1 commission, bureau, or task force every 10 years to study the collection, compilation and dissemination of statistics. Agencies were assigned that task in 1844, 1866, 1877, 1903, 1907, 1918, 1922, 1931, 1933, 1942, 1948, 1961, and 1971. In fiscal year 1971, 40 government agencies spent a dollar for each American on the collection and publication of statistics.

Evacuate. Two hurricanes hit the United States in an average year.

Better get that kite down and get inside. Florida averages 80 to 100 thunderstorms a year. The Pacific Coast averages 2 to 5.

In a typical year, lightning kills some 150 people in the United States, injures more than 1,000 and causes property damage of more than $100 million.

The guilty, the innocent and the still pending. Of every 100 people charged with a crime in the United States, 36 are convicted, 12 are acquitted, and 34 are referred to juvenile court. The cases of the other 18 are still pending.

Nobody asked the animals. The horse is the favorite animal of 1 American child in 11. The average girl is 3 times more likely to love horses than is the average boy.

Snakes are the animals kids like least. One in 3 6-year-old hates snakes, and boys hate them almost as much as girls do.

Which way to the ocean? One American in 2 lives within 50 miles of a coastline.

The age of fame. *The Big Book of Halls of Fame in the United States and Canada* (Bowker, 1977) says that the average age at which people are enshrined in a hall of fame is 66.37 years.

Waiting for the foal, cub, kitten, fawn, pup, calf, lamb, bunny, gosling, duckling, and other young'uns to be born. Here are some average gestation or incubation periods for animals:

pigeon	11 to 19 days
golden hamster	15 to 17 days
mouse	19 to 31 days
rat	21 days
chicken	22 days
duck	28 days
rabbit	31 days
ground hog	31 to 32 days
kangaroo	32 to 39 days
squirrel	44 days
fox	51 to 63 days
wolf	60 to 63 days
cat	63 days
dog	63 days
guinea pig	68 days
lion	108 days
pig	115 days
monkey	139 to 270 days
goat	151 days
sheep	151 days
bear	180 to 240 days
deer	197 to 300 days
hippopotamus	240 days
human	253 to 303 days
horse	336 days
ass	365 days
whale	365 to 547 days
elephant	624 days

You can't fool Granny. The average older woman can tell synthetic fibers from real fibers better than the average younger woman can.

How pigs work. As a food factory, the pig is far more efficient than the cow. Pigs transform about 35 per cent of what they eat into live weight, while cattle convert only 11 per cent.

Money that ain't. In an average year, counterfeiters gyp Americans out of about $3 million.

The weatherman's batting average. In forecasting high and low temperatures a day ahead of time in the 48 contiguous states, the Weather Service was off by an average of 4.9 per cent in 1966. Ten years later, it had reduced its margin of error to 3.6 per cent.

But the Service's long-range forecasting was hardly better than guesswork. In predicting whether the next season would be warmer or cooler, wetter or drier than normal, the weatherman was right only 60 per cent of the time.

Precip. On average, it rains only once every 2 weeks in Las Vegas, and 1 day out of 10 in Phoenix and Los Angeles. In Juneau, Alaska, it rains or snows 3 days out of five.

In San Francisco, it rains 1 day out of 5 or 6. Pittsburgh, Portland, Oregon, and Seattle get rain or snow 2 days out of 5—almost twice as often as in Dallas.

It precipitates 1 day out of 3 in New York, Chicago, Lakeland, Florida, Missoula, Montana, and Cape Hatteras, North Carolina. The average is 1 wet day of every 4 in Tulsa, Salt Lake City, Boise, Aberdeen, South Dakota, and Fort Smith, Arkansas.

What the government knows. According to Robert Ellis Smith, author of *Privacy: How to Protect What's Left of It* (Doubleday, 1979), the government has an average of 18 computer files for everyone in America and buys 1 out of every 22 computers made.

1040 and more. Americans spend about 785 million hours a year filling out government forms, according to the U. S. Office of Management and Budget. That works out to 5 hours, 12 minutes for every person over 18.

Wet, on average. In an average year, an average place in the continental United States gets 29 inches of precipitation.

Americans from elsewhere. At the time of the 1970 Census, 4 of every 100 Americans had immigrated to the U.S.

Of every 100 foreign-born Americans, 13 came from Italy, 11 from Germany, 9 from Canada, 7 from Mexico, 7 from Great Britain, 7 from Poland, 6 from the Soviet Union, 5 from Asia (1 each from China and Japan), 4 from Ireland, and the rest from other places.

Let's have a beer at the Legion hall. Of every 100 men in America over age 18, 41 have been in the armed services. This ratio hasn't varied much since the early 1960s.

Middle America. If the United States were a flat sheet of plastic, and you balanced it on your fingertip, your finger would be under Butte County, South Dakota. That's the geographic center of the country.

The center of population is another story. It moves a little bit west every year, and sometimes a bit north or south, as well. In 1970, it was on a farm 5 miles east-southeast of Mascoutah, Illinois, and about 30 miles east of St. Louis.

The center of population moved from Maryland into Virginia in 1810, to West Virginia in 1830, to Ohio in 1860, to Indiana in 1890, and to Illinois in 1950.

Two events that jolted the population center farther west than usual were the California gold rush of the 1850s, and, a century later, the admission to statehood of Alaska and Hawaii.

It doesn't look as though the population center and the geographic center will ever coincide. If the population center keeps on its present course, it will pass several hundred miles to the south of Butte County, South Dakota.

Back to nature. Since 1970, our rural population has been growing faster than that of urban America.

Most of the movement has been to the countryside and villages rather than to farms. But even the farm population, steadily declining for decades, took a tiny hike in 1978.

Elbow room. At the time of the 1970 Census, there were 58 people for every square mile of the United States. The world as a whole averaged 68 people for every square mile. There were 200 for every square mile in China, 720 in Japan, and 819 in Holland.

New Jersey averaged 953 people for every square mile. Nevada averaged 4.

Fewer immigrants. In 1910, an average neighborhood of 10 families included one that had come to this country within the previous decade. Today, fewer than 1 of every 50 Americans has immigrated during the past 10 years.

The average immigrant in 1910 was a laborer. The typical immigrant today is a skilled worker.

But still diverse. One American in 8 is black, 1 in 16 is Hispanic, 1 in 10 is over 65, and 1 in 3 is a child.

And mostly city folks. Seven of every 10 Americans live in metropolitan areas, 3 of them in the cities and 4 in the suburbs.

In the sticks. A white American is much more likely to live in a small town or the country than is a black, and a black is much more likely to live there than a Hispanic.

Asian Americans. One American in 100 is of Asian descent. Of every 100 Asian Americans in 1970, 62 were born in the U.S. and 38 immigrated.

Seven in 10 Asian Americans live in the West. Thirty-eight per cent live in California, and 27 per cent live in Hawaii, where they constitute 47 per cent of that state's population.

Among Asian Americans, only Chinese Americans have

moved East in large numbers. Six Chinese Americans in 10 live in the East, most of them in New York State.

Asian Americans earn more, on average, than their fellow Americans. Japanese Americans earn about 20 per cent more than Chinese Americans.

More Asian Americans are owners of small businesses than members of any other minority group.

Asian Americans are twice as likely as other Americans to have a college degree.

Where those new folks come from. Of every 99 persons immigrating to America between 1971 and 1977:

20 came from Europe (4 of them from Italy)
32 came from Asia or the Mideast (6 of them from Korea)
45 came from this hemisphere (a third of them from Mexico)
2 came from Africa.

American Babel. Spanish is the mother tongue of 1 American in 27—that's 8 million people. For every 8 Americans brought up on Spanish, 6 were brought up on German, 4 on Italian, 2.5 on French, 2.5 on Polish, and 1.5 on Yiddish. One American in 872 grows up speaking Serbo-Croatian.

Of the 800,000 native American Indians, 1 in 3 speaks an Indian language as her or his mother tongue. More than half of those people speak Navajo. One Alaskan in 13 grows up speaking Eskimo.

The first Americans. Indians come in last by most measures of well being. For every $100 earned by the average American family, the Indian family earns $61. The typical Indian lives to be 44, a third less than the average American. Suicides among Indian teen-agers are 3 times the national rate. The average educational level for Indians under federal supervision is 5 years of schooling. According to *Our Brother's Keeper: The Indian in White America,* the federal Bureau of Indian Affairs has 1 employee for every 18 Indians in the United States.

Between 1890 and 1970, the Indian population increased by 320 per cent. So did the total U.S. population.

In the first census to count them accurately, in 1890, there were 248,253 American Indians in the United States; in 1970, that figure had grown to 792,730. Indians live in every state—229 of them in Vermont—but the majority live in 5: Oklahoma, Arizona, California, New Mexico, and North Carolina. One Indian in 3 lives on a reservation.

It's 54 in Kansas City. At an average time on an average day or night at an average place in the continental United States, the temperature is 53.2 degrees Fahrenheit and the wind is blowing at 8 to 12 miles an hour.

The average temperature is 79 in San Juan, 77 in Honolulu, 76 in Miami, 74 in Yuma, Arizona, 72 in Corpus Christi and Orlando, 70 in Phoenix, 69 in Houston, 68 in New Orleans, 66 in Dallas and Las Vegas, 65 in Los Angeles and Mobile, 64 in Columbia, South Carolina, 63 in San Diego, 60 in Tulsa, Chattanooga, and Sacramento, 59 in Raleigh, 57 in Washington, D.C., Albuquerque, and San Francisco, 56 in St. Louis and Louisville, and 55 in Charleston, West Virginia, and Philadelphia.

It's 54 in Kansas City, Newark, New Jersey, and Wilmington, Delaware, 53 in Pittsburgh, Seattle, and Portland, Oregon, 52 in Dayton, Ohio, and Omaha, and 51 in Boston, Chicago, Salt Lake City, and Boise. It's 50 in Denver, Providence, Detroit, and Akron, 48 in Des Moines, 46 in Concord, New Hampshire, and 45 in Sioux Falls, Sheridan, Wyoming, and Portland, Maine.

The average temperature is 44 in Minneapolis, Burlington, Vermont, and Green Bay. It's 43 in Helena, 41 in Fargo, 39 in Duluth, and 35 in Anchorage.

Missing the boat. Every year since 1945, an average of 15 ships per annum have vanished at sea. That's about 1 ship for every 10 million square miles of regularly traveled ocean.

Geologist Robert F. Schmalz of Penn State says that on the basis of its size and of those statistics, the Bermuda Triangle—the patch of ocean where more than a hundred ships and planes have reportedly vanished—is actually one of the safest stretches of water.

"Statistically," he says, "we would expect that at least 16 ships would have vanished in the 5-million-square-mile Bermuda Triangle since World War II—perhaps more if we consider the fact that the 'Triangle' is one of the most heavily traveled areas of the world's oceans. Since the actual disappearances fall far short of this number, I think the 'Triangle' must be considered one of the safest regions of the sea."

Can't they stay afloat? The Coast Guard says the average pleasure-boating fatality occurs when a boat capsizes on a calm lake or pond, with little or no wind, in broad daylight, with good visibility, on a Saturday or Sunday during summer.

Antifreeze. In an average year, the temperature *never* gets below freezing in Los Angeles, San Diego, San Francisco, Miami, Key West, or Honolulu.

At the other end of the scale, it gets below freezing 323 days of an average year in Barrow, Alaska, and 198 days of an average year in International Falls, Minnesota.

The average number of freezing days is 124 in Detroit, 119 in Chicago, 101 in Philadelphia, 98 in Pittsburgh, 96 in Boston, 81 in New York, 60 in Atlanta, 44 in Portland, Oregon, and 39 in Dallas.

Elementary, my dear Watson. Three out of 4 murders and 3 out of 5 assaults result in the arrest of a suspect, the FBI says. A suspect is arrested in half the rapes and a quarter of the robberies. But only 1 out of 6 burglaries and 1 out of 7 car thefts lead to arrests.

A sentence isn't always what it says. According to government statistics, the average adult released from a federal prison in 1977 had been sentenced to 31.1 months and had actually served 15.8 months before being released (usually on parole).

Violators of the immigration laws served 81.6 per cent of their sentences. Kidnapers served 38.5 per cent. Car thieves served 59.3 per cent, robbers 36.7 per cent, counterfeiters 46.8

per cent, drug-law violators 49.5 per cent, embezzlers 54.8 per cent, persons who escaped prison or harbored a fugitive 53.7 per cent, forgers 54.9 per cent, and income-tax violators 60.5 per cent of the sentences imposed on them.

oR not noT TO bE OR OR or NoT To qUicK bRown be be nOt tO foXx be not NOt bE Be. You remember that old hypothesis that if enough monkeys pecked away at typewriters long enough they would eventually write the complete works of Shakespeare?

Well, the New York *Times* reports that Dr. William R. Bennett, Jr., a professor of physics at Yale, did some computations.

"He calculates," according to the *Times*, "that if a trillion monkeys were to type 10 randomly chosen characters a second it would take, on the average, more than a trillion times as long as the universe has been in existence just to produce the sentence: 'To be or not to be, that is the question.' "

Down with crime. Of every 100 Americans, 75 favor gun control, 64 favor the death penalty for murderers, 70 support more government spending to fight crime, and 85 would like to see harsher treatment of criminals by the courts.

Wake up, Harry! I hear something! The average American burglar is a teen-age boy. So is the average car thief.

Sunny cities. Believe it or not, the National Climatic Center keeps detailed records, city by city, on number of hours of sunlight. These statistics, which the NCC calls "Sunshine—Average Percentage of Possible," work down from 100 per cent for every hour the sun fails to shine, whether it's blocked by clouds, fog, smog, or what have you.

On an average day of an average year, it's sunny 9 of every 10 daylight hours in Yuma, Arizona, but only a little over 4 out of 10 daytime hours in Pittsburgh.

Here's how cities compare by "Average Percentage of Possible Sunshine":

75% or more

Yuma
Phoenix
Tucson
Las Vegas
Sacramento
Key West
Albuquerque
El Paso

70% to 74%

Los Angeles
Denver
Dodge City
Salt Lake City

65% to 69%

Boise
Wichita
Kansas City
Charlotte
Oklahoma City
Charleston,
    South Carolina
Memphis
San Francisco
Honolulu
Tampa

60% to 64%

Jacksonville
Atlanta
Des Moines
Sioux City
Topeka
New Orleans
Boston
Billings
Lincoln, Nebraska
Omaha
Cheyenne

Richmond
Norfolk
Tulsa

55% to 59%

Hartford
Washington, D.C.
Chicago
Peoria
Indianapolis
Louisville
Portland, Maine
Baltimore
Minneapolis
St. Louis
Atlantic City
New York
Fargo
Cincinnati
Philadelphia
Providence
Nashville
Houston
Milwaukee

50% to 54%

Detroit
Duluth
Concord
Buffalo
Cleveland
Columbus, Ohio

49% or less

Sault Ste. Marie,
    Michigan
Portland, Oregon
Parkersburg,
    West Virginia
Seattle
Pittsburgh

Tornado alley. The average tornado moves east or northeast at 25 to 40 miles an hour, carving a path of destruction 250 yards wide. It injures 3 people and causes $305,343 worth of damage. Someone is killed by 1 out of every 5½ tornadoes.

Your average tornado is most likely to hit between 2 and 7 P.M. in April, May, or June, in Kansas, Oklahoma, or Texas.

In an average year, 655 tornadoes strike the United States, with at least 1 tornado touching down on 161 days of the year. Another 450 funnel clouds never hit the ground, and therefore don't count as tornadoes.

Bang. Banger. Bangest. America produces an average of 3 nuclear devices a day, every day.

A Niagara for each of us. America disposes of 150 gallons of water a day for each of us. Here's where it goes:

Homes: The average American uses 60 gallons a day at home for cooking, laundry, drinking, taking baths, flushing, washing the car, and watering the lawn.

Industry: Fifty gallons per American per day.

Commercial users: Grocers, barber shops, restaurants, and the like use 20 gallons per American.

Government: Public uses—cleaning streets, fighting fires, filling pools—account for 10 gallons per person daily.

Vanished: Another 10 gallons per day per person are lost, according to the American Water Works Association, "much of it through leaks and breaks in underground pipelines."

Where art thou? About 12 per cent of the U.S. population lives in either the New York, Chicago, or Los Angeles metropolitan areas, but 24 per cent of the nation's actors, architects, dancers, designers, musicians, composers, painters, sculptors, photographers, radio-TV announcers and teachers of drama, art, and music—in a word, artists—live in one of those three areas.

Your average state. If you consider only population and land area, Iowa's the most average state—twenty-fifth in population and twenty-fourth in land area.

Where the troops are. Of every 100 members of the U.S. armed forces, 22 are stationed on foreign soil.

Of every 100 sailors, 89 are shore-based and 11 are at sea.

Where the boys and girls are. One in 5 Americans is 14 to 24 years old.

But they aren't evenly distributed. Disproportionately young states are Alaska, Utah, South Carolina, and Hawaii, where at least 22 per cent of the population is in that age group. Youths are underrepresented in New Jersey (17.6 per cent) and Florida (17.7 per cent).

Sources

ABC Leisure Magazine
ABC Television
Actors' Equity Association
AFL-CIO
Aircraft Owners' and Pilots' Association
Gerald Albaum, Experimental Center for the Advancement of Invention and Innovation, University of Oregon
Alcoholics Anonymous
American Association of Fund-Raising Counsel
American Association of Professional Bridal Consultants
American Association of Retired People
American Association of Sex Educators, Counselors, and Therapists
American Bankers' Association
American Bus Association
American Cancer Society
American Council on Education
American Council of Life Insurance
American Dental Association
American Diabetes Association
American Dietetic Association
American Federation of Musicians
American Home Economics Association
American Hotel and Motel Association
American Humane Association
American Journal of Home Economics
American Library Association
American Medical Association
American Newspaper Publishers Association
American Psychiatric Association
American Public Transit Association

American Society of Dowsers, Inc.
The American Sunbathing Association, Inc.
American Telephone & Telegraph Co.
American Water Works Association
American Way
Amtrak
Annals of the New York Academy of Science
Anne Anastasi, *Psychological Testing,* Macmillan, 1976
Rep. John Anderson, Republican of Illinois
April-Marcus, Inc.
Arbitron
Army magazine
Arthritis Foundation
Rep. Les Aspin, Democrat of Wisconsin
Associated Master Barbers and Beauticians of America
The Associated Press
The Association for Voluntary Sterilization
Association of Home Appliance Manufacturers
Atlanta *Journal*
Atlantic magazine
Automotive Information Council

B&B Caterers, Washington, D.C.
Ball Corp.
Barron's
The Baseball Encyclopedia, Macmillan, 1976
Alan P. Bell and Martin S. Weinberg, *Homosexuality: A Study of Human Diversity,* Simon & Schuster, 1978
Better Homes & Gardens
Beverage Industry
Bicycle Manufacturers Association of America
The Big Book of Halls of Fame in the United States and Canada, Jacques Cattell Press, Bowker, 1977
"The Biology of Human Variation," *Annals of the New York Academy of Science*
Book Industry Study Group
Boston *Globe*
Boy Scouts of America
Brewers' Almanac
John A. Brittain, Brookings Institution
R. H. Bruskin Associates
Business Insurance

California Department of Motor Vehicles
Candy Marketer magazine
Jackson Carroll, Douglas Johnson, and Martin E. Marty, *Religion in America, 1950 to Present,* Harper & Row, 1979
Craig Carter and William A. Borst
Catholic University of America
Center for the American Woman and Politics, Rutgers University
Center for Science in the Public Interest
Center for Study of Responsive Law
Central Opera Service
Cereal Institute of America
Chain Store Age
Champion Spark Plugs
Changing Times, the Kiplinger Magazine
Charcoal Briquet Institute
Chemical and Engineering News, American Chemical Association
Chicago *Sun-Times*
Citibank
Civil Service Journal
Clark University
Clearinghouse on Smoking and Health
Clinical Disorders of Fluid and Electrolyte Metabolism, ed. by Charles R. Kleeman and Morton H. Maxwell, McGraw-Hill, 1972
Coda
John Coleman, ed., *Introducing Psychology: A Textbook for Health Students* (pub. info. unavailable)
The College Board
Communications of the Association for Computing Machinery
Congressional Record
Consumer Reports
Cornell University, New York State College of Home Economics Center for Housing and Environmental Studies, Department of Housing and Design
Corporation for Public Broadcasting
Cosmetic, Toiletry, and Fragrance Association
Cotton Council

Daily News Record
Robert Davids, Society for American Baseball Research
Detroit *News*
Digest of Educational Statistics
Distilled Spirits Industry

Documenta Geigy Scientific Tables, sixth ed., ed. by Konrad Diem, published by Geigy Pharmaceuticals
Dome Simplified Home Budget Book
Leslie Alan Dunkling, *First Names First,* Universe, 1977
Donald Durost, U. S. Department of Agriculture

Economic Report of the President, 1979, 1980
Daniel J. Edelman, Inc.
Education Commission of the States
Bill Eisner
Epilepsy Foundation of America
Esperanto League for North America
Esquire magazine
Professor Clinton J. Esser, Northern Illinois University

Harvey Faberman and Erich Goode, *Social Reality*
Family Circle magazine
Family Economics Review, U. S. Department of Agriculture
Elaine Poliakoff Fenton
James Fixx, *The Complete Runner's Day-by-day Log and Calendar, 1979,* Random House, 1978
Food Marketing Institute
Henry Ford III
Ford Motor Co.
Jonathan L. Freedman, *Happy People: What Happiness Is, Who Has It, and Why* (pub. info. unavailable)

The Gallup Organization, Inc.
Gardens for All, Inc.
Stan Gellers
General Mills
"General Mills American Family Report, 1978–79," Yankelovich, Skelly and White, Inc.
General Motors
Georgetown University
Steve Gerstel
Arnold Gesell
The Gillette Co.
Givaudan Corporation
Paul Glick, U. S. Census Bureau
The Gold Institute
Golf Digest magazine

Dr. David B. P. Goodman
Peggy Grant, U. S. Postal Service
Great Waters of France
Alan Guttmacher Institute

Stan Hall
Philip G. Hammer, Jr., and F. Stuart Chapin, Jr., *Human Time Allocation: A Case Study of Washington, D.C.,* Center for Urban and Regional Studies, University of North Carolina
The Handbook of Prescription Drugs
Louis Harris and Associates, Inc.
Harshe-Rotman & Druck, Inc.
Harvard University Medical School, Laboratory of Neurophysiology, Department of Psychology
John H. Harvey and William P. Smith, *Social Psychology: An Attributional Approach,* Mosby, 1977
Denis Hayes, *Rays of Hope,* Norton, 1977
Health Insurance Institute
R. J. Herrnstein, *I. Q. in the Meritocracy,* Little, Brown, 1973
Highway Users' Institute
Shere Hite, *The Hite Report,* Macmillan, 1976
Hoffman-LaRoche, Inc.
Home Economics Research Journal
Honeywell, Inc.
Human Behavior magazine
Human Sexuality, American Medical Association
The Humane Society
Morton Hunt, *Sexual Behavior in the 1970s,* reprinted with permission of Playboy Press, Copyright © 1974 by Morton Hunt

Improving Productivity in Solid Waste Collection, the National Center for Productivity and Quality of Working Life
Information Please Almanac, 1979
Institute for Family Research and Education
Insurance Information Institute
International City Management Association
International Civil Aviation Organization
International Fabricare Institute
Iowa State University
Theodore Irwin, Public Affairs Committee

Journal of the American Dental Association
Journal of American Insurance

Journal of Home Economics
Journal of Pediatric Psychology
Journal of Sex Research

Clifford S. Kachline, historian, National Baseball Hall of Fame and Museum, Inc.
Major Paul Kahl, Kelly Air Force Base, Texas
Dr. Armand M. Karow, Jr., consultant, Medical College of Georgia
Kentucky Fried Chicken
Kentucky Fried Chicken Time-out Institute
Alexander Kira, *The Bathroom: Criteria for Design,* Penguin, 1976
Jeane Kirkpatrick, *Political Woman,* Basic Books, 1974
Charles R. Kleeman and Morton H. Maxwell, eds., *Clinical Disorders of Fluid and Electrolyte Metabolism,* McGraw-Hill, 1972
Robert Kloss, Ron E. Roberts, and Dean S. Dorn, *Sociology with a Human Face,* Mosby, 1976
Knight-Ridder newspapers

Ladies' Home Journal
Ladies' Professional Golf Association
Charles Lave, University of California at Irvine
The League of New York Theaters and Producers
Harvey C. Lehman
Nat Lehrman, *Masters and Johnson Explained,* Playbook Press, 1976
Fred Lindsey, *Years of Change,* published by *Nation's Business,* U.S. Chamber of Commerce
Los Angeles *Times*

Dorothea McCarthy and Elizabeth B. Hurlock
Sen. George S. McGovern, Democrat of South Dakota
Gorman McMullen, Independent Telephone Association
Alex Mackenzie and Associates, Inc.
Magazine Publishers Association
Major League Baseball Players' Association
Manufactured Housing Institute
E. Martinez, Air Line Pilots' Association
William H. Masters, M.D., and Virginia E. Johnson, *Human Sexual Response,* Little, Brown, 1966
Maxwell Associates
Medical College of Georgia

Medical Economics magazine
Meetings and Conventions magazine
Men's Wear magazine
Metropolitan Life Insurance Co.
Frank Miles
Minnesota Department of Public Safety
Dr. Gabe Mirkin
Money magazine
Monthly Labor Review, U. S. Department of Labor
Desmond Morris, *Intimate Behavior,* Random House, 1972
Desmond Morris, *The Naked Ape,* McGraw-Hill, 1967
Motion Picture Association of America
Motor Vehicle Manufacturers Association
Mutual of Omaha

National Assessment of Educational Progress
National Association of Investment Clubs
National Automobile Dealers Association
National Bureau of Economic Research
National Collegiate Athletic Association
National Commission on Working Women
National Council of Churches
National Council of Churches of Christ
National Education Association
National Football League
National Football League Players' Association
National Geographic Society
National Guild of Piano Teachers
National Hockey League Players' Association
National Hot Dog and Sausage Council
National Household Cleaning and Laundry Census, Market Research Corp.
National Institute for the Food Service Industry
National Live Stock and Beef Board
National Organization for the Reform of Marijuana Laws
National Restaurant Association
National Safety Council
National School Transportation Association
National Soft Drink Association
Nation's Restaurant News
Marilyn Neckes
New England Journal of Medicine

Jeff Newmeyer
Newsweek
New York Convention and Visitors' Bureau
New York *Daily News*
The New Yorker
New York State Department of Social Hygiene
New York *Times*
John Newton, University of Delaware
Frank Nicholas, chairman, Beech-Nut Baby Foods
A. C. Nielsen Co.

Dr. Ann Oakley, *The Sociology of Housework,* Pantheon, 1975
Ohio Agricultural Research and Development Center
Ohio State University
Opinion Research Corp.
Oppenheimer Management Corp.
Woodrow Orner

Craig Palmer
Pete Palmer and Irv Matus in *Baseball Research Journal,* Society
    for American Baseball Research, 1978
Parade magazine
Parker Brothers
Neal R. Peirce
The Pennsylvania State University
Pet Food Institute
Pharmaceutical Manufacturers Association
Pitney Bowes
Proceedings of the National Conference on Dog and Cat Control
Progressive Grocer
Proprietary Association
Psychological Reports
Psychology Today magazine
Public Affairs Committee
Public Citizen, Inc.
Publishers Weekly

Railroad Retirement Board
J. D. Ratcliff, *Your Body and How It Works,* Delacorte, 1975
Readings in Marriage and Family, 1978/79, Duskin Publish, 1978
Resort Management magazine
Retail Week (formerly *Clothes, Etc.*)

Mike Reynolds, U. S. Canoe Association
Sandi Risser
Professor John P. Robinson, Cleveland State University
Root and deRochemont, *Eating in America,* Morrow, 1976
Roper Surveys
Harry F. Rosenthal
Benjamin Ruhe

Russell Sage Foundation
Gerald R. St. Onge, Associated Master Barbers and Beauticians of
   America
St. Petersburg *Independent*
St. Petersburg *Times*
The Savings and Loan Foundation
Sentry Insurance
Tom Seppy
Gail Sheehy, *Hustling,* Delacorte, 1973
Gail Sheehy, *Passages,* Dutton, 1976
The Silver Institute
Simplicity Pattern Company
James H. Smith, Jr.
Soap and Detergent Association
Social Science Frontiers, Russell Sage Foundation
Sociological Abstracts
Frank Stafford and Greg Duncan, University of Michigan
Stanford University
Star-Kist
State Farm Insurance Company
Statistical Abstract of the United States, U. S. Department of Commerce, 1978, 1979
Steelcase, Inc.
The Sugar Association, Inc.
Supermarketing magazine
Survey of Current Business, U. S. Department of Commerce
Peter Swerdloff, *Men and Women,* Time-Life Books, 1975
Adrian W. Sybor, U. S. Public Health Service

Television and Growing Up: The Impact of Televised Violence, report to the surgeon general of the United States
Tennis magazine
Texas Real Estate Research Center
Time magazine

The Tobacco Institute
"Today" show, NBC
Today's Health magazine
The Travel Agent magazine
Travel Weekly magazine
Marcello Truzzi, ed., *Sociology for Pleasure,* Prentice-Hall, 1974
Tufts University

Unitarian Universalist Service Committee
United Nations
United Press International
University of Arizona Department of Anthropology
University of California
University of California at Los Angeles
University of Iowa
University of Iowa Health Center
University of Kentucky Department of Behavioral Science and To-
    bacco and Health Research Institute
University of Michigan Survey Research Center
University of Notre Dame
University of Tennessee
University of Texas
University of Washington
U.S.A. Pocket Data Book, U. S. Department of Commerce
U. S. Brewers' Association
U. S. Catholic Conference
U. S. Chamber of Commerce
U. S. League of Savings Associations
U. S. Government
    ACTION
    Alcohol, Drug Abuse and Mental Health Administration
    Air Force
    Army
    Army Corps of Engineers
    Army Natick Development Center
    Bureau of the Census
    Bureau of Labor Statistics
    Bureau of Mines
    Bureau of Prisons
    Civil Service Commission
    Coast Guard
    Commission on the Review of the National Policy Toward Gam-
        bling

Community Services Administration
Congressional Budget Office
Consumer Product Safety Commission
Department of Agriculture
Department of Commerce
Department of Health and Human Services
Department of Labor
Department of Transportation
Federal Bureau of Investigation
Federal Communications Commission
Federal Highway Administration
Federal Home Loan Bank Board
Federal Reserve Board
Federal Trade Commission
Food and Drug Administration
Forest Service
General Accounting Office
Heritage, Conservation and Recreation Service
Internal Revenue Service
Interstate Commerce Commission
National Center for Education Statistics
National Center for Health Statistics
National Center for Productivity and Quality of Working Life
National Commission for Productivity and Quality of Working
   Life
National Endowment for the Arts
National Heart and Lung Institute
National Highway Traffic Safety Board
National Institute on Aging
National Institute on Alcohol Abuse and Alcoholism
National Institute on Drug Abuse
National Institute of Mental Health
National Institutes of Health
National Oceanic and Atmospheric Administration
National Park Service
National Transportation Safety Board
National Weather Service
Office of Education
Office of Personnel Management
Outdoor Resources Review Commission
Passport Office
Postal Service
President's Council on Physical Fitness and Health

Public Health Service
Senate Press Gallery
Senate Subcommittee on Education, Arts, and the Humanities
Social Security Administration
Treasury Department
Veterans' Administration
White House Council of Economic Advisers
U.S. News & World Report
U. S. Parachute Association

Viva magazine

The Wall Street Journal
David Wallechinsky and Irving Wallace, *The People's Almanac,*
    Doubleday, 1975
WASH radio
Washington *Post*
Washington *Star*
David Wechsler, *Measurement and Appraisal of Adult Intelligence*
Wegman Food Market, Inc.
Weight Watchers
Harold Wentworth and Stuart Berg Flexner, compilers and eds.,
    Dictionary of American Slang, Thomas Y. Crowell, 1975
William Patterson College
The Wine Institute
Woman's Day magazine
WomenSport magazine
Work in America Institute Inc.
World Almanac
Worldwatch Institute
Writer's Digest magazine
WTOP radio

Xerox Corporation

Yale University
Yale University School of Medicine
Yankelovich, Skelly, and White, Inc.

Professor Marvin Zuckerman, University of Delaware